Benjamin W Hitchcock

Hitchcock's Chronological Record of the American Civil War,

giving every event in the order of its occurrence, from November 8th, 1860, to June 3d, 1865. Also, a complete list of vessels captured by the Confederate navy

Benjamin W Hitchcock

Hitchcock's Chronological Record of the American Civil War,
giving every event in the order of its occurrence, from November 8th, 1860, to June 3d, 1865. Also, a complete list of vessels captured by the Confederate navy

ISBN/EAN: 9783337409517

Printed in Europe, USA, Canada, Australia, Japan

Cover: Foto ©ninafisch / pixelio.de

More available books at **www.hansebooks.com**

HITCHCOCK'S

CHRONOLOGICAL RECORD

OF THE

AMERICAN CIVIL WAR,

GIVING

EVERY EVENT IN THE ORDER OF ITS OCCURRENCE,

FROM

NOVEMBER 8TH, 1860, TO JUNE 3D, 1865.

ALSO, A COMPLETE LIST OF

VESSELS CAPTURED BY THE CONFEDERATE NAVY.

CHRONOLOGY.

1860.

Nov. 8. The election of Abraham Lincoln and Hannibal Hamlin, as President and Vice President of the United States, was announced at Washington.

9–11. James Chesnut, Jr., and James H. Hammond, U. S. Senators from South Carolina, resigned their seats in the Senate.

Dec. 3. The Second Session of the 36th Congress opened at Washington.

10. U. S. House of Representatives appointed a Committee of 33 on the State of the Union.

10. Howell Cobb, of Georgia, Secretary of the U. S. Treasury, resigned his office. John A. Dix, of New York, was appointed his successor.

14. Lewis Cass, of Michigan, Secretary of State, resigned.

17. Meeting of the South Carolina State Convention at Columbus, and adjournment to Charleston.

20. The South Carolina "Ordinance of Secession" passed.

23. Discovery of a large embezzlement of the Indian Trust Funds, in charge of Jacob Thompson, Secretary of the Department of the Interior.

24. Resignation of the South Carolina Representatives in Congress.

25. Intervention of citizens of Pittsburgh, Pa., to prevent the removal to the South of ordnance in Alleghany Arsenal.

26. Major Anderson removed his command from Fort Moultrie to Fort Sumter.

26. Messrs. Barnwell, Orr, and Adams, Commissioners appointed by South Carolina to treat with the Federal Government, arrived at Washington.

27. Captain N. L. Coste, U.S.R. service, in command of the cutter William Aiken, betrayed his vessel into the hands of the State authorities of South Carolina.

28. The palmetto flag was raised over the custom-house and post-office in Charleston, S. C., and Castle Pinckney and Fort Moultrie were occupied by the South Carolina military.

28. Enthusiastic Union meeting at Memphis, Tenn.

28. Twenty one guns were fired at Wilmington, Del., in honor of Major Anderson and his men.

29. John B. Floyd resigned his position as Secretary of War.

30. South Carolina troops took possession of the U.S. Arsenal at Charleston, containing many thousand stand of arms and valuable military stores.

1861.

Jan. 2. Gov. Ellis, of North Carolina, dispatched troops to seize Fort Macon, the forts at Wilmington, and the U.S. Arsenal at Fayetteville.

3. Fort Pulaski, at Savannah, Ga., taken possession of by Georgia troops, by order of the Governor.

3. South Carolina Commissioners left Washington for Charleston, the President declining to receive any official communication from them.

4. United States Arsenal at Mobile seized by secessionists. No defence.

4. Fast day, by proclamation of President Buchanan.

4. Fort Morgan, at the entrance of Mobile Bay, taken and garrisoned by 200 Alabama troops.

5. Steamship Star of the West sailed from New York with troops and provisions for Fort Sumter.

7. Meeting of Alabama State Convention.

7. Meeting of Mississippi State Convention.

7. Meeting of Virginia Legislature.

7. Meeting of Tennessee Legislature.

8. Jacob Thompson resigned his place in the Cabinet, as Secretary of the Interior.

8. United States sub-Treasury at Charleston seized.

9. Mississippi Ordinance of Secession passed.

9. Steamship Star of the West, with supplies for Fort Sumter, fired into from Morris' Island and Fort Moultrie, and driven from Charleston harbor.

11. Louisiana State troops, under Captain Bradford, took possession of the U.S. marine hospital, two miles below New Orleans, and ordered the removal of the patients, 216 in number.

Jan. 11. Florida Convention adopted an Ordinance of Secession by a vote of 62 to 7.

11. Alabama Convention adopted an Ordinance of Secession by a vote of 61 to 39.

11. Abolition meeting at Rochester, N. Y., broken up by a mob.

12. Senator Seward's great Union speech in the U.S. Senate.

12. Fort Barrancas and the Navy Yard at Pensacola, Fla., seized by rebel troops.

15. Col. Hayne, Commissioner from South Carolina to Washington, demanded the withdrawal of the garrison of Fort Sumter.

15. U. S. coast survey schooner Dana seized by Florida State authorities.

18. Massachusetts Legislature unanimously tendered to the President of the U.S. such aid in men and money as he might request to maintain the authority of the general government.

19. Convention of Georgia adopted a secession ordinance by a vote of 208 to 89.

21. Jefferson Davis, of Mississippi, withdrew from U.S. Senate.

24. U. S. arsenal at Augusta, Ga., surrendered to the State authorities.

26. Louisiana Convention passed an ordinance of secession by a vote of 113 to 17. The popular vote afterwards taken was 20,448 for; 17,296 against.

29. U. S. revenue cutter Robert McClelland, Captain Breshwood, surrendered to State of Louisiana.

29. Secretary Dix's dispatch to Hemphill Jones at New Orleans, "If any one attempts to haul down the American flag, shoot him on the spot."

31. South Carolina authorities offered to buy Fort Sumter.

31. U. S. branch mint and custom-house at New Orleans seized by State authorities.

Feb. 1. Texas Convention at Galveston passed an ordinance of secession, to be voted on by the people on the 23d of February, and to take effect March 2.

1. U. S. revenue cutter Lewis Cass, Capt. Morrison, surrendered to the State of Louisiana.

4. A convention of delegates from the seceded States organized at Montgomery, Alabama; Howell Cobb, President, J. F. Hooper, Secretary.

5. Peace Convention at Washington organized; John Tyler, of Va., Chairman, J. C. Wright, of Ohio, Secretary.

8. Congress at Montgomery adopted a Constitution for a provisional government, to go into immediate operation; Jefferson Davis, President, Alex. H. Stephens, Vice President.

8. U. S. arsenal at Little Rock, Ark., with 9,000 stand of arms and 40 cannon, &c., was surrendered to State authorities.

13. The election of Lincoln and Hamlin, as President and V. President of the U. S., formally declared in the Senate by John C. Breckinridge, V. President.

18. Jefferson Davis inaugurated as President of the Southern Confederacy.

22. John Ross, principal Cherokee Chief, rejected a proposition of Gov. H. M. Rector, of Ark., to entice his nation to take part in the rebellion.

23. Hon. Abraham Lincoln, President elect, arrived in Washington.

23. U. S. property to a great amount, together with the various army posts in Texas, surrendered to the rebels by General Twiggs. Property valued at $1,500,000, besides buildings.

27. Peace Convention, at Washington, submitted to the Senate a plan of adjustment of the national difficulties, involving seven amendments to the Constitution.

March 1. General Twiggs expelled from the army of the United States.

2. Revenue cutter Dodge seized in Galveston Bay by Texas authorities.

4. Abraham Lincoln inaugurated 16th President of the U. S., at Washington.

4. A State Convention declared Texas out of the Union.

5. Gen. P. T. Beauregard took command of the forces investing Fort Sumter, S. C.

6. Fort Brown, Texas, surrendered to State troops.

18. Supplies cut off from Fort Pickens and the Federal fleet in the Gulf of Mexico, by rebel authorities at Pensacola.

20. Sloop Isabel, at Pensacola, with provision for the Federal fleet, was seized by the rebels.

21. Great speech of A. H. Stephens, V. President of the Southern Confederacy, at Savannah, Ga.

30. Mississippi State Convention ratified the Constitution of the C. S., by a vote of 78 to 7.

April 3. South Carolina Convention ratified the Constitution of the C. S. by a vote of 114 to 16.

10. Militia organized in District of Columbia for defence of the capital.

11. Steamship Coatzacoalcos arrived in N. York, bringing Federal troops from Texas.

11. Confederate States Commissioners left Washington.

12. Attack on Fort Sumter.

12. Reinforcement of Fort Pickens.

14. Evacuation of Fort Sumter.

15. Seventeen vessels from Southern ports, without U. S. clearances, were seized at New York and fined $100 each.

15. President's proclamation, calling for 75,000 volunteers to suppress insurrection, and also calling an extra session of U. S. Congress on July 4.

16. The government of the Southern Confederacy called for 32,000 men.

16. New York Legislature appropriated $3,000,000 for war purposes.

16. At New York, Philadelphia, Trenton and other places, journals were compelled to display the American flag.

17. State Convention of Va., in secret session, passed an ordinance of secession.

18. 500 volunteers from Pennsylvania, and 300 regulars, arrived at Washington.

18. Lieut. Jones, in charge of Harper's Ferry arsenal, hearing of the advance of a large Virginia force to seize the establishment, set fire to it, and retreated to Carlisle, Pa.

18. Great Union meeting at Wheeling, Va.

19. Seizure of the U. S. transport Star of the West, at Indianola, by Texas troops under Col. Van Dorn.

19. Sixth Massachusetts regiment on its way to Washington, attacked by a mob in Baltimore, and 3 killed and 7 wounded. In defending themselves, 7 rebels were killed and 8 wounded.

19. The N. Y. 7th militia, Mass. 4th and 8th militia, and R. I. Providence Artillery left New York on their way to Washington.

19. Clearances refused to vessels in northern ports to ports south of Maryland.

20. Eighth Mass. regiment reached Annapolis, Md.

20. Great Union mass meeting of citizens in Union Square, N. Y.

20. 600 kegs of gunpowder, destined for New Orleans, seized by the U. S. Marshal at New York.

21. American Flag publicly buried at Memphis, Tenn.

20. U. S. arsenal at Liberty, Mo., seized.

20. Steamship Star of the West, having been seized by secessionists, was taken into New Orleans.

20. The ports of South Carolina, Georgia, Alabama, Florida, Mississippi, Louisiana, and Texas ordered to be blockaded by the President, as those States were in a state of insurrection against the government.

20. Bridges on Pennsylvania Northern and Philadelphia railway, near Baltimore, burned by a mob from that city.

21. Gosport Navy Yard, opposite Norfolk, Va., set on fire, and vessels scuttled and sunk, by U. S. officers in charge, to prevent their seizure by the rebels.

21. Branch Mint of the U. S. at Charlotte, N. C., seized by order of the Governor of that State.

21. Philadelphia and Baltimore railway taken possession of by U.S. government.

21. The N. Y. 6th, 12th, and 71st, and one R. I. and one Mass. regiment, with a battery, left New York on transports for the Chesapeake.

21. Fourth Mass. regiment arrived at Fortress Monroe.

21. Andrew Johnson, U. S. Senator from Tennessee, mobbed at Lynchburg, Va.

22. U. S. arsenal at Fayetteville, N. C., containing 37,000 stand of arms, 3,000 kegs of powder, and a large quantity of shot and shell, seized by State authority.

22. Depot of U. S stores at Napoleon, Ark., seized under orders of Henry M. Rector, Governor of that State.

22 3,200 Pennsylvania troops at Cockeysville, 14 miles from Baltimore.

22. Seventh N. Y. regiment land at Annapolis, Md.

23. N. Y. 8th, 13th, 28th, and 69th regiments embarked for Washington.

22. Embargo laid, by the Mayor and Police Board of Baltimore, on provisions and steamboats, thus withholding the government stores in that city.

23. First South Carolina regiment left Charleston for the Potomac.

24. Fort Smith, Ark., seized by a rebel force under Col. Borland.

24. N. Y. 7th and Mass. 8th arrived in Washington.

25. A large amount of arms removed to Alton, Ill., from St. Louis arsenal, by Illinois volunteers, to prevent their seizure by rebels.

25. Col. Van Dorn, of Texas State troops, captured 450 U. S. troops at Saluria.

25. Transport Empire City, from Texas, arrived in N.Y. with 600 men of the 3d Infantry and 2d Cavalry, U.S.A., from that State.

25 Gov. Letcher, of Va., by proclamation, transferred that Commonwealth to the Southern Confederacy.

26. Gov. Brown, of Georgia, by proclamation, prohibited the payment of all debts to Northern creditors till the end of hostilities.

26. Bridges over Gunpowder Creek, on Philadelphia and Baltimore railway, and bridge over Bush river, on the same route, destroyed by the rebels.

26. Gov. Burton, of Delaware, issued a proclamation calling for volunteers to defend the Union.

27. Military Department of Washington assigned to Col. Mansfield; Department of Annapolis to Gen. Butler; Department of Pennsylvania to Maj-Gen. Patterson.

April 27. Five men arrested at the Navy Yard, Washington, for filling bomb-shells with sand and sawdust.

27. A number of Southerners employed in the Departments at Washington, refused the oath of allegiance prescribed by the Government, and resigned.

27. The ports of Virginia and North Carolina were included in the blockade by the President.

28. U. S. frigate Constitution arrived at New York from Annapolis.

29. Secession defeated in Maryland House of Delegates by a vote of 53 to 13.

29. Ellsworth's Fire Zouaves left New York for Annapolis.

29. Daily communication between Baltimore and Philadelphia re-established.

May 1. Brig.-Gen. Harney addressed a strong Union letter to his friends in Missouri.

2. N. Y. 69th (Irish) regiment arrived at Washington.

2. Col. F. P. Blair, Jr., announced that the four regiments called for from the State of Missouri, by the President, were enrolled, armed, and mustered into the service within one week from the call.

3. Gov. Jackson, of Missouri, in a message to the Legislature, recommended arming the State, and a union of sympathy and destiny with the slaveholding States.

3. Four New Jersey regiments, fully equipped, under General Runyon, started for the seat of war.

3. President Lincoln issued a proclamation calling into service 42,000 volunteers for three years, and directing the increase of the regular army and navy of the United States.

3. Privateer Savannah captured by the U. S. brig Perry.

4. Steamship Star of the West was put into commission as the receiving ship of the Confederate navy, at New Orleans.

5. Brig.-Gen. Butler, with 6th Massachusetts and 8th New York regiments, took possession of the Relay House, at the junction of the Baltimore, Washington and Ohio railways, nine miles south of Baltimore.

6. The six regiments called for from Indiana, were mustered into service in one week from date of the call.

6. Virginia admitted into the Southern Confederacy in secret session of Confederate Congress.

6. Police Commissioners of St. Louis, Mo., demanded of Capt. Lyon the removal of U. S. troops from all places and buildings occupied by them in that city outside the Arsenal grounds.

6. City military of Baltimore disbanded by order of Major Trimble, commander.

6. Confederate States Congress recognized war with United States, and authorized issue of letters of marque and reprisal.

6. Legislature of Arkansas passed an unconditional ordinance of secession, 69 to 1.

7. Major Anderson, with consent of Sec.-of-War, accepted command of Kentucky state military.

7. Serious riot at Knoxville, Tenn., caused by hoisting a Union flag.

7. League between Tennessee authorities and Confederate States.

7. The late U. S. garrison of Fort Davis, Texas, consisting of 11 officers and 300 men, made prisoners of war by a force of 1,800 rebels near Eastonville. They all refused to enlist in the rebel army.

9. U. S. troops landed at Locust Point, in Baltimore, and were conveyed by the Balt. and Ohio branch railroad through the city.

9. The Confederate Congress authorized President Davis to raise such force for the war as he should deem expedient.

9. U. S. ships Cumberland, Pawnee, Monticello and Yankee enforcing the blockade off Fortress Monroe.

9. Steamers Philadelphia, Baltimore, Powhatan and Mount Vernon, armed by U. S. Government, and cruising on the Potomac.

9. Virginians have batteries in Norfolk harbor, at Craney Island, Sandy Point, the Hospital, Fort Norfolk, and the Bluffs, three miles from the Hospital.

10. Maj.-Gen. R. E. Lee appointed to command the rebel forces in Virginia.

10. Maj.-Gen. McClellan appointed to command the Department of Ohio.

10. The President directed that all officers in the army should take anew the oath of allegiance to the United States.

10. The secession military, under Gen. Frost, at St. Louis, Mo., surrendered to Capt. Lyon, commanding U. S. forces. A mob assailed the U. S. military after the surrender, and were fired on by them and many killed and wounded.

10. The Winans steam gun captured by Gen. Butler, three miles from the Relay House, Md.

10. The Maryland Legislature passed a resolution imploring the President of the United States to cease the present war.

11. U. S. steam frigate Niagara off Charleston, S. C., and began the blockade of that port.

11. Gen. Harney issued a proclamation exhorting the people of Missouri, to maintain peace, and announced his determination

to use the authority of the Government for that purpose.

11. A company of Home Guards, at St. Louis, Mo., mostly German, were fired on by a mob, and returned the fire. Three of the Guards and 14 of the citizens were killed.

13. The 6th Mass. and 8th N. Y. regiments, under Gen. Butler, occupied Federal Hill, near Baltimore.

13. Convention of Union delegates from 35 counties in W. Virginia, met in Wheeling.

13. A lady from New Haven, Conn., teacher of a Grammar School in New Orleans, denuded, tarred and feathered in Lafayette Square, amid an immense crowd of people, being accused of expressing abolition sentiments.

14. Gov. Hicks, of Maryland, issued a proclamation, calling for four regiments of troops, to serve within Maryland, or for the defence of the capital of the United States.

14. Gen. Butler seized a large quantity of arms stored in Baltimore, and a schooner loaded with arms.

15. A proclamation of neutrality with respect to the civil war in the U. S. was issued by Queen Victoria, in which the subjects of Great Britain were forbidden to take part in the contest, or endeavor to break a blockade "lawfully and effectually established."

15. The town of Potosi, Washington co., Mo., taken possession of by U. S. troops, and rebel prisoners and munitions of war taken to St. Louis.

16. Gen. Butler appointed Maj.-Gen. of Volunteers.

18. Arkansas admitted to the Southern Confederacy.

18. Military Department of Virginia organized, embracing E. Virginia, N. Carolina and Tennessee, Maj.-Gen. Butler in command.

18. John Ross, principal Cherokee Chief, in two admirable letters rejects the efforts of the rebels in Arkansas to draw his nation into rebellion.

19. Shots exchanged between U. S. steamers Freeborn and Monticello, and the rebel battery at Sewall's Point, Va.

19. Eight thousand rebel troops at Harper's Ferry.

20. Death of Col. Vosburgh, N. Y. 71st, at Washington.

20. Seizure by the Government of principal telegraph offices throughout the free States, and of the accumulated dispatches for twelve months.

20. Ordinance of secession, and ordinance assenting to the Confederate Constitution passed by North Carolina State Convention.

20. Seizure of 1,600 muskets and 4,000 pikes by Federal troops in Baltimore.

20. Gen. Cadwallader, successor to Gen. Butler, occupied Federal Hill, Baltimore.

20. Fort McHenry reinforced.

20. Prize ship Gen. Parkhill, of Liverpool, arrived at Philadelphia, with a crew from the frigate Niagara.

21 Confederate Congress at Montgomery adjourned to meet at Richmond, July 20.

22. Erection of rebel batteries at Aquia Creek.

22. Maj. Gen. Butler arrived at Fortress Monroe.

22. Fort at Ship Island, Miss., destroyed to prevent its falling into rebel hands.

22. Steamer J. C. Swan, 30 miles below St. Louis, seized by order of Gen. Lyon.

22. Five thousand pounds of lead seized at Ironton, Mo., *en route* for the South.

23. Strong secession speech by A. H. Stephens, at Atlanta, Ga.

23. A battery of Whitworth guns, 12-pounders, arrived in N. Y. city, a present to the Government from patriotic Americans abroad.

23. At Clarksburgh, Harrison co., Va., two companies of secession troops surrendered their arms and dispersed at the demand of Union companies under Capts. Moore and Vance.

24. All vessels from the Northern States at New Orleans, which arrived after the 6th inst., were seized by the Confederate States Marshal.

24. Jeff. Davis appointed the 13th of June to be observed as a day of fasting and prayer.

24. Thirteen thousand Union troops crossed the Potomac and entered Virginia, occupying Alexandria and Arlington Heights.

24. Assassination of Col. Ellsworth, at Alexandria, Va.

25. Destruction of seven bridges and five miles of rails from Alexandria to Leesburg, Va., by the 69th N. Y. S. M.

26. Confederate privateer Calhoun arrived at New Orleans with three whaling vessels and cargoes as prizes.

26. Arrival of 600 U. S. troops at Havana, from Texas.

27. A writ of *habeas corpus* was issued at Baltimore, Md., by Chief Justice Taney, in the case of John Merryman. Gen. Cadwallader declined surrendering him, and an attachment was issued for the General's arrest, which was not served.

27. U. S. steamer Brooklyn commenced the blockade of the Mississippi river.

May 27. Brig.-Gen. McDowell took command of the Federal forces in Virginia.

27. The blockade of Mobile, Ala., commenced.

28. Blockade of Savannah initiated by U. S. gunboat Union.

28. The rebels erected barricades at Harper's Ferry and Point of Rocks; Manassas Junction fortified.

28. Strength of the Rebels in Virginia reported at 90,000 men.

28. Jeff. Davis arrived at Richmond.

28. Services of Miss D. L. Dix accepted by the War Department, for organizing military hospitals, and procuring nurses.

29. Advance of Ohio and Pennsylvania troops through Maryland, towards Harper's Ferry; rebels fall back to Martinsburg.

29. Federal troops occupied Grafton, Va.

30. Concentration of Federal troops at Chambersburg, Pa.

31. Steamers Freeborn and Anacosta attacked rebel batteries at Aquia Creek, Va.

31. Gen. Harney superseded by Gen. Lyon in Missouri.

31. Gens. Banks and Fremont commissioned as Major-Generals.

Ex-Gov. Pratt of Maryland, arrested and taken to Washington Navy Yard.

June 1. British Government prohibited U. S. and rebel armed vessels from bringing any prizes to British ports.

1. Charge of U. S. cavalry at Fairfax Court House, Va., Lieut. Tompkins, commanding.

2. Federal batteries erected at the Rip Raps, near Fortress Monroe.

2. Gen. Twiggs appointed Maj.-Gen. Confederate army.

3. Gen. Beauregard took command of the rebel forces at Manassas Junction.

3. Surprise of rebel troops at Phillippi, Va., by U. S. forces under Cols. Dumont, Kelly and Lander. Col. Kelly was severely wounded.

3. Hon. Stephen A. Douglas died at Chicago. His dying message to his sons was, "Tell them to obey the laws and support the Constitution of the United States."

3. Border State Convention met at Frankfort, Ky.

4. Chief-Justice Taney's protest published against the suspension of the *habeas corpus* by the President.

5. Gun factory and arms of Merrill and Thomas, Baltimore, seized by U. S. Government.

6. Gov. Pickens, of S. C., forbade the remittance of funds to Northern creditors.

6. Thirty-five Virginia cavalry were captured at Alexandria. They took the oath of allegiance and were released.

6. Treasonable dispatches to the rebel Government discovered in the telegraph office at Washington, from Jas. E. Harvey, appointed minister to Portugal.

6. Secession camp at Ellicott's Mills, Ky., ten miles from Cairo, broken up by troops sent from latter station by Gen. Prentiss.

8. Bridges at Point of Rocks and Berlin, on the Potomac river, burned by order of rebel Gen. Johnston.

8. Sanitary Commission authorized and appointed by the Government.

8. Four bridges on the Alexandria and Hampshire railway, Va., burned by disunion troops.

8. Gen. Patterson's troops marched from Chambersburg towards Harper's Ferry.

8. Seizure of arms at Easton, Md., by U. S. troops from Annapolis.

8. Vote of Tennessee reported in favor of secession.

10. Gen. Banks assumed command in Baltimore.

10. Gov. Harris, of Tenn., authorized the raising of troops for the rebel army.

10. Repulse of Federal troops at Great Bethel, near Fortress Monroe.

11. Surprise and rout of armed rebels at Romney, Va., by Col. Wallace's Indiana regiment.

12. Gov. Jackson, of Missouri, issued a proclamation calling 50,000 State militia into service, to protect the "lives, liberty and property of the citizens of the State."

12. Meeting of W. Virginia State Convention at Wheeling. They resolved to elect loyal State officers.

13. Fast day in seceded States, by order of Pres. Davis.

13. Skirmish at Seneca Mills, on the Potomac, 28 miles above Washington, between U. S. District Volunteers and rebel cavalry.

14. Gen. J. A. Dix, of New York, appointed Maj.-Gen. of U. S. Volunteers.

14. Harper's Ferry evacuated by the rebel forces, who destroyed all the available property.

14. Flight of Gov. Jackson and Gen. Price from Jefferson City, capital of Missouri. The telegraph lines and bridges destroyed by them on their route to Booneville.

14. The great Union gun arrived at Fortress Monroe.

14. Miss Dix and a number of nurses arrived at Fortress Monroe.

14. Maryland election resulted in the triumph of all the Union candidates but Winter Davis.

15. Mr. Woodall, of Baltimore, hung by rebels at Harper's Ferry.

15. Jefferson City, Mo., occupied by U.S. troops, under Gen. Lyon.

16. Skirmish at Seneca Mills, Md. Rebel captain and 2 men killed by Major Everett's command.

17. Skirmish at Edward's Ferry, on the Potomac, between the 1st Pennsylvania regiment and a body of rebels.

17. Six persons killed in St. Louis, by soldiers of Col. Kallman's regiment discharging a volley at the Recorder's Court-building, in retaliation of a shot fired into their ranks.

17. Surprise at Vienna, Va. First Ohio regiment fired into by a masked battery, 8 killed, 6 wounded.

17. Western Virginia Convention unanimously declared their independence of the eastern section of the State.

17. Rebel forces at Booneville, Mo., defeated by Gen. Lyon. 35 rebels killed or wounded, and 30 prisoners. Federal loss, 2 killed and 8 wounded. A large quantity of arms and camp equipage captured.

17. Gov. Hicks, of Md., in a message repelled the attempt of the Legislature to search his executive records for supposed correspondence with the Government.

18. U.S. troops at Hagerstown and Williamsport, Md., crossed the Potomac, under command of Gen. Patterson.

18. First balloon ascension for U.S. military purposes, by Prof. Lowe, at Washington.

18. Surprise of 800 Union Home Guards under Capt. Cook, at Camp Cole, Mo., by rebels from Warsaw. 25 killed, 52 wounded, 23 prisoners: 45 of the enemy killed or wounded.

18. Thirty-five rebels, with arms and ammunition, captured at Liberty, Mo., by U.S. regulars from Kansas City.

18. Railway bridge over New Creek, Va., burned by rebels from Romney.

20. Senator Lane, of Kansas, appointed brigadier-general.

20. Gen. McClellan took command of the Federal army in Western Virginia.

20. Cornelius Vanderbilt offered all the steamships of the Atlantic and Pacific Steamship Company, for the service of the Government.

21. East Tennessee Union Convention held at Greenville.

22. The exequator of Mr. Trappman, Prussian Consul at Charleston, revoked by the President, for complicity with the rebels.

23. Balloon observations by Prof. Lowe, at Falls Church, Va.

23. Forty-eight locomotives, and a large quantity of other railway property of the Baltimore and Ohio railway, destroyed by rebels at Martinsburgh, Va.

24. Great fire in Richmond, Va.

24. Riot in Milwaukee, Wis., occasioned by the banks refusing to receive on deposit certain bills comprising an important part of the currency, and their consequent depreciation.

24. Rebel batteries at Mathias Point, Va., shelled by U. S. steamers Pawnee and Freeborn.

24. Engagement of U. S. steamer Monticello, with rebels, at Carter's Creek, Va.

24. Secession of Tennessee proclaimed by Gov. Harris. Vote, 104,913 for, to 47,238 against.

25. Virginia vote announced to be 128,884 for, and 32,134 against secession.

25. Western Virginia government recognized by the President.

26. Address of the Sanitary Commission to the citizens of the United States.

26. Brilliant skirmish of Corp. Hayes and 12 men of Col. Wallace's Indiana regiment, scouting on Patterson Creek, Md.

27. John C. Fremont arrived at Boston from Liverpool, bringing a large quantity of arms for the government.

27. Marshal Kane, of Baltimore, arrested by order of Gen. Banks, and John R. Kenly appointed provost marshal.

27. Engagement between gunboat Freeborn and rebel batteries at Mathias Point. Captain Ward of the Freeborn killed.

27. Cols. Magruder and Hardee appointed brigadier-generals in Confederate army.

27. East Tennessee Union Convention meet at Nashville. Hon. Thomas A. R. Nelson presiding.

28. Skirmish at Shorter's Hill, Virginia. Union loss, 1 killed and 1 wounded; rebel loss, 2 killed.

29. Steamer St. Nicholas and three brigs captured by secessionists on the Chesapeake.

July 1. Gen. Banks arrested Messrs. Howard, Getchell, Hincks, and Davis, late members of Police Board, Baltimore.

1. Skirmish at Farmington, Mo. A large body of rebels routed by 50 Home Guards, under Capt. Cooke.

2. Rebels driven from Martinsburgh, Va., by Abercrombie's brigade, Gen. Patterson's division. Union loss, 3 killed and 10 wounded; rebel loss, 30 killed and wounded, 20 prisoners.

2. Organization of Virginia Legislature, at Wheeling.

3. Gen. Lyon, with 2,000 Federal troops, left Booneville, Mo., for the southwest.

3. Arkansas Military Board called out 10,000 men to repel invasion.

July 4. U. S. Congress met in special session.

4. Passenger trains on Louisville and Nashville railway seized by rebels.

4. Skirmish at Harper's Ferry between N.Y. 9th and rebels. Federal loss, 2 killed and 3 wounded.

4. Rebel battery erected at Mathias Point, Va.

4. Great Union meeting at San Francisco.

5. Battle at Carthage, Mo. Union forces, under Col. Sigel, 1,500; rebels, 4,000. Union loss, 13 killed and 31 wounded; rebel loss, 250 killed and wounded. Successful retreat of Sigel.

5. Skirmish at Newport News, Va., between a detachment of Hawkins' Zouaves and rebels.

4–7. U. S. steamer South Carolina captured or destroyed 11 vessels off Galveston.

6. Western Military Department constituted: Illinois, and the States and Territories west of the Mississippi to the Rocky Mountains, including New Mexico. Maj.-Gen. Fremont commanding.

6. Skirmish of 45 men, 3d Ohio, at Middle Fork Bridge, 12 miles east of Buckhannon, Va. 1 killed and 3 wounded of the Federals, and 7 rebels killed and wounded.

7. " Infernal " machines detected floating in the Potomac.

7. Skirmish at Great Falls, Va. Major Gerhardt's 8th German battalion have 2 men killed. Several rebels killed.

7. Congressman Vallandigham assaulted in the camp of 2d Ohio regiment.

8. Telegraphic dispatches of military operations placed under censorship.

8. Skirmish at Bealington, Western Va., 14th Ohio, and 7th and 9th Indiana, and Col. Barnett's 1st Ohio battery. Rebels defeated with loss of 20 killed, 40 wounded; Union loss, 2 killed, 6 wounded.

10. Loan bill passed by House of Representatives, authorizing the Secretary of the Treasury to borrow $250,000,000, redeemable in 20 years.

10. Postal service discontinued in Middle and West Tennessee.

10. Bill authorizing $500,000 000 and and 500,000 volunteers, to suppress the rebellion passed the Senate.

10. Gen. Banks appointed George R. Dodge police marshal of Baltimore, *vice* Col. Kenly, and removed all the military to positions in the suburbs.

10. House of Representatives empowered the President to close the ports of seceded States.

10. Skirmish at Monroe Station, Mo., between Federal troops, under Col. Smith, and rebels, commanded by Gen. Harris. Rebels routed on the following day, after they had burned 25 railway cars and station house, by Union forces sent to relieve Col. Smith. Several Federals wounded; rebel loss, 30 killed and wounded, and 70 prisoners.

10. Rebel General Wise issued a proclamation to citizens of Western Va., calling for volunteers, and offering pardon for past offences.

10. Skirmish at Laurel Hill, Va. Federal troops under Cols. McCook and Andrews, rebels under Col. Pegram. Rebels defeated. Union loss 1 killed 3 wounded.

11. Alex. H. Stephens' speech, at Augusta, Ga., defending secession, and soliciting contributions to aid the Confederacy.

11. The *State Journal*, at St. Louis, Mo., suppressed by Gen. Lyon for disloyal sentiments.

11. Battle of Rich Mountain, Va. Defeat of the rebels under Col. Pegram, 60 killed, 150 wounded, and 150 prisoners. Capture of 200 tents, 60 wagons, 6 cannon, and other stores. Union loss 11 killed and 35 wounded.

12. Fight at Barboursville, Va. Six companies of Col. Woodruff's 2d Kentucky attack and defeat 600 rebels. 1 Kentuckian and 10 or 12 rebels killed.

12. 600 rebels, under Col. Pegram, surrendered to Gen. McClellan, at Beverly, Va.

12. Twelve of Col. Bendix's N. Y. regiment captured at Newport News.

13. John B. Clark, of Mo., expelled from the House of Representatives, having been found in arms against the Government.

13. Great Union speech of Joseph Holt, at Louisville, Ky.

13. Battle of Carrick's Ford, Va., and death of Gen. Garnett, rebel commander. Defeat and rout of the rebels, with a loss of 150 killed and wounded, and 800 prisoners. Federal loss 13 killed, 40 wounded.

15. Skirmish at Bunker Hill, Va. Rout of rebel cavalry by fire of R. I. battery. The rebels pursued by 2d U S. cavalry.

15. Peace meeting at Nyack, N. Y.

16. Railway cars, containing Union troops, fired into at Millsville, Mo. 3 soldiers killed, 7 wounded; 7 rebels killed.

16. Federal army under Gen. McDowell marched toward Manassas.

16. Bill authorizing the President to call out militia to suppress the rebellion, passed the House of Representatives, and the bill to accept services of 500,000 volunteers.

16. Speech of J. C. Breckinridge in the Senate in opposition to the Union Defence Bill.

16. Tilghman, a negro, killed 3 of a rebel prize crew on the schooner S. J. Wa

ring, and brought the vessel into N. York on the 22d.

17. Advance column of national army occupied Fairfax Court House, Va.

17 Battle at Searytown, Va. Repulse of Federals with loss of 9 killed. 38 wounded. 9 missing. Rebel loss less. 3 Federal colonels and 2 captains captured.

17. Gen. Patterson's army marched from Bunker Hill, Va., to Charlestown.

17. Skirmish at Fulton, Mo. Rebels driven back with loss.

18. Kansas City, Mo., Home Guards, under Major Van Horn, attacked near Harrisonville by a superior force of rebels, whom they defeated, killing and wounding 20. Union loss 1 killed.

18. Battle at Blackburn's Ford. Attack on the rebel entrenchments at Bull Run by a portion of Gen. Tyler's Division, who were repulsed with a loss of 83 men killed, wounded and missing. Rebel loss 68, killed and wounded.

19. Six Federal officers, near Hampton, Va., fired on by rebels in ambush. Major Rawlings killed, and Lieut. Johnson and Mr. Shurtliffe wounded and captured.

19. By Gen. Order No. 46 of War Department, Maj.-Gen. Patterson was honorably discharged, and Maj. Gen. Banks appointed his successor in the Department of the "Shenandoah," and Gen. Dix appointed to succeed Gen. Banks in the Department of Maryland.

19. The Captain-General of Cuba liberated all the vessels brought into Cuban ports by privateer Sumter as prizes.

20. Rebel Congress met at Richmond, Va.

21. Battle of Bull Run.

22. Brig.-Gen. Beauregard promoted to the rank of "General" in the rebel army, the highest grade.

22. Rebel Congress appointed a day of thanksgiving for the victory at Manassas.

22. Maj. Gen. McClellan assigned to command the Department of the Potomac.

22. Missouri State Convention met at Jefferson City.

22. Rebels attacked and dispersed at Forsythe, Mo., by Federal troops under Gen. Sweeny, with loss of two wounded. Rebel loss, 5 killed, 10 wounded.

24. Naval expedition from Fortress Monroe to Black river, by Lieut. Crosby and 300 men. Nine sloops and schooners of the rebels burnt, and one schooner with bacon and corn captured.

25. U. S. steamer Resolute, Lieut. Budd, brought two schooners and one sloop prizes to Washington.

25. Gen. McClellan arrived at Washington, and Gen. Fremont at St. Louis, and Gen. Banks at Harper's Ferry, to take charge of their respective departments.

25. Robert Toombs resigned the Secretaryship of State of the Confederacy, to take office in the army, and R. M. T. Hunter, of Va., was appointed to succeed him.

26. Fifteen Home Guards from Rolla, Mo., were attacked at Lane's Prairie by a superior force of rebels, who were repulsed with the loss of 1 lieutenant killed and 3 men wounded. Two guards were slightly wounded.

26. Three rebels captured by Col. McLeod Murphy, of New York, in Virginia, scouting alone.

28. Flight of Gen. Wise's army from Gauley Bridge, Va., pursued by Gen. Cox, who captured 1000 muskets and a quantity of powder.

28. A detachment of Col. Mulligan's Chicago regiment, aided by Home Guards, captured 28 rebels, 40 horses and 2 teams, at Hickory Hill, Mo.

29. A rebel battery at Aquia Creek, Va., engaged by four U. S. steamers for three hours, with slight damage.

30. Six Government clerks at Washington resigned, owing to a Virginia ordinance of disfranchisement.

30. Three hundred kegs of powder and 6 cannon were captured from the rebels near Warsaw, Mo.

30. The Confederate forces occupied and fortified New Madrid, Mo.

30–31. Missouri State Convention abolished the State Legislature, declared the offices of Governor, Lieut.-Gov. and Sec. of State vacant, appointed special State officers, and provided for a special election by the people in Aug. 1862.

Aug. 1. Rebel privateer Petrel, formerly U. S. revenue cutter Aiken, sunk by U. S. frigate St. Lawrence, near Charleston. Thirty-six out of 40 of her crew were rescued by the frigate's boats.

1. Gov. Gamble, of Mo., delivered his inaugural to the State Convention.

1. Departure of Gen. Fremont's expedition from St. Louis to Cairo and Bird's Point.

2. Fort Fillmore, New Mexico, with 750 men, traitorously surrendered by Major Lynde, U. S. A.

2. Schooner Enchantress, with a valuable cargo, recaptured by U. S. steamer Albatross, Capt. Prentiss, off Charleston, S. C.

2. Defeat of rebel forces at Dug Spring, Mo., by Gen. Lyon. Federal loss, 9 killed, 30 wounded. Rebel loss, 40 killed, 80 wounded.

3. Lieut.-Col. Baylor, commanding the

rebel forces in Arizona, issued a proclamation taking possession of New Mexico, in the name of the Confederate States, declaring all Federal offices vacant, and appointing a secretary, attorney-general and other officers.

Aug. 3. Engagement at Mesila, N. M., between Federal troops and 700 rebels. Capt. McNeely and Lieut. Brooks, of Federal army, were wounded, and 12 rebels killed.

5. The bark Alvarado, having a rebel prize crew, chased ashore near Fernandina, Fla., and burned by sailors from U. S. ship Vincennes.

5. Skirmish at Point of Rocks, Md. Sixty men of New York 28th attacked rebel cavalry, killing 3, wounding 2 and capturing 7 men and 20 horses, without loss themselves.

5. Skirmish at Athens, Mo. 800 Home Guards, under Col. Moore, defeated a force of 1000 rebels, killing 23 and wounding 50. 10 Federals killed and 10 wounded. 5 wagon loads of supplies and 40 horses were captured by the Guards.

5. Election in Kentucky for members of the Legislature, the returns showing a large Union majority.

6. Adjournment *sine die* of Special Congress at Washington.

7. The village of Hampton, Va., was burned by rebel forces under Gen. Magruder. They were prevented from burning the bridge by skirmishers of Max Weber's New York regiment.

7. The privateer York was burned by gunboat Union, which also recaptured the schooner G. V. Baker.

8. Rebel cavalry routed at Lorrettsville, Va., with loss of 1 killed and 5 wounded, by 100 men of 19th N. Y., under Capt. Kennedy.

8 Messrs. Breckinridge and Vallandigham partook of a banquet at the Eutaw House, Baltimore. Mr. Breckinridge, in an attempt to address the people, was prevented by popular clamor.

9. Skirmish at Potosi, Mo. Rebels driven off with loss of 2 killed, 3 wounded.

10. Battle of Wilson's Creek, Mo. The Federal army under Gen. Lyon, 5,200 men, was defeated by the combined forces of Gens. Price and McCulloch, 20,000. Gen. Lyon was killed. Federal loss, 223 killed, 721 wounded, 292 missing. Rebel loss, (McCulloch's report,) 265 killed, 800 wounded, 30 missing; Price's report of Missouri troops, 156 killed, 517 wounded.

12. "Bangor (Me.) Democrat" office destroyed by a mob.

12. C. J. Faulkener, ex-minister of U. S. to France, arrested on a charge of treason.

13. Skirmish near Grafton, Va. 200 rebels routed, 21 killed and wounded, by Capt. Dayton's company of 4th Virginia, without loss.

14. Mutiny in New York 79th regiment, near Washington.

14 Gen. Fremont declares martial law in St. Louis, Mo.

14 "War Bulletin" and "Missourian" journals suppressed at St. Louis.

14. Mutiny of 60 men of 2d Maine at Arlington, Va.; who were arrested and sentenced to be sent to the Dry Tortugas.

14. All loyal men notified by Jeff. Davis to leave the Confederate States in 40 days.

15. Two Federal sailors killed and 2 wounded, of the U. S. steamer Resolute, in a skirmish at Mathias Point, Va.

16. Col Hecker's regiment surprised 400 rebels at Fredericktown, Mo., capturing 12 men and all the camp equipage.

16. Five New York newspapers were presented by the Grand Jury as hostile to the Government.

16. A "Peace" meeting at Saybrook, Conn., broken up.

16. $58,000 seized by U. S. troops at Genevieve, Mo., and taken to St. Louis.

16. Proclamation of Pres. Lincoln, declaring commercial intercourse with the eleven States in rebellion unlawful, excepting such parts thereof as have or may become restored to loyal government, and forfeiting all vessels therefrom or bound to the same, after 15 days.

17. Railway train near Palmyra, Mo., fired into by rebels. One soldier was killed, and several wounded.

18. Privateer Jeff. Davis wrecked on the bar at St. Augustine, Fla.

18. Gen. Wool assumed command at Fortress Monroe.

19. Capt. Haleman with 50 mounted men left Bird's Point for Charleston, Mo., and encountered a body of rebels, killing 2 and capturing 33 men and 35 horses, without any casualty themselves.

19. Skirmish at Charleston, Mo. Two hundred and fifty of 22d Illinois under Col. Dougherty, and Lieut.-Col. Ransom of 11th Illinois defeated 300 rebels under Col. Hunter of Jeff. Thompson's army. 20 rebels were killed and wounded, and 17 prisoners taken. The Union loss was 1 killed and 6 wounded.

19. Two hundred and forty Union fugitives from E. Tenn. arrived at Danville, Ky., and were fed in the Seminary yard.

19. Office of the "Sentinel," Easton, Pa., destroyed by a Union mob.

19. A. L. Kimball, editor of the "Essex Co. Democrat," Haverhill, Mass., was tarred

and feathered, and ridden on a rail by a Union mob.

19. "Passports" required, by notice from the Department of State, from all persons leaving or arriving within the United States.

19. Office of the "Jeffersonian," Westchester, Pa., destroyed by a Union mob.

19. Office of "The People's Friend," at Covington, Ind., destroyed by a Union mob.

20. Skirmish at Hawk's Nest, in the Kanawha Valley, Va. A body of rebels attacked the 11th Ohio, but were driven back with loss. Union loss, 2 wounded and 1 missing.

20. The Wheeling (Va.) Convention passed an ordinance to erect a new State, to be called Kanawha.

20. A railway train from Jefferson City, Mo., when near Lookout Station, was fired into by rebels, and 1 soldier killed and 6 wounded. 2 rebels were killed, several wounded, and 5 prisoners taken.

20. Gen. McClellan assumed command of the army of the Potomac.

20. Gen. Butler assumed command of U.S. Volunteer forces near Fortress Monroe.

21. Surprise of part of company K, Ohio 7th, near Cross Lane, W. Virginia, 2 killed and 9 wounded, 5 of whom were taken prisoners, including Capt. Shutte.

22. Disloyal papers were rejected from the U. S. mails. Large bundles of papers were seized by the U. S. Marshals in Philadelphia and other cities.

22. The "Stark County Democrat" office, in Canton, Ohio, was destroyed by a Union mob.

22. The steamer "Samuel Orr" was seized at Paducah, Ky., by rebels, and taken up the Tennessee river.

24. A portion of the Cherokee Indians made an alliance with the "Southern Confederacy." The Cherokees and Creeks raised 2,000 men for the rebel army, and were promised payment of their annuities by the Confed. Commissioners.

24. Arrest of Mayor Berret, of Washington.

24. The office of the Bridgeport (Conn.,) "Farmer" was destroyed by a Union mob.

24. Office of the "Alleghanian," Cumberland, Md., was destroyed by a Union mob.

25. A band of rebels at Wayne Court-House, Va., was routed by 53 Federals under Capt. Smith, from Camp Pierpont, Ceredo, Wayne co., Va. 4 rebels were killed, and 8 taken prisoners.

25. All vessels and boats on the Potomac seized by Government authorities.

25. Gov. H. R. Gamble, of Mo., issued a call for 42,000 State militia, to serve six months, unless sooner discharged.

26. Surprise of 7th Ohio, Col. Tyler, at Cross Lanes, near Summersville, W. Virginia, by a large force of rebels. 15 killed, 40 wounded, and 30 prisoners. Rebel loss not known.

26. The War Department prohibited the transmission or publication of any intelligence of army or naval movements calculated to give information to the enemy.

26. The Postmaster-General directed postal agents to arrest express agents or others engaged in transmitting letters to seceded States in violation of the President's proclamation of 16th inst.

26. Com. Foote ordered to the command of U. S. naval forces on the Western waters.

26. A naval and military expedition to N. Carolina coast sailed from Hampton Roads, Va., under command of Com. Stringham and Maj.-Gen. Butler.

26. Skirmish of two companies of N. Y. 23d, with a large force of rebels at Ball's Cross Roads, Va. One Federal killed, and one wounded.

28. A party of Federal troops under Capt. Smith attacked and dispersed a force of rebels at Wayne Court-House, W. Virginia, and returned to Ceredo without loss. Five or 6 of the rebels were killed or wounded, and 8 captured.

28–29. Bombardment and capture of Forts Hatteras and Clark, at Hatteras Inlet, N. C. 30 pieces of cannon, 1,000 stand of arms, 3 vessels with valuable cargoes, and 750 prisoners were taken.

29. Fight at Lexington, Mo. The rebels, under Col. Reed, were driven off with loss of 8 killed and several wounded. The Federals had 5 or 6 wounded, and several loyal citizens were captured.

30. Martial law was proclaimed throughout Missouri, by Gen. Fremont, and the slaves of all persons found in arms against the U. S. declared free.

Sept. 1. Skirmish at Bennett's Mills, Mo. Attack on Home Guards commanded by Lieut. Chandler, by a large force of rebels. Federal loss, 3 killed, 6 wounded. Rebel loss unknown.

1. Fight at Boone Court-House, Va. Rebels defeated, with a loss of 30. Six Federal soldiers wounded.

2. Fight near Fort Scott, Mo. 600 rebels under Gen. Rains, were attacked and pursued by 500 Federals under Col. Montgomery. The rebels falling back on reinforcements, Montgomery retreated.

2. The Mass. 13th captured 20 Charleston, S. C., cavalry, after killing 3 and wounding 5, 2½ miles from Harper's Ferry.

2. Col. Crossman, of Gen. Kelly's staff, with two companies, attacked 400 rebels,

at Worthington, Marion co., Va., by whom he was repulsed with the loss of two men.

Sept. 3. Passenger train on the Hannibal and St. Joseph railway, Mo., was thrown into the Platte river, by the giving way of a bridge, partly burned by the rebels. 17 persons were killed, and 60 wounded.

4. An engagement on the Mississippi river occurred, near Hickman, Ky., between national gunboats Tyler and Lexington and the rebel gunboat Yankee and shore batteries.

6. Paducah, Ky., was occupied by Federal forces under Gen. Grant.

7. Gens. Pillow and Polk occupied Columbus, Ky., with 7,000 rebels.

7. Five schooners were captured by Federal officers at Hatteras Inlet.

8. Gen. Pope broke up a camp of 3,000 rebels near Hunneville, Mo., under Gen. Green, and captured a large quantity of stores.

9. A revolt occurred among the N. Y. Rifles, at Willett's Point, N. Y. Two men were killed and 5 wounded.

9. A government steamer conveying prisoners from Lexington, Mo., to Fort Leavenworth, broke her rudder, and being obliged to land, the vessel was seized by the rebels, the prisoners liberated, and 40 Federal soldiers captured.

10. 156 Union prisoners, among them all the principal officers held captive by the rebels at Richmond, were sent to Castle Pinckney, in Charleston harbor.

10. Battle of Carnifex Ferry, near Summersville, Va. Federal commander, Rosecranz, rebel, Floyd, who retreated with small loss. Federal loss, 16 killed, 102 wounded.

11. Skirmish at Lewinsville, Va. Federal loss, 6 killed, 10 wounded.

11. The President modified Gen. Fremont's emancipation proclamation.

11. The Kentucky Legislature, by a vote of 71 to 26, ordered the Confederate troops to leave the State.

12. A rebel camp at Petersburg, Hardy co., Va., was broken up by Capt. Kid's cavalry, and large amount of stores captured.

12. Skirmish at Black river, near Ironton, Mo. A detachment of Indiana cavalry, under Major Gavitt, defeated a body of rebels, under Ben. Talbot, killing 5, capturing 4, and 25 horses and a quantity of arms.

12. The Legislature of Kentucky authorized the Governor to call out the State military to repel the Southern invaders.

12. Two slaves, the property of T. L. Snead, a secessionist of St. Louis, were manumitted by Gen. Fremont.

13. A large body of rebels, under Col. Brown, were repulsed from Booneville, Mo., with a loss of 12 killed and 30 wounded, by Home Guards under Capt. Eppstein, who lost 1 killed and 4 wounded.

12–14. Two engagements occurred on Cheat Mountain, Western Va., in which the rebels, under Gen. R. E. Lee, were defeated with a loss of 100 killed and wounded, among the former, Col. J. A. Washington, and 20 prisoners. The Federal forces, under Gen. J. J. Reynolds, lost 13 killed, 20 wounded, and 60 prisoners.

13–18. The provost marshal of Baltimore, Md., arrested Mayor Brown, Ross Winans, and Messrs. Pitts, Sangster, Wallis, Scott, Dennison, Quinlan, Lynch, Warfield, Hanson, and J. C. Brune, of the Legislature, also editors Howard and Hall, by order of the War Department.

13. An expedition from the U.S. frigate Colorado, under Lieut. J. H. Russell, cut out and destroyed the privateer Judah, under the rebel guns at Pensacola. The Federal loss was 3 killed and 15 wounded.

14. A rebel camp near Kansas City, Mo., was broken up; 7 men killed and 6 taken prisoners.

18. Col. F. P. Blair, Jr, was arrested at St. Louis for disrespectful language when alluding to superior officers.

15. A body of rebels attacked Col. Geary's 28th Pennsylvania regiment, stationed on the Potomac, three miles above Harper's Ferry, and were repulsed with severe loss. One of Col. Geary's men was killed, and several slightly wounded.

16. A naval expedition from Hatteras Inlet under command of Lieut. J. Y. Maxwell, destroyed Fort Ocracoke, on Beacon Island, N. C.

16. The Federal gunboat Conestoga captured the steamers V. R. Stephenson and Gazelle, on Cumberland river, Ky.

16. Ship Island, near the mouth of the Mississippi river, was occupied by Federal forces from the steamer Massachusetts.

17. A fight took place at Mariatown, Mo., between 600 Federals, under Cols. Montgomery and Johnson, and 400 rebels, who were defeated with a loss of 7 killed, and 100 horses and their tents and supplies captured. Col. Johnson and 2 Federal privates were killed, and 6 wounded.

17. A train on the Ohio and Mississippi railway, with a part of the 19th Illinois regiment, broke through a bridge near Huron, Ind., by which 26 soldiers were killed and 112 wounded.

17. 500 of the 3d Iowa, under Lieut.-Col. Scott, attacked and were repulsed by 3,000 rebels, under Gen. D. R. Atchison, at

Blue Mills Landing, Mo. The Federal loss was over 100 in killed and wounded.

18. Skirmish at Barboursville, Ky., between the Home Guard and Zollicoffer's men. 7 rebels were killed, and 1 guard wounded and another taken prisoner.

18. Eighteen secession members of the Maryland Legislature were arrested and lodged in Fort McHenry.

19. Ex-Governor Morehead and others, of Louisville, Ky., were arrested by the U. S. marshal on charges of treason, or complicity with treason.

20. Surrender of Col. Mulligan's command, at Lexington, Mo., to the rebel Gen. Price, after 4 days' siege.

21. Gen. Lane's command surprised a superior force of rebels at Papinsville, Mo., routing them with a Union loss of 17 killed and 10 wounded; rebel loss, 40 killed, 100 prisoners, and all their tents and supplies.

21. Two detachments of troops from Union gunboats, near Glasgow, Mo., encountered each other, while reconnoitering at night, and by mistake four were killed and several wounded.

21. Gen. Robert Anderson assumed command of Federal and State troops in Ky.

21. J. C. Breckinridge fled from Frankfort, Ky., and openly joined the rebels.

22. Skirmish of the 7th Iowa, at Elliott's Mills, Ky., with rebel cavalry, who were defeated with the loss of three of their number.

23. Ross Winans, of Md., took the oath of allegiance.

23. Capt. Goldsborough succeeded Com. Stringham in command of the Chesapeake blockading fleet.

23. Detachments of 8th and 4th Ohio, and Ringgold's cavalry, under Cols. Parke and Cantwell, advancing from New Creek toward Romney, Va., attacked and drove out 700 rebels from Mechanicsville Gap, and pursued their combined forces of 1,400 from Romney to the mountains. Federal loss 3 killed, 10 wounded; rebel loss 15 killed, 30 wounded.

24. The Comte de Paris and the Duc de Chartres, grandsons of Louis Philippe of France, were attached as aids to Gen. McClellan's staff, and commissioned as captains.

25. Successful expedition of 3,000 men, under Gen. W. F. Smith, for reconnoitering and forage, from Chain Bridge to Lewinsville, Va. A large quantity of stores were captured.

25. Engagement at Chapmansville, Western Va. Col. Pratt, with 560 of the 34th Ohio, defeated a body of rebels under Col. J. W. Davis, killing 29, including their commander, and wounding a large number. Col. Pratt's loss was 4 killed, 8 wounded.

25. A body of rebels were defeated near Osceola, Mo., by Federal troops under Col. Montgomery, who set fire to the town. 10 rebels killed; 1 Federal killed, 4 wounded.

25. James B. Clay (son of the illustrious Henry,) and 16 other rebels were captured near Danville, Ky., while on their way to Zollicoffer's camp.

26. At Lucas Bend, Ky., 75 of Captain Stewart's cavalry attacked and routed 40 rebel cavalry, killing 4 and capturing 5, without loss themselves.

26. By Presidential proclamation of August 12, this day was observed as a day of fasting and prayer throughout the loyal States.

27. A body of Kansas troops, under Montgomery and Jamison, engaged the advance guard of McCulloch's rebel army near Shanghai, in Benton co., Mo., and drove them back with loss.

27. Gen. Fremont, with 15 steamers and 15,000 men, sailed from St. Louis up the Missouri river.

27. The rebels evacuated Munson's Hill, Va., which was occupied by Federal troops.

28. Baker's California regiment, and Baxter's Philadelphia volunteers mistook each other for rebels, at Fall's Church, Va., and fired, killing 15 and wounding 30.

Oct. 1. The U. S. steamer Fanny, with 35 men of the 9th N. Y. volunteers, was captured by the rebels on the north coast of Hatteras Inlet. She was loaded with government stores.

2. A secessionist camp at Charleston, Mo., was broken up, and 40 rebels captured.

2. $33,000, deposited in the St. Louis Building and Savings Association, for the part payment of a U. S. annuity to the Cherokee Indians, declared confiscated to the Government in consequence of the secession of that tribe.

3. Attack on an entrenched camp commanded by Gen. H. A. Jackson, at Greenbrier, Western Va., by Union forces under Gen. J. J. Reynolds. Union loss 8 killed, 32 wounded; rebel loss greater. A drawn battle.

3. Gen. Price, and the rebel army under his command, withdrew from Lexington, Mo., leaving a brigade as a guard.

3. Gustavus Smith, formerly Street Commissioner of New York, was appointed a Major-General in the rebel army.

4. Commander Alden, U. S. steamer South Carolina, captured two schooners off the S.W. Pass of the Mississippi, with four to five thousand stand of arms.

4. A company of 110 Texas rangers were

defeated by 100 U. S. troops from Fort Craig, at Alimosa, N. M. 10 Texans and their captain killed, and 30 wounded.

Oct. 4. Two boats from U. S. steamer Louisiana, Lieut. A. Murray, destroyed a rebel schooner, being fitted out for a privateer, at Chincoteague Inlet, Va. They engaged and repulsed the rebels with a loss of 4 U. S. seamen wounded.

4. A large force of rebels, under Col. Wright, attacked the 20th Indiana, Col. Brown, at Chicamacomico, near Hatteras Inlet. Federals retreated, leaving their pickets, wounded, and camp equipage in the hands of the enemy.

4. Gen. Butler, commanding the Military Department of New England, had his head-quarters at Boston.

5. The rebel forces under Col. Wright were driven from the Chicamacomico with severe loss, by U.S. steamer Monticello.

7. John Ross, principal Chief of the Cherokee Indians, negotiated a treaty of alliance on behalf of that people with the Confederate Government.

7. 57 released prisoners, taken by the rebels at the battle of Bull Run, arrived at Fortress Monroe from Richmond.

7. U. S. gunboats Tyler and Lexington exchanged shots with rebel batteries at Iron Bend, 3 miles above Columbus, Ky.

8. Brig.-Gen. William T. Sherman appointed to command the Department of the Cumberland (Kentucky), in place of Brig.-Gen. R. Anderson, retired from ill-health.

8. 200 rebels under Capt. Holliday, encamped two miles from Hillsboro', Ky., were attacked and defeated by a body of Home Guards, under Lieut. Sadler. Rebel loss 11 killed, 29 wounded, 22 prisoners; also 127 rifles and other arms. Federal loss 3 killed, 3 wounded.

9. Attack upon Wilson's N. Y. Zouaves, at Santa Rosa Island, four miles from Fort Pickens, at 2 A. M., by 1,500 rebels under Gen. Anderson. The regulars from Fort Pickens, and the Zouaves, defeated the rebels, killing and wounding about 100, and taking 35 prisoners. Federal loss 13 killed, 21 wounded.

9. Federal troops under Gen. Smith advanced from Chain Bridge, and occupied Lewinsville, Va.

10. Cavalry skirmish 4 miles from Paducah, Ky. 2 of the 4th U. S. cavalry mortally wounded, and 2 taken prisoners.

11. The rebel steamer Nashville, commanded by Lieut. R. B. Pegram, escaped from Charleston, S. C.

11. Lieut. Harrell, of U. S. steamer Union, with three boats' crews, cut out and burnt a rebel schooner in Dumfries Creek, on the Potomac, and escaped without loss.

11. Missouri State Convention met at St. Louis.

11. Marshal Kane was transferred from Fort McHenry to Fort Lafayette.

12. Rebel steamer Theodora ran the blockade at Charleston, S. C., having on board Messrs. Mason and Slidell, Commissioners to England and France, with their secretaries.

12. Capt. P. G. Morton captured a train of 21 wagons, 425 cattle, and 35 prisoners, with stores for hostile Cherokees, at Chelsea, Kansas.

12. Cavalry skirmish south of Cameron, Ray co., Mo. A company of Major James' cavalry routed a large body of rebels, who lost 8 killed and 5 prisoners. One Federal was killed and 4 wounded.

12. Six rebel gunboats, the ram Manassas, and a fleet of fireships, attacked the U. S. fleet at the mouth of the Mississippi, and were repulsed by them with slight loss on either side.

12. A party of 12 of a N.Y. Zouave regiment, under Lieut. Zeller, were captured by the rebels near Newport News, Va.

12. Forty men of the 39th Indiana attacked and defeated a superior force of rebels, 8 miles from Green river, Western Va., without loss themselves, killing 5 and wounding 3 of the enemy.

12. Night skirmish near the residence of Cy. Hutchinson, Barren co., Ky. Ten Federal horsemen, under Cols. Hobson and Pennebraker, and Capt. S. Taylor, encountered 100 rebel cavalry, of whom 4 were killed and several wounded. Federal loss, 3 killed.

12. 500 men of the Piatt (Cincinnati) Zouaves, under Lieut.-Col. Toland, and two companies of the 4th Va., drove out a large body of rebels from Winfield, 20 miles below Charleston, on the Kanawha, Western Va., who had been committing depredations. The Federals captured a large quantity of military stores.

12. Skirmish between a detachment of the 39th Indiana, under Lieut.-Col. Jones, and 58 rebel cavalry, near Upton's, 14 miles below Camp Nevin, Ky. The rebels were repulsed with a loss of 5 killed and 3 wounded.

12. A woman and five children, from families of U. S. soldiers from Utah, were drowned while attempting to cross the Platte river on a raft, near St. Josephs, Mo., the rope having been cut by an enemy.

13. Eighteen miles N.E. of Lebanon, Mo., Major Wright, with two companies of U.S. cavalry, routed 300 mounted rebels, under Capts. Lorrels and Wright. 62 of the reb-

els were killed and wounded, and 30 taken prisoners. One Federal trooper was killed.

13. Skirmish at Beckwith's farm, 12 miles S.E. of Bird's Point, Mo. 20 men under Lieut. Tufts, encountered a superior force of rebels, and after engaging them retired. 2 were killed, 5 wounded, and 3 missing, of the national force; 12 were killed and wounded of the rebels.

13. Brig Grenada, of New York, was captured by the privateer "Sallie," of Charleston, which ran the blockade on the 10th instant.

14. 150 voters of Chincoteague Island, Accomac co., Va., took the oath of allegiance to the U. S., in the presence of Lieut. Murray, of U. S. ship Louisiana. The inhabitants of the island, 1,000 in number, were loyal; no other flag than the national had thus far been allowed to float on the island.

14. Major White, with one company of Missouri Scouts, captured 45 rebels at Linn Creek, Mo., commanded by Capt. Roberts.

14. The U. S. Secretary of State, Wm. H. Seward, issued a circular to the Governors of all States bordering on the ocean and the lakes, recommending that their defences should be put in effective condition to meet the contingency of foreign war, instigated by rebel emissaries.

15. U. S. steamer Roanoke, off Charleston, captured and burnt the ship Thomas Watson, which ran on Stono reef while attempting to evade the blockade.

15. Ten of the N. Y. 14th killed 2 rebels in a skirmish near Lewinsville, Va.

15. Gen. Wool, at Fortress Monroe, declined to receive a flag of truce from Norfolk.

15. 600 rebels, under Gen. Jeff. Thompson, attacked and captured 40 U. S. soldiers guarding the Big river bridge, near Potosi, Mo. Federal loss 1 killed, 6 wounded; rebel loss 5 killed, 4 wounded. The rebels paroled the U. S. soldiers and burnt the bridge.

15. The rebel batteries at Aquia creek and Shipping Point, on the Potomac, fired on all vessels passing, but inflicted no serious damage.

15. Three U. S. steamers sailed from New York in pursuit of the privateer Nashville.

16. Col. J. W. Geary, of the Penn. 28th, with 400 men from his own, the 13th Mass. and 3d Wis., crossed the Potomac at Harper's Ferry, and captured 21,000 bushels of wheat, stored in a mill near Bolivar Heights. A severe skirmish occurred with a body of rebels who disputed the ground, from whom the Federals captured a 32-pounder, and made good their retreat, accomplishing the object of the expedition. Federal loss, 4 killed, 8 wounded.

16. Major F. J. White, with 220 Missouri scouts, surprised the rebels at Lexington, Mo., and without loss, captured 60 or 70 prisoners, released Cols. White and Grover, and 12 other captives, and seized 2 steamboats, with arms, ammunition and stores.

16. 1,000 rebels under Gen. Thompson and Col. Lowe, near Ironton, Mo., were defeated with a loss of 36 killed and wounded, by Maj. Gavitt's Indiana cavalry, and 5 companies of Col. Alexander's 21st Illinois. Union loss, 11.

19. Col. Morgan, with 220 men of the 18th Missouri regiment, and two pieces of artillery, defeated 400 rebels on Big Hurricane Creek, Carroll co., Mo., killing 14, and taking 8 prisoners. Col. Morgan had 14 men wounded—two mortally.

19. Twenty rebel N. C. prisoners were sent to Fortress Monroe, to be released on taking an oath not to bear arms against the Government.

21. Battle of Edward's Ferry, Va. 1,900 men from Gen. C. P. Stone's division, under command of Col. E. D. Baker, U. S. senator from Oregon, were ordered to cross the Potomac at Harrison's Island, or Ball's Bluff, to support reconnoissances above and below that point. At 4 P. M. they were attacked by 3,000 rebels under Gen. Evans, and driven to the river bank, where, there being no adequate provision for crossing, they suffered severe loss, by the enemy's fire, and by drowning. Killed, 223, wounded, 250, taken prisoners, 500. Rebel loss about 200 in killed and wounded.

21. About 2,500 rebels, near Fredericktown, Mo., under Jeff. Thompson and Col. Lowe, were attacked by 3,500 Federal troops, commanded by Col. J. B. Plummer, of 11th Missouri, with Missouri, Illinois, Wisconsin and Indiana troops, under Cols. Ross, Marsh, Hovey, Baker, Lieut.-Col. Pennabaker, Maj. Schofield, Capt. Stewart and Lieut. White. The rebels were defeated with great loss, and Col. Lowe was killed. They left 175 bodies on the field, and had a large number wounded. Eighty were taken prisoners, and 4 heavy guns were captured. The Federal loss was 7 killed and 60 wounded.

21. A portion of the rebel General Zollicoffer's command was repulsed from an advanced position of General Schoepf's brigade, near Camp Wild Cat, Laurel co., Ky. The Federal loss was 4 killed and 21 wounded.

22. Flag-officer Craven, of the Potomac flotilla, reported the Potomac river com-

manded by rebel batteries, at all important points below Alexandria.

Oct. 22. A detachment of U. S. cavalry broke up a rebel camp at Buffalo Mills, Benton co., Mo., killing and wounding 20, taking 60 prisoners, 22 wagons and a number of horses.

23. Col. Len. Harris, with the 2d Ohio, two guns of Capt. Konkle's Ohio battery and Capt. Laughlin's cavalry, drove out a body of 200 rebels from West Liberty, Morgan co., Ky., after a skirmish in which 10 were killed, 5 wounded, and 6 made prisoners, of the rebels, with no loss on the part of the Federals. A small quantity of stores was captured.

23. Fifty men of the 6th Indiana while skirmishing near Hodgesvillé, Ky., were attacked by a superior force of rebels, whom they repulsed, killing 3 and wounding 5. Three of the Federals were severely wounded, including Lieut. Grayson, their commander.

23 Gen. Fred. W. Lander was appointed to command the brigade of the late Col. Baker.

24. President Lincoln suspended the writ of *habeas corpus*, so far as related to military arrests, in the District of Columbia.

24. The steamer Salvor was captured while attempting to run the blockade at Tampa Bay, Fla.

24. Western Virginia voted almost unanimously in favor of a division of the State.

24 The western section of the California telegraph was completed to Salt Lake City, connecting the wires from the Pacific to the Atlantic ocean.

24. Skirmish between the pickets of Gen. Wm. T. Ward and a scouting party of rebels near Campbellsville, Ky. Several of the rebels were killed and wounded, and their captain taken prisoner.

25. 160 of Gen. Fremont's Body-guard, under command of Major Zagonyi, charged 2,000 rebels, drawn up to receive them, near Springfield, Mo., routed them, and occupied the town. Rebel loss, 106 killed, many wounded, and 27 prisoners. Zagonyi's loss, 15 killed, 27 wounded, 10 missing. The Missouri "Prairie Scouts," under Maj. F. J. White, attacked the rear of the rebel force, at the same time, making three successful charges, and inflicting severe loss on the enemy. The loss of the "Scouts" was 33 in killed, wounded and missing.

26. An artillery fight across the Potomac, at Edward's Ferry, for several hours. Two killed in Gen. Banks' encampment, and 3 wounded. Both parties were compelled to move back their encampments.

26. Gen. B. F. Kelly, with 2,500 Virginia and Ohio Volunteers, from New Creek, Va., attacked an inferior rebel force near Romney, who were routed and pursued through that town with severe loss. Col. Thos. Johns, of 2d regiment, Potomac Home Brigade, made a diversion of the enemy's force, by marching to the rear of Romney, by way of Frankfort, and engaged and held in check a regiment of the rebels. The expedition was successful in capturing a large supply of military stores and provisions. Federal loss, 2 killed, 14 wounded. Rebel loss, 10 killed, 15 wounded, and a number of prisoners, including Col. Angus McDonald, their commander: their artillery wagons, camps, etc., were captured.

26. Parson Brownlow was forced to suspend the publication of the Knoxville (Tenn.) *Whig*.

26. A wagon train was established between Baltimore and Washington, for want of sufficient railway facilities, consequent on the danger from rebel batteries in navigating the Potomac.

26. Major Phillips, with 300 of the 9th Illinois, from Paducah, sailed on the steamer Conestoga to West Eddyville, Ky., on the Cumberland river, where they landed and marched 6 miles to Saratoga, and surprised a detachment of rebel cavalry, under Capt. Wilcox. After a brief resistance the enemy fled, losing 13 killed, many wounded, 24 prisoners, and 52 horses. Four of the Illinois men were wounded.

26. Surprise of a rebel encampment at Plattsburg, Clinton co., Mo., by a superior force of Federals. Rebel loss, 8 killed, 12 prisoners, one cannon, and a quantity of small arms.

28. Three rebel vessels were surprised and burnt at Chincoteague Inlet, Va., by a portion of the crew of U. S. gunboat Louisiana, under Lieut. A Hopkins.

28. D. Davis, of Ill., J. Holt, of Ky., and H. Campbell, of Mo., were appointed Commissioners by Pres. Lincoln to audit all unsettled military claims in Missouri.

29. 250 U.S. Kentucky volunteers, under Col. Burbridge, marched from Owensboro' to Morgantown, Ky., crossed the river at that point, defeated a superior rebel force and destroyed their camp. Federal loss, 2 wounded.

28. Gen. J. B. Henderson, with a superior force, surrounded and captured 400 rebels at Dyer's Mills, near Concord, Mo. They were allowed to lay down their arms and return home.

29. Nearly 100 "contrabands" arrived at Fortress Monroe in two days.

29. Rebel State "Conference" at Russellville, Ky.

29. The great naval expedition sailed from Fortress Monroe, under the command of Flag-officer Com. Samuel F. Dupont, comprising 77 vessels of all classes. The land forces, numbering 20,000 men, were commanded by Brig.-Gen. Thos. W. Sherman.

31. Skirmish at Morgantown, Green River, Ky. Col. McHenry's command drove a party of rebels attached to Buckner's camp across the river, with loss.

31. At N. York, the jury empaneled for the trial of the sailors captured on the privateer Savannah, the first rebel armed vessel that was commissioned, failed to agree.

Nov. 1. Lieut.-Gen. Winfield Scott, at his own request, was retired from active service, and Maj.-Gen. George B. McClellan was appointed to succeed him as Commander-in-chief of the U. S. army.

1. Lieut.-Col. Morse, with 450 cavalry and infantry, surprised and routed a rebel force 800 strong, under Col. Sweeny, in camp near Renick, Randolph co., Mo.

1. Rebels from Gen. Floyd's command attacked a Federal camp at Gauley Bridge, Va., by cannonading from the opposite shore. They were driven into the hills by 3 companies from Gen. Benham's camp, at Hawk's Nest.

1. A violent storm overtook the naval expedition off the N. C. coast 3 vessels were disabled and returned, 2 were driven ashore, and 2 foundered. Seven lives lost.

2. Gen. Fremont, at Springfield, received an order from Washington, relieving him from command of the Department of Missouri. Gen. Hunter was appointed temporarily to the command.

2. An address was issued by Gov. Harris, of Tenn., calling upon the people to furnish every shot-gun and rifle to defend the soil.

2. Major Joseph's Missouri militia, numbering 129, were attacked at Platte City, Mo., by Silas Gordon with 300 rebels, who were repulsed with a loss of 13 killed and wounded, 30 prisoners, many guns, and all their equipments.

2. The English steamer Bermuda ran the blockade at Charleston, S. C., with 2,000 bales of cotton.

2. Prestonburg, Ky., was occupied by Union troops under Gen. Nelson, without opposition.

3. *et seq.* Rising of Union men in E. Tenn., who burned or broke down several important railroad bridges.

3. Five rebel boats made an attack on Fort Hatteras, N. C., but were repulsed by the U. S. gunboat National, and the Fort.

3 Col. Greensle drove rebel troops from Houston, Mo., and returned to Rolla with several prisoners and a large amount of property.

4. Enthusiastic Union meeting in Baltimore Co., Md., addressed by Reverdy Johnson.

4. Barbourville, Ky., was occupied by 1,500 Federals without opposition.

6. Extra session of South Carolina Legislature adjourned, after choosing Presidential electors and ordering the banks to loan the State $300,000.

5. Colonel Corcoran and 15 other national officers who were prisoners, were selected by lot by the rebels, as hostages, to be hung in the event of that punishment being awarded to the privateers held by the national government.

6. Two parties of rebel troops met above Newport News, Va., and by mistake fired on each other, killing and wounding a number. Among the killed was Major Bailey, of Mobile.

6. The grand jury at Frankfort, Ky., found indictments for treason against 32 prominent citizens, among whom were R. J. Breckinridge, Jr., J. C. Breckinridge, Humphrey Marshall, and Benj. Desha.

6. Electors for President and V. President were chosen throughout the revolted States, and also members of Congress.

6. 120 Federals, under Capt. Shields, were captured by 500 rebels near Little Santa Fé, Mo. They were on their way to join Gen. Fremont's column.

6. The 13th Indiana regiment, Col. J. J. Sullivan, and Capt. Robinson's Ohio cavalry, returned to Huttonsville, Va., from an extensive march through Webster Co. Several rebels were killed and wounded in scouting, and 13 prisoners taken.

7. Battle of Belmont, Mo., Gens. Grant and McClernand with 2,850 men, landed at Belmont at 8 A.M., drove in the rebel pickets and captured their camp, which was burnt. A battery of 12 guns was taken, and about 200 prisoners. Meantime, a large reinforcement of rebels was landed from Columbus, on the opposite side of the river, which intercepted Gen. Grant's army in their return to their boats. The Federals cut their way through a much superior force of the enemy, losing 150 of their number prisoners, together with their killed and wounded, who fell into the hands of the rebels. Federal loss, 89 killed, 150 wounded, 150 missing. The rebel loss was greater, 155 were taken prisoners.

7. Gen. Hunter, Fremont's successor in Missouri, repudiated the agreement just made between Gens. Fremont and Price, the rebel commander, concerning the privi-

leges of unarmed citizens, and the disarming of unrecognized bodies of men.

Nov. 7. Skirmishing on New river, near Gauley Bridge, Va. Federal forces under Gen. Rosecrans, drove off a body of rebels who had besieged his camp for several days. Several rebels and one private of 13th Ohio killed.

7. The Federal fleet under Com. Dupont captured Forts Warren and Beauregard at Port Royal entrance, and took the town of Beaufort, S. C., with a loss of 8 killed, 6 badly wounded, and 17 slightly. None of the national vessels seriously damaged. Rebel loss unknown, but not large.

7. Two launches and 40 men, commanded by Lieut. Jas. E. Jouett, from the U.S. frigate Santee, off Galveston, Texas, surprised and burnt the rebel privateer Royal Yacht, by night, after a sharp conflict, killing several of the rebels, and capturing 13. Federal loss 2 killed and 7 wounded.

8. U. S. gunboat Resene shelled out a rebel battery at Urbana Creek, on the Rappahannock, Va., and captured a large schooner with stores.

8. Five railway bridges were burned in E. Tennessee by Unionists.

8. Capt. Wilkes, with the U. S. steam sloop-of-war San Jacinto, overhauled the English mail steamer Trent in the Bahama channel, and took from her the rebel emissaries Mason and Slidell, with their secretaries, who had taken passage for England.

8. Col. Greusle returned with his command to Rolla, Mo., from an expedition against the rebels in Texas co., bringing 9 prisoners, 500 head of cattle and 40 horses and mules.

8. A portion of Gen. Nelson's Ky. brigade were ambuscaded while on their way to Piketon, Ky., by 200 rebels in a strong position. The rebels were dispersed with the loss of 10 killed, 15 wounded. Gen. Nelson had 6 killed and 24 wounded. Another portion of Gen. Nelson's brigade under command of Col. Sill, reached Piketon by a circuitous route, and attacked a body of rebels, defeating them with a small loss, and having one Federal soldier killed.

8. A bridge on the E. Tenn. railway, 200 feet span, was destroyed by Unionists. Also 4 on the line N. of Knoxville, and a heavy wooden bridge at Charleston, Bradley co., Tenn.

9. Maj.-Gen. Henry W. Halleck, of Cal., was ordered to take command of the Department of Missouri, in place of Gen. Fremont: Brig.-Gen. Don Carlos Buell, of Ind., was appointed to command the Department of Kentucky: Maj.-Gen. Hunter to command the Department of Kansas: Col. E. R. S. Canley, the Department of N. Mexico.

10. A band of rebel marauders was captured by Lieut. Shriver, with a squad of 1st Iowa cavalry, near Clark's Station, Mo.

10. A portion of Gen. Cox's brigade crossed the New river near Gauley, Va., and attacked Floyd's forces posted there, who retreated after a severe skirmish, in which the 11th Ohio regiment lost 8 killed and 10 wounded.

10. 150 of the 9th Virginia regiment, Col. K. V. Whaley, were surprised at Guyandotte, Va., on the Ohio river, by a superior force of rebels, and after a sharp skirmish, in which 8 of the Federals were killed and 12 wounded, and nearly the same loss sustained by the rebels, Col. Whaley and 45 of his men were captured, and the rest escaped. About two-thirds of the town was burned next day by the Union Virginia and Ohio troops who arrived there, in retaliation for the treachery and cruelty of the rebel inhabitants evinced in the scenes of the engagement.

11. At Columbus, Ky., two rebel lieutenants and six privates were killed by the explosion of a Dahlgren gun. Rev. Maj.-Gen. Polk narrowly escaped.

11. 110 of Col. Anthony's regiment attacked a rebel camp on the Little Blue river, near Kansas City, Mo., which proved too strong for them, and after severe fight, Col. Anthony's men were drawn off in good order, losing 8 killed and 8 wounded.

12. Reconnoissance in force by Gen. Heintzelman, with 6,000 men, to Occoquan Creek, Va., 18 miles from Alexandria. Capt. Todd's company of Lincoln cavalry were surprised by a superior force of rebels, 3 killed, 1 wounded and 3 taken prisoners, including the captain,

12. Attack on the U.S. fleet at the Passes of the Mississippi, by the Manassas Ram, 5 gunboats and several fire ships, under command of Capt. Hollins. U. S. ship Vincennes grounded, and the Richmond was damaged by the ram and also grounded: but the enemy were driven off without obtaining any advantage.

12. The privateer Beauregard, of Charleston, S. C., with 27 men, was captured 100 miles E. N. E. of Abaco, by the U. S. sloop-of war W. G. Anderson, Lieut. W. C. Rogers, commanding.

12. Skirmish on Laurel Creek by portions of Gen. Benham's with Gen. Floyd's forces, in which the rebels retreated after small loss.

12. Skirmish of Gen. Kelly's pickets near Romney, Va., losing 2 killed and several wounded. 12 rebels taken prisoners.

13. Rebel Gen. Zollicoffer retreated from Cumberland Ford to Cumberland Gap, Tenn.

14. The privateer schooner Neva, from China, was seized at San Francisco, Cal., by Capt Pease, of U. S. cutter Mary.

14. Lieut J. H. Rigby, with 20 men of the Gist Artillery, on an expedition from Salisbury, Md., to Wilmington and Newcastle, Md., seized 3 brass 6 pounders and 100 muskets, in possession of secessionists in those places.

14. The Gov. of Florida, by proclamation, forbade the enlistment of citizens of that State to serve in any other portion of the Confederacy.

14. $30,000 had been raised by Southern people for the widow of "the martyr Jackson," who killed Col. Ellsworth, at Alexandria, Va.

14. Gen. Benham, in pursuit of the army of Gen Floyd, in W. Va., overtook the rear guard near McCoy's Mills, and defeated it, killing 15 rebels, among them Col. Croghan. Floyd, in his retreat, destroyed 200 of his tents, and lost 10 wagon-loads of ammunition and arms.

14. Fast-day was observed in the rebel States.

14. Steamship Champion arrived at New York from Aspinwall, bringing Gen. Sumner and several companies of regular soldiers from San Francisco, having under arrest ex-Senators Gwin and Brent, and C. Benham, late Attorney General of California, charged with complicity with the rebels.

16. A party of 57 of the N. Y. 30th, attached to Gen. Keyes' brigade on the Potomac, while out foraging west of Upton's Hill, Va., were betrayed and surrounded by 200 rebel cavalry, and one half their number, with the teams and wagons, captured.

16. 50 wagons and 500 oxen, with the teamsters and stores, were captured near Pleasant Hill, Cass co., Mo., by the rebels.

16. 68 Federal prisoners, the crews of fishing smacks captured off the Florida coast, were taken to Tallahassee, Fla.

17. Union troops under Col. Alcorn, defeated Hawkins' regiment at Cypress Bridge, McClean co., Ky., routing them with severe loss, and taking 25 prisoners, 300 horses, etc. Federal loss, 10 killed, 15 wounded.

17. A party of Union troops recaptured nearly all the wagons and cattle seized the day before near Pleasant Hill, Mo.

17. U. S. gunboat Connecticut captured British schooner Adelaide, with military stores and supplies for rebels, near Cape Carnaveral, and took her into Key West.

17. Lieut. G. W. Snyder, U. S. A., a valuable engineer officer, died at Washington, of typhoid fever.

17. The 3d Missouri cavalry routed a large number of rebels near Palmyra, Mo., while on their way to join Price's army, killing 3, wounding 5, taking 16 prisoners.

18. The rebel Congress met at Richmond, V., Howell Cobb, of Ga., in the chair.

18. Capt. A. H Foote was appointed Flag-officer of the fleet of the Western Military Department.

18. Gen. Halleck assumed charge of the Missouri Department, *vice* Gen. Hunter.

18. Information was received at Washington of the imposition practised upon the Indians west of Arkansas, by Albert Pike, rebel Commissioner.

18. Rebel troops in Accomac and Northampton cos., Va., disbanded, and Union troops, under Gen. Lockwood, seized their arms and took possession of the peninsula.

18. 150 rebels were taken prisoners by Federal cavalry, near Warrensburg, Mo.

19. Missouri rebel legislature, at Neosho, Newton co., passed an ordinance of secession.

19. N. Y. ship Harvey Birch was captured and burnt in the British channel by the rebel steamer Nashville.

19. The principal part of Warsaw, capital of Benton co., Mo., was burnt by rebels.

19. Lieut. Worden, U.S.N., held prisoner by the rebels, was exchanged for Lieut. Short, of the Confederate army.

19. U. S. gunboat Conestoga engaged rebel batteries on the Tennessee river, and silenced them, receiving but slight damage herself.

19. First flotilla of the "Stone Fleet" sailed for the South, from Conn. and Mass.

20. Col. Burchard, with Lieut. Gregg and 24 men, attacked a large company of rebels under Capts. Hays and Gregg, near Kansas City, Mo., and defeated them, killing 5 and wounding 8. The Col. and Lieut. were slightly wounded.

20. A special Committee from the Virginia State Convention to consider proposed amendments to the State Constitution, reported in opposition to free schools and free suffrage for poor whites.

20. Secession State Convention at Russelville, Ky., adopted an ordinance of secession, and appointed Commissions to the rebel government.

22. Two U. S. gunboats, Cambridge and Hertzel, from Fortress Monroe, shelled out the camps of the 2d Louisiana and 10th Georgia regiments, at the junction of James and Warwick rivers.

22. Fort Pickens opened fire on the rebel encampments and forts, near Pensacola, Fla.,

which was replied to by them, and a severe cannonade ensued for two days. Much damage was experienced by Fort McRae, the Navy Yard, and town of Warrington—loss of life slight on either side. The U. S. fleet in the harbor took part. The Richmond was badly damaged by a shot. 1 killed, 6 wounded at Fort Pickens: 1 killed, 7 wounded on the Richmond.

Nov. 23. The Confederate gunboat Tuscorora accidentally took fire and was destroyed on the Mississippi, near Helena, Ark.

24. An explosion took place at Fort Pickens, Fla., by the careless handling of a shell, by which 5 men were killed, and 7 wounded.

24. A skirmish in Lancaster, Mo., between 450 Federals under Col. Moore, and 420 rebels commanded by Lieut.-Col. Blanton. The rebels were routed with the loss of 13 killed, and many wounded and prisoners. Union loss, 1 killed and 2 wounded.

24. Tybee Island, in Savannah harbor, was occupied by U. S. forces under Flag-officer Dupont.

24. Rebel Commissioners Mason and Slidell were imprisoned in Fort Warren, Mass.

25. Col. Bayard with the 1st Pa. Cavalry made a reconnoissance from Langley to Dranesville, Va., and in a skirmish killed 2 and captured 4 rebels. 3 or 4 were wounded. 6 secessionists were also arrested. 2 of the Cavalry were wounded.

25. Com. Tatnall, with 3 steamers and a gunboat, attacked the Federal fleet in Cockspur Roads, Ga., but withdrew without injury, after 40 or 50 shots were exchanged.

25. The State of Missouri, as represented by the late Governor Jackson and the Commissioners from the rebel members of the Legislature, was unanimously received by the Richmond Congress as a member of the Confederacy.

26. The house of Mr. Bell, near Franklin, Tenn., was attacked by an armed party of rebels, the building fired, and the inmates, some 10 or 12, all killed or burned but two, who escaped.

26. Skirmish at Black Oak Point, Hickory co., Mo. Capt. Cosgrove and Lieut. Bobbitt, with 25 men, surprised a rebel camp, killed 5, captured 8, and took 75 tents, 6 wagons, 10 horses, 35 guns, and other property, and released 6 loyal prisoners.

26. A squadron of the 3d Pa. Cavalry, near Vienna, Va., were attacked on three sides by a superior force of cavalry and infantry, and retreated after a short engagement. 29 of their men were missing.

26. The Convention to form a new State in W. Va., met at Wheeling.

27. Federal troops, from Gen. Sherman's command, visited Bear Island and Edisto Island, near the mouth of the Ashepoo river, S. C.

27. Henry R. Jackson was appointed a Maj.-Gen. in the Georgia army.

27. Gen. McClellan appointed the hour of 11 each Sabbath for religious worship throughout the U. S. army, and directed that all officers and men off duty should have opportunity to attend.

27. Transport Constitution sailed from Fortress Monroe to Ship Island, Mississippi Sound, with a portion of Gen. Butler's expedition, under Brig. Gen. Phelps.

28. Capts. Robb and White, and Lieut. Moonlight, three U. S. officers, were captured from the railway train at Weston, Mo., by Sy. Gordon.

28. S. C. planters on the seaboard burnt their cotton, to prevent its capture by the Federal forces or the coast.

29. The English Government forbade temporarily the exportation of cotton.

29. Major Hough, with 4 companies of Missouri cavalry, in defence of the Sedalia railway train, had an engagement at Black Walnut Creek, Mo., in which 17 rebels were killed and wounded, and 5 taken prisoners. 5 of the cavalry, including the Major, were wounded.

29. Col. De Kay, Maj. Sharpf and other Federal officers, and 40 men, had a skirmish about a mile beyond New Market, Va., in which the rebels were routed, leaving 2 dead, and carrying off their wounded.

Dec. 1. The U. S. steamer Penguin arrived at Brooklyn with the prize "Albion," captured while attempting to run the blockade at Charleston, S. C., with arms, ammunition, provisions, &c., worth $100,000.

1. A party of Federals attacked the rebel pickets at Morristown, E. Tenn., killing a large number and putting the rest to flight.

1. Skirmish near Hunter's Chapel, Va., between a squadron of Gen. Blenker's horsemen and a squadron of rebel cavalry, who were defeated, losing 3 or 4 killed and wounded, and 2 prisoners. 1 Federal killed.

2. The first regular session of the 37th Congress commenced at Washington.

2. A party of citizens in Mo., near Dunksburg, 20 miles west of Sedalia, attacked a body of rebels under Capts. Young and Wheatley, killing 7 and wounding 10 of them. Several citizens slightly wounded.

3. Skirmish at Salem, Dent co., Mo. A party of Federal soldiers, commanded by Maj. Bowen, were surprised and fired on, while sleeping in a house near headquarters, by 300 rebels under Cols. Freeman and Turner, and 15 killed and wounded. The

main body of the Federals were drawn out by Maj. Bowen, who attacked the rebels in turn and drove them from the town. 1 Federal killed and 4 wounded. Rebel loss unknown.

3. H. C. Burnett of Ky. and J. W. Reed of Mo. were expelled from U. S. House of Representatives as traitors.

4. Col. Taylor with 30 men of the 3d New Jersey had a skirmish with a number of rebel cavalry near Annandale, Va., three or four of whom were captured, and several killed and wounded without Federal loss.

4. Gen. Phelps, with 2,000 men, attached to Gen. Butler's expedition, occupied Ship Island, Mississippi Sound.

4. A detachment of Federal cavalry surprised the rebel guard at Whip-poor-will Bridge, on the Memphis Branch railway, Ky., taking 11 prisoners. 5 or 6 Confederates were killed or wounded. 4 Federals were wounded.

4. J. C. Breckinridge was expelled from the U. S. Senate.

5. Reports of the Secs. of War and Navy show the Government had in service for the war 682,971 men.

5. Skirmish at Brownsville, Ky. 100 Home Guards defeated a superior rebel force under Gen. T. C. Hindman, of Ark. Rebel loss, 3 killed, 5 wounded; the Guards sustaining no loss.

6. Successful foray of the 13th Mass., Col. Leonard, from the Potomac to Berkley Springs, Va., capturing a large quantity of provisions.

5. Riot at Nashville, Tenn., occasioned by the attempt of the rebel authorities to enforce the the endraftment of the militia. Two persons were killed and several wounded.

7. At Sedalia, Mo., 106 mule teams and the teamsters were seized by rebels.

7. Capt. Sweeney, with 35 rebel guerrillas, were captured near Glasgow, Mo., by Capt. Merrill's cavalry.

7. Skirmish near Dam No. 5 on the Potomac. Rebels driven off, losing 12 men.

7. Skirmish near Olathe, Mo. 2 Federals killed. 3 rebels killed and 5 wounded.

8. Capt. McGuire's company of 27th Mo., captured 14 rebels at Sedalia, Mo.

8. U. S. steamer Augusta captured schr. E. Waterman, loaded with provisions, coal and war munitions, off Savannah, Ga.

9. Gen. Halleck required all municipal officers at St. Louis, Mo., as well as State officials, to subscribe to the oath of allegiance prescribed by the State Convention in October previous.

9. The U. S. steamer Harriet Lane, and 6 steamers attached to the upper Potomac flotilla, shelled the woods at Budd's Ferry, and exchanged shots with the rebel batteries opposite, at Shipping Point. Some large buildings, containing rebel stores, were burnt, by boatmen from the Jacob Bell and Anacosta.

9. Gov. Pickens of S. C. proclaimed the State invaded, by land and sea, and called for 12,000 twelve-month volunteers.

9. A detachment of the "Stone Fleet" left New Bedford, Mass., for a southern port.

9. Garret Davis was elected a senator from Ky., in place of J. C. Breckinridge.

9. The rebel Congress "admitted" Kentucky to the Confederacy.

11. Federal troops, under Lieut.-Col. Rhodes, had a skirmish near Bertrand, Mo., losing 1 man. They took 16 prisoners and a number of horses and fire-arms.

11 Five vessels of the Stone Fleet, and the ships George Green and Bullion, of Gen Butler's expedition, sailed from Boston, Mass.

11. Skirmish at Dam No. 4, on the Potomac, near Sharpsburg, Md. Seven rebels on the Virginia shore were killed, and many wounded. Capt. Williams and 6 men having crossed the river were captured by the rebels.

11. Great fire at Charleston, S. C. 600 houses destroyed.

12. A squad of men from Col. Whitaker's regiment were defeated in an attempt to arrest secessionists near Bagdad, Shelby co., Ky., and retreated with one wounded.

12. Col. Merrill's cavalry regiment returned to Sedalia, Mo., from Waverley, bringing as prisoners 4 rebel capts., 2 lieuts. and 40 men, a mortar, and many horses.

12. Co. I, of 15th Ohio, were attacked on the banks of the Green river, Ky., by a superior force of rebel cavalry, whom they repulsed, wounding several of the cavalry, without loss themselves.

13. Villages of Papinsville and Butler, Bates co., Mo., rebel rendezvous, were burned by Maj. Williams of the 3d Kansas.

13. Wm. H. Johnson, of the Lincoln Cavalry, a deserter, who was captured, under military order was shot.

13. The British ship Admiral was captured off Savannah, Ga., while attempting to run in, by the Augusta.

13. Rebel Gov. Jackson, of Mo., issued a proclamation, from New Madrid, praising the valor, fortitude and success of the rebel army, and calling for more volunteers.

13. Battle of Camp Alleghany, Va. 2,000 Federal troops, under Brig.-Gen. R. H. Milroy, marched from Cheat Mountain Summit to attack a rebel camp on Alleghany Summit, of 2,000 troops, under Col. E. Johnson. The Federals approached in 2 divisions, of

750 each, from different directions, but did not arrive simultaneously, and alternately attacked the whole rebel force. They retired after a well contested fight of 8 hours, losing 20 killed, 107 wounded, and 10 missing. The rebels reported about the same loss.

Dec. 14. Ex-minister Faulkner was released on parole, to be exchanged for Congressman Ely.

14. Reconnoissance by Federal troops, within 28 miles of Charleston, S. C. The rebels, as they retreated, burnt their cotton.

15. Skirmish on the Virginia shore, opposite Berlin, Md. A detachment from the 28th Penn. were attacked by 120 rebels in ambush, but cut their way through to their boat, and escaped, having 1 wounded, and 2 taken prisoners. 2 of the enemy were killed and 5 wounded.

15. Many Union refugees escaped from Arkansas. Capt. Ware, late of the Ark. Legislature, organized a military company of Ark. Union men at Rolla, Mo.

16. Platte City, Mo., was fired by rebels, and the principal public buildings destroyed.

16. The *Europa* arrived from England, with news of the excitement among the British people occasioned by the arrest of Messrs. Mason and Slidell, and also the ultimatum of the British Government, demanding a surrender of the rebel commissioners, and an apology for their seizure. Mr. Seward's dispatch to Mr. Adams, dated Nov. 30, having settled the matter in anticipation, there was but little excitement in the public mind.

16. Gen. Zollicoffer established a camp on the banks of the Cumberland river, six miles from Somerset, Ky.

16. A party of 8 men from the 2d and 4th N. J. advanced to Annandale, on the south bank of the Potomac. They were surprised by the enemy and 3 of them captured.

17. Battle at Munfordsville, Green river, Ky. The rebels defeated; 33 killed and 60 wounded. Federal loss, 10 killed and 17 wounded.

17. Gen. Pope captured 300 rebels near Osceola, Mo.

17. Entrance to the harbor at Savannah, Ga., blockaded by sinking 7 vessels laden with stone.

18. A part of Gen. Pope's forces under Col. J. C. Davis and Col. F. Steele, surprised a rebel camp near Milford, north of Warrensburg, Mo., and captured nearly 1300 men, 70 wagons loaded with stores, and all their camp equipage and arms. Federal loss, 2 killed, 17 wounded.

18. Gen. Barnard, Chief-engineer of the U. S. army, reported to Congress that the defences around Washington consisted of 48 works, the perimeter of which was 48 miles, mounting above 300 guns.

18. The Island City sailed from Boston for Fortress Monroe with 240 rebel prisoners, to be exchanged.

18. Rebel Gen. Jackson attempted a movement against Williamsport, Md., but Gen. Williams being on the alert, the rebel force retired.

18. News from Ky., that Gen. McCook, was at Munfordsville, Gen. Mitchell at Bacon Creek, and Gen. Zollicoffer, (rebel) at Cumberland river, near Mill Springs.

19. Skirmishing at Point of Rocks, Md. Rebels from Va. shore commenced shelling the encampment of Col. Geary's Pennsylvania regiment, but were repulsed after half an hour's fight, without loss on the Federal side.

19. A band of 25 rebels visited the town of Ripley, Jackson Co., Va., and seized all the arms in the place, some ammunition and clothing. They also robbed the post-office and the principal store in the place.

20. George W. Jones, late U. S. Minister to Bogota, was arrested in New York on a charge of treason.

20. Battle of Dranesville, Va. Federal forces, under Gen. E. O. C. Ord, defeated about 2,800 Confederates from South Carolina, Alabama, and Virginia. Federal force about 4,000 men, of whom 7 were killed and 61 wounded. Rebel loss, 75 killed 150 wounded and 30 prisoners, together with a large supply of forage.

20. A scouting party under Capt. Wood, captured 100 rebels near Springfield, Mo., who were released upon taking the oath of allegiance.

20. A party of rebels from Gen. Price's army committed extensive ravages on the N. Missouri railway, between Hudson and Warrenton. The bridges, wood-piles, water tanks, ties and rails were destroyed along the route for 80 miles.

20. 103 Federal soldiers, under Major McKee, repulsed a superior force of rebels four miles S. of Hudson, Mo., killing 10 and capturing 17 prisoners and 30 horses, at the same time rescuing a stock train which had just been seized by the rebels.

20. The main ship channel at Charleston harbor, was obstructed by sinking 16 vessels of the "stone fleet."

22. Reconnoissance in the vicinity of Tybee Island and Broad river, Ga., from Gen. Sherman's command.

22. Skirmish near New Market bridge, Newport News, Va. Two companies of

20th N. Y. regiment, under Major Schoepf, were attacked by 700 rebel cavalry and infantry, and escaped with loss of 6 wounded. Ten of the enemy were killed and a number wounded, when they retreated.

23. Gen. Pope sent an expedition to Lexington, Mo. Two boats of the rebels were captured and burnt.

26. A skirmish took place at Camp Boyle, Columbia, Ky. A body of rebels were attacked by a detachment of Col. Hazzard's regiment, under Major Ousley, who dispersed them, killing 5 and wounding others, without loss themselves.

26. Gen. McCall sent a reconnoitering party towards Dranesville, Va., which was driven back by the rebels, who had a force of 10,000 men there.

26. A Cabinet Council at Washington, decided to give up Mason and Slidell, on the ground that they could not be held consistently with the doctrine of neutral rights always maintained by the U. S. Government.

26. Gen. Scott arrived at New York, in the Arago, from France.

26. Bluffton, S. C., was occupied by Federal troops under Gen. Stevens.

26. The Lighthouse on Morris Island, Charleston, S. C. harbor, was blown up by order of rebel authorities.

26. Major Gower, with a squadron of 1st Iowa cavalry, arrived at Jefferson City, Mo., bringing as prisoners, 1 capt., 13 men, and 10 wagon loads of stores.

26. Philip St. George Cook, a Brig.-Gen. in the rebel army, shot himself, at his residence in Powhatan Co., Va.

26. A fire occurred in the government stables at Washington, D. C., in which nearly 200 horses were burned.

27. Lord Lyons, the British minister at Washington, was notified that Mason and Slidell awaited his disposal.

27. Alfred Ely, U. S. representative from Rochester, N. Y., taken prisoner at Manassas Plains, was released in exchange for C. J. Faulkner.

27. The rebel privateer Isabel, ran the blockade off Charleston, S. C.

27. The bridges over Fabias river on the Palmyra railway, Mo., destroyed by rebels.

28. Gen. Buell's army in Ky., was reported by the War Department to number 60,000 men.

28. The rebels at Bowling Green, Ky., were reported to number 30,000, under Gens. A. S. Johnston, Buckner, and Hindman.

28. Gen. Prentiss, with 5 companies 3rd Missouri cavalry, under Col. John Glover, and 5 companies of Col. Birge's sharpshooters, 470 in all, attacked a rebel camp at Mount Zion, in Boone Co., Mo., numbering nearly 900 men. The rebels were routed, losing 25 killed, 150 wounded, and 40 prisoners. 90 of their horses and 105 stand of arms were captured. The Federal loss was 3 killed and 46 wounded.

28. A squadron of Federal cavalry, from Col. Jackson's regiment, commanded by Major Murray, left their camp near Calhoun, Ky., on a scouting expedition across Green river. They were attacked near Sacramento, by a large force of rebels under Col. De Forrest, and after a short engagement compelled to retire. Capt. A. G. Bacon was killed, and Lieut. R. H. King, of Frankfort, and 8 privates wounded. Capt. Merriweather and two privates of the rebels were killed, and a number wounded.

30. The rebel Gen. H. H. Sibley having entered New Mexico with a military force without opposition, took possession of it, and annexed it to the Southern Confederacy by proclamation.

30. Messrs. Thomas and Burnett, of Ky., were "qualified" and took their seats in the rebel Congress at Richmond, Va.

31. Two boats under Acting-Masters A. Allen, and H. L. Sturges, from the U. S. steamer, Mount Vernon, destroyed a light ship off Wilmington, N.C., which the rebels had fitted up for a gunboat. The expedition was at night, and the boats were under fire from Fort Caswell, but escaped injury.

31. Capt. Shillinglaw and Mason, N. Y. 79th, and Lieutenants Dickinson, 3rd U. S. infantry, J. W. Hart, 20th Indiana, and other officers and men were released by the rebels from Richmond, Va.

31. Capture of the town of Biloxi, Miss. by U. S. gunboats Lewis, Water Witch, and New London, with national forces from Ship Island. The town and fort surrendered without a fight. The guns were removed by Commander Smith, and the Federals retired.

1862.

Jan. 1. The rebel Commissioners Mason and Slidell, with their Secretaries, left Boston for England, via Provincetown, Mass., where the British war steamer Rinaldo received them.

1. Col. H. Brown opened fire from Fort Pickens on the rebel vessels and fortifications within range of his guns, which was returned by the enemy.

1. The British bark Empress arrived at New York as a prize, with 6,500 bags of coffee, captured by the U. S. sloop-of-war Vincennes, off New Orleans bar.

Jan. 1. Part of the Louisville and Nashville railway was destroyed by order of the rebel Gen. Buckner.

1. Skirmish at Port Royal Ferry, S. C. Federal troops under Gen. Stevens, with the assistance of five gunboats, crossed from Beaufort to the mainland and attacked batteries erected by the rebels, who retreated towards Grahamville. Federal loss, 3 killed, 11 wounded. Rebels, 6 killed, 12 wounded.

1. Jeff. Owens, Col. Jones, and 50 rebel bridge-burners were captured near Martinsburg, Adrian Co., Mo., by State militia under General Schofield.

1. Four Federal soldiers were captured, 1 killed, and 10 guns taken by a party of rebels on Green river, Ky., near Morgantown.

2. The U. S. gunboats Yankee and Anacosta, exchanged shots with the rebel batteries at Cockpit Point, on the Potomac.

2. Daniel P. White of Ky., qualified and took his seat in the Confederate Congress.

3. Col. Glover, with 300 Federal troops, attacked a rebel camp 9 miles N. of Hunnewell, Mo., taking 8 prisoners, putting the rest to flight, and capturing a quantity of arms, &c.

3. 240 released Federal prisoners arrived at Fortress Monroe from Richmond.

4. The 84th Pa., 39th Ill., 500 cavalry and other troops were driven from Bath, Va., by a superior rebel force under Gen. Jackson, who took 30 Federals prisoners. The Federals retreated to Hancock, Md. 7 rebels were killed and a number wounded. 3 of the Federals were killed, several wounded.

4. Skirmish at Huntersville, W. Va. A portion of the 25th Ohio, 2d Va., and Bracken's Ind. cavalry, all under Major Webster, attacked a rebel force of 400 cavalry and 350 infantry who were guarding the rebel supplies at that depot. They were routed with a loss of 2 killed and 7 wounded, leaving $50,000 worth of army stores which were destroyed by Unionists.

5. Skirmish on the mainland near Port Royal, S. C. 7 rebels were captured.

5. Rebel army under Gen. Jackson bombarded Hancock, Md. from the opposite Va. shore, but were driven away by artillery forces under Gen. Lander without a close engagement.

5. Five Federal soldiers were killed by rebels in ambush in Johnson Co., Kansas.

6. 4,000 Cherokee Indians were driven from their homes by Texas rebels.

7. Destruction of bridges and culverts on the Balt. and Ohio railway, near the Cacapon river, by rebel Gen. Jackson.

7. Engagement at Blue's Gap, near Romney, W. Va. Federal troops under Col. Dunning, of the 5th Ohio, attacked 2,000 of the enemy, routing them with the loss of 15 killed, 20 prisoners, 2 pieces of cannon, their wagons, &c. No Federal loss.

7. 300 of the 32d Ohio, under Capt. Lacey, were sent by Gen. Milroy into Tucker Co., Va., where they dispersed 400 rebels, capturing 2 officers and a private, and a large quantity of stores. 4 rebels were found dead and many were wounded.

7. Three brigades of Gen. Smith's division, S. side of the Potomac, proceeded toward Peacock Hill, Lewinsville, Fairfax Court House and Vienna, and captured an immense quantity of hay, oats, corn, &c.

7. A band of rebels having seized a quantity of army stores from the depot at Sutton, Braxton Co., W. Va., information was sent to Col. H. Anisansel, commanding 1st Virginia Cavalry, at Clarksburg. The Col. overtook the rebels 30 miles E. of Sutton, and, attacking them, killed or wounded 22, took 15 horses and 56 head of cattle, and recaptured the greater part of the stores.

7. Skirmish at Paintsville, near Prestonburg, Ky. Col. Garfield dispersed 2,500 rebels under Humphrey Marshall, killing 3, wounding a large number, and capturing 15. Federal loss 2 killed and 1 wounded.

8. The newspapers of Missouri were put under military censorship, and their editors ordered to send two copies of each issue to the Provost Marshal.

8. Riot at Warsaw, Mo. Two secessionists were shot.

8. Reconnoissance of gunboats towards Savannah, Ga., under command of Capt. Davis.

8. Capt. Latham and 17 men of 2d Virginia regiment, encountered about 30 rebel guerrillas on the Dry Fork of Cheat river, W. Va., and after a severe fight of an hour's duration, the rebels were driven from the field with the loss of 6 killed and several wounded. Federal loss 6 wounded. Capt. Latham destroyed the rebel tents and provisions.

8. The 1st Kansas regiment, on its march from Sedalia to Lexington, Mo., was fired upon from ambush, and a sergeant and 2 horses killed.

8. A. W. Bradford was inaugurated as Governor of Maryland, and made an eloquent address, expressing in the strongest terms devotion to the Union and the Constitution.

8. Major W. M. G. Torrence of the 1st Iowa cavalry, assisted by detachments of the 1st Missouri cavalry, Major Hubbard, 4th Ohio and Merrill's Horse, in all 500

mounted men, attacked a rebel camp at Silver Creek, Howard Co., Mo., where six or eight hundred men were stationed, under Col. Poindexter. The enemy were routed with a loss of 12 killed, 22 wounded, and 15 prisoners, leaving their horses, guns, and camp and garrison equipage. The material was destroyed by Major Torrence. Federal loss 3 killed and 10 wounded.

9. A division of the Chamber of Commerce at St. Louis, Mo., was occasioned by disloyal sentiments. A new and loyal Chamber was formed.

10. A reconnoitering force of 5,000 men under the command of Brig. Gen. McClernand, left Cairo, Ill., and proceeded toward Columbus and Mayfield.

10. Waldo P. Johnson and Trusten Polk, U. S. Senators from Missouri, were expelled from the Senate for disloyalty.

10. Skirmish at Pohick Church, Va. The 5th Michigan dispersed a body of rebels.

10. Skirmish at Bath, Va., between a detachment of Federals under Capt. Russell and rebels from Gen. Jackson's division.

10. Battle near Prestonburg, Ky. Gen. Garfield, with 1,500 Federal troops, overtook Humphrey Marshall with 3,000 rebels, compelling him to destroy his stores and putting him to flight. Rebel loss 50 killed many wounded and 25 prisoners. Federal loss, 2 killed, 25 wounded.

11. The 1st Kansas regiment arrived at Lexington, Mo., and arrested several prominent rebels. They also seized a large quantity of stores designed for the use of Gen. Price.

11. Fifty rebels belonging to Col. Alexander's regiment were captured 6 miles from Sedalia, Mo.

12. The Burnside Expedition sailed from Fortress Monroe, under command of Com. Goldsborough and Gen. Burnside, for Albemarle Sound, N. C.

12. Secretary Seward telegraphed the British Consul at Portland, Me., that British troops might pass through U. S. territory on their way to Canada.

12. The rebels in Kentucky burned the houses, and carried off or destroyed the property of loyal men at Horse Cave and in Cave City and vicinity, and the people sought refuge at Munfordsville.

13. Hon. Simeon Cameron, Secretary-of-War, resigned his position, and Edwin F. Stanton was appointed in his stead on the 15th inst.

13. The steamship Constitution, with the Maine 12th regiment, and the Bay State regiment, sailed from Boston for Ship Island, Miss., via. Fortress Monroe.

15. Gen. McClernand's column advanced to Mayfield, Ky., and Gen. Grant to Fort Jefferson. 20,000 rebels reported at Columbus, Ky., under Gen. Polk.

16. Hon. Edwin B. Stanton, the new Secretary-of-War, assumed the duties of his office.

17. 150 wounded Federal prisoners arrived at Fortress Monroe from Richmond, Va. Eight rebel officers were released from the Fortress the same day.

17. Capture of British schooner Stephen Hart, loaded with arms, ammunition and stores for the rebels, by the U. S. storeship Supply.

17. Ex President John Tyler died at Richmond Va.

17. Skirmish near Ironton, Mo. Rebels under Jeff. Thompson were defeated by Col. Miles.

17. Two companies of the 1st Kansas cavalry, under Major Halderman, arrested Capt. Whitney, Joe Shelby and several other rebel officers, and also recovered a number of horses, mules, wagons, etc., taken from Col. Mulligan's command at Lexington, Mo.

17. The Fortification Bill passed the U. S. House of Representatives, appropriating $5,960,000 for fort and harbor defences.

18. Gen. Grant made a reconnoissance in force towards Columbus, Ky.

18. Gen. Halleck levied an assessment on the wealthy secessionists of St. Louis, Mo., to provide for the wants of loyal refugees in the city who had been driven from their homes in the S. W. section of the State by rebels.

18. Capts. Murdock and Webster, with their commands, returned to Cairo from an expedition to Bloomfield, Mo. They captured Lieut. Col. Farmer and 11 other rebel officers and 68 privates, with a quantity of army stores.

19. Battle of Mill Spring, Ky. The rebels completely routed, with loss of 192 killed, and 140 prisoners. Gen. Zollicoffer, their commander, was killed. The Federal troops were under Gen. Thomas. 1,200 horses and mules, over 100 large wagons, and 14 cannon, 2,000 muskets, etc., were captured. Federal loss 39 killed, 207 wounded.

19. The U. S. gunboat Itasca captured the rebel schooner Lizzie Weston, off Florida, laden with 293 bales of cotton, 152,500 pounds, for Jamaica.

23. The property of several wealthy secessionists at St. Louis was seized under execution by Gen Halleck, and sold to pay the assessment to support Union refugees.

23. The second stone fleet was sunk in Maffit's Channel, Charleston, S. C., harbor

JAN. 24. The Federal light-boat off Cape Henry, [illegible] Chesapeake, [illegible] captured by the rebels [illegible].

[illegible] wer [illegible] were [illegible] the [illegible]

[illegible] Burnside Expedition reached [illegible].

[illegible] Federal [illegible] occupied [illegible] M. [illegible] Hamilton [illegible] were [illegible] were [illegible] negro [illegible]

[illegible] near [illegible] The Federals were [illegible]

[illegible] battery Monitor was launched at Greenpoint, N. Y.

[illegible] Savannah river [illegible] Fort Pulaski [illegible] Savannah was demonstrated.

[illegible] Gen. Beauregard took command of rebel troops in Tennessee.

[illegible] The rebel commissioners Mason and Slidell arrived at Southampton, England.

[illegible] Murray [illegible] near [illegible] church [illegible] effected his escape.

3. [illegible] the Secretary of State [illegible] were captured [illegible] vessel attempting to violate the blockade.

[illegible] were captured [illegible]

[illegible] during [illegible] to prevent [illegible] belligerent.

FEB. 1. [illegible] Federal [illegible]

[illegible] The [illegible] steamer [illegible] arrived at Liverpool, England, from [illegible] the [illegible] and [illegible] been [illegible] by the privateer Sumter.

[illegible] House of Representatives [illegible] 151, [illegible] contract.

[illegible] The President of the [illegible] powered [illegible] Congress to take possession of all the railway and telegraph lines [illegible] purpose [illegible] of the rebellion.

[illegible] wer [illegible] and [illegible] in which the [illegible] their home.

[illegible] occurred [illegible] cavalry, under Lieut. [illegible] Federal infantry under Captain Duncan, in which the Federals were defeated with a loss of seven men.

[illegible] officer [illegible] were [illegible] Federal prisoners.

[illegible] were transferred [illegible] Fort Lafayette [illegible] prisoners.

[illegible] privateer Nashville [illegible] England, and the U. S. gunboat Tuscarora [illegible] space of 24 hours.

[illegible] Gen. McDowell [illegible] document from [illegible] Davis to [illegible] Lincoln [illegible] prisoners in their hands [illegible] Missouri.

[illegible] The Federal army under Gen. Grant were within [illegible] miles of Fort Henry, on the Tennessee river.

[illegible] Capt. [illegible] rebels near [illegible] were [illegible] Federals.

4. A scouting party under [illegible] Hart

ness, of Col. Miles' 81st Pa. regiment, returned from the vicinity of Fairfax Court House, Va., bringing several rebel prisoners.

4. Steamship Constitution, with the Mass. Bay State, and the Maine 12th regiments, and other troops, under Gen. Phelps, left Fortress Monroe for Ship Island, Miss.

5. Attack on Fort Henry, Tenn. commenced by Federal gunboats under Com. Foote.

5. Queen Victoria, of England, removed the prohibitions relating to the export of material of war from the British dominions declared on the 30th Nov. and 4th Dec., 1861.

6. Jesse D. Bright, of Indiana, was expelled from the U. S. Senate, for complicity with treason.

7. A band of rebels concealed near the landing at Harper's Ferry, Va., having, by means of a flag of truce, decoyed a boat from the Maryland shore, and then fired on its occupants, by order of Col. Geary, the block of large buildings facing the landing were burned. But seven families, 40 persons in all, then resided in the town.

7. Unconditional surrender of Fort Henry to Com. Foote, with Gen. Tilghman and staff, one colonel, two captains, and 80 privates. Com. Foote transferred the fort to Gen. Grant.

7. Federal troops took possession of the Memphis and Ohio railway.

7. The rebels driven from Romney, Va., by Gen. Lander, who occupied the town.

7. Successful skirmish with rebel cavalry near Fairfax Court House, Va., by Col. Friedman, with the Cameron Dragoons; 1 rebel killed, and 12 captured, with 12 horses, &c. 2 Federals wounded.

8. Portions of Gen. Butler's expedition sailed from Boston and from Fortress Monroe, for Ship Island, Miss.

8. Capture of rebel forts and garrisons on Roanoke Island, N. C., by the Federal forces under Com. Goldsborough and Gen. Burnside. 2,500 prisoners, 6 forts, 40 guns, 3,000 small arms. Federal loss, 50 killed, 150 wounded.

8. Capt. Smith, of the 5th Virginia (loyal) with 21 men, surprised 32 of Jenkins' cavalry on Linn Creek, Logan County, Va., killing 8, wounding 7, and capturing the remainder, with 32 horses. One Federal was killed and 1 wounded.

9. Skirmish of a body of Federal cavalry with rebels near Fort Henry, Tenn. 5 rebels killed, and 30 taken prisoners.

9. Edenton, N. C., occupied by Federal troops.

10. Destruction of rebel gunboats in the Pasquotank river, N. C., also of the rebel battery at Cobb's Point, and the occupation of Elizabeth City by Federal forces from 14 gunboats, commanded by Capt. Rowan.

10. Gen. Charles P. Stone, U. S. A., was arrested by Gov't. order, and imprisoned in Fort Lafayette.

10. Arrest of several male and female secessionists in Washington. Also, of Dr. Ives, N. Y. *Herald* correspondent.

10. Capt. Phelps, of Com. Foote's squadron, commanding the gunboats Conestoga, Taylor and Lexington, captured a new rebel gunboat, and destroyed all the rebel craft between Fort Henry and Florence, Ala.

11. Bursting of the "Sawyer" gun at Newport News, Va., by which 2 Federal soldiers were killed and 2 wounded.

12. An expedition under the command of Col. Reggin returned to Fort Henry, Tenn., from up the Tennessee river, having captured $75,000 worth of contraband goods at Paris, Tenn., and also the tents and camp equipage of the rebel troops that retreated from Fort Henry.

13. Evacuation of Springfield, Mo., by the rebel army under Gen. Price. Occupation of the town by Federal troops of Gen. Curtis' army. 600 of the rebel sick, and many forage wagons were left behind.

14. The rebel camp at Blooming Gap, Va., was surprised by forces under Gen. Lander. 65 prisoners were taken, including 17 officers, and 13 killed and 20 wounded. Federal loss, 7 in killed and wounded.

14. Fort Donelson was invested and attacked by the Federal army under Gen. Grant.

14. E. M. Stanton, Sec.-of-War, issued an order releasing all political prisoners upon their taking an oath of allegiance.

14. A skirmish took place near Flat Lick Ford, on the Cumberland river, Ky., between two companies of cavalry, under Col. Munday, two companies of the 49th Indiana, and some rebel pickets, in which the latter lost 4 killed, 4 wounded, and 3 taken prisoners. There was no Federal loss.

14. Com. Foote, with 6 gunboats, attacked Fort Donelson, but was repulsed, the Commodore being severely wounded. Federal loss 60 in killed and wounded.

14. The rear guard of Gen. Price's army in S. W. Missouri was attacked by Gen. Curtis' command, and many prisoners taken.

14. Bowling Green, Ky., was evacuated by rebel troops, who destroyed most of the available property in the town that could not be removed.

Feb. 14. Three rebel schooners and one sloop, laden with rice, were destroyed by the crews of armed boats from the U. S. bark Restless, Lieut. E. Conroy, in Bull's Bay, S. C.

15. The national batteries at Venus Point, on the Savannah river, were attacked by 4 rebel gunboats, which were repulsed, one of them being severely injured.

15. The railway bridge crossing the Tennessee river at Decatur, Ala., was destroyed by Union men.

15. Gen. Burnside administered the oath of allegiance to the inhabitants of Roanoke Island.

15. The iron-clad steam gunboat Galena was launched at Mystic, Conn.

16. Gen. Price was driven from Missouri by Gen. Curtis, who followed him into Arkansas, capturing many prisoners.

16. Gen. Mitchell's troops occupied Bowling-Green, Ky.

16. Fort Donelson surrendered to the Federal army, under Gen. Grant, after three days' desperate resistance. 15,000 prisoners were captured, including Brig.-Gen. Buckner, and an immense quantity of war material. Gens. Floyd and Pillow escaped, with a portion of the garrison.

16. Destruction of the "Tennessee Iron works," owned by John Bell and Messrs. Lewis & Wood, on the Cumberland river, six miles above Dover, by order of Com. Foote.

17. The First Missouri cavalry fell into an ambush of rebels at Sugar Creek, Ark., by which 13 of their number were killed and wounded.

18. Gov. Rector of Arkansas, by proclamation, called every man subject to military duty into service within 20 days.

18. First session of the Congress of the "permanent" Government of the Confederate States opened at Richmond, Va.

18. The wire and suspension bridges over the Cumberland river at Nashville, Tenn., were destroyed by Gen. Floyd, despite the remonstrances of the citizens.

18. A skirmish at Independence, Mo., between a detachment of Ohio cavalry and a band of rebels under Quantrel and Parker. 3 rebels killed, several wounded and taken prisoners. 1 Federal killed, 3 wounded.

19. 1,000 additional rebel prisoners were taken at Fort Donelson, they having come down the river to reinforce Gen. Buckner.

19. Evacuation of Clarksville, Tenn., by the rebels. The Federal forces, under Com. Foote, took possession of the town, and captured a large quantity of army stores.

19. Bentonville, Ark., was captured by Gen. Curtis, after a short engagement with the rebels, in which more prisoners and supplies were taken.

20. The rebel steamer Magnolia, with 1,050 bales of cotton, was captured in the Gulf of Mexico, by the U. S. steamers Brooklyn and South Carolina. An attempt to fire the vessel was frustrated by the Federal seamen.

20. The town of Winton, N. C., was partially burned by the national forces.

20. The track of the Memphis and Ohio railway was torn up, and the bridges burned in many places, by order of rebel Gen. Polk.

21. Battle of Valvende, N. M. 1,500 Federals, under Col. Canby, were defeated by an equal force of rebels, under Col. Steele. Federal loss, 55 killed, 140 wounded. Rebel loss, about the same.

22. Inauguration of Jefferson Davis, of Miss., as President of the "Confederate States," at Richmond, Va., and Alex. H. Stevens, of Ga., as Vice-President, they having received the unanimous vote of 109 delegates representing 11 States, viz.: Ala., Ark., Fla., Ga., La., Miss., N. C., S. C., Tenn., Texas, Va., for the permanent organization of the Confederate States.

22. The U. S. sloop-of-war Adironac was launched at Brooklyn, N. Y.

23. 347 released Federal prisoners arrived at Fortress Monroe, among them Cols. Lee, Wood and Cogswell.

23. Lieut. Guin, of Com. Foote's command, made a reconnoissance up the Tenn. river as high as Eastport, Miss., being well received by the inhabitants. At Clifton, Tenn., he took possession of 1500 sacks and barrels of flour and 6,000 bush. of wheat.

23. Gallatin, Tenn., occupied by Gen. Buell's forces.

23. A skirmish at Mason's Neck, near Occoquan, Va., between Texas rangers, and part of the N. Y. 37th, in which 2 of the latter were killed and 1 wounded.

24. Harpers' Ferry, Va., occupied by the 28th Pa. regiment.

25. Nashville, Tenn., was occupied by Federal forces of Gen. Buell's command.

25. The 9th Ohio and 2d Minnesota regiments received handsome flags from ladies of Louisville, Ky., in compliment of their valor at Mill Spring, Jan. 19.

25. The remainder of Gen. Bank's division crossed the Potomac and occupied Bolivar and Charlestown, Va.

25. All the telegraphic lines that could be used by government were taken under military control, and the transmission of reports of military operations forbidden, without permission of the military censor

26. Cotton and tobacco planters of Va.,

at a meeting held at Richmond, refused to consent to the destruction of their crops.

26. The command of Capt. Montgomery, was surprised by a large force of rebels at Keittsville, Barry Co., Mo. 2 Federals were killed, 1 wounded, and 40 of their horses captured.

26. The U. S. gunboat R. B. Forbes ran ashore near Nag's Head, N. C., was set on fire and destroyed.

27. Fayetteville, Ark., was occupied by Gen. Curtis, who captured a number of prisoners, stores, &c. The rebels retreated across the Boston Mountains.

27. 42 Federal soldiers were poisoned at Mud Town, Ark., by eating food which had been left for them by rebels.

27. Col. Wood's cavalry drove rebels out of Dent, Texas and Howell Cos., Mo., capturing 60 prisoners.

27. U. S. iron clad battery Monitor, Lieut. Worden, sailed from N. York for Fortress Monroe.

28. The British ship Labuan, with a valuable cargo, arrived at N. York, captured by the U. S. sloop-of-war Portsmouth off Rio Grande river.

28. The rebel steamer Nashville ran the blockade of Beaufort, N. C., and reached the town.

28. Capt. Nolen with 64 of the 7th Ill. cavalry attacked 90 of Jeff. Thompson's cavalry and a battery, west of Charlestown, Mo., and captured 4 guns, losing 1 man.

March 1. The U. S. gunboats Tyler, Lieut. Gwin, commanding, and Lexington, Lieut. Shirk, on an expedition up the Tenn. river, engaged and silenced a rebel battery at Pittsburg, Tenn., 7 miles above Savannah.

1. Evacuation of Columbus Ky., by rebel troops, leaving their heavy guns, and a large quantity of war material. 400 of the 2d Illinois cavalry occupied the town next day, and troops from Com. Foote's flotilla the day after.

1. U. S. steamer Mount Vernon, captured the schooner British Queen, at the blockade of Wilmington, N. C.

1. John Minor Botts, Valentine Hecker, Franklin Stearns, and others were arrested at Richmond Va., on a charge of "treason."

2. Death of Brig.-Gen. Lander, at Camp Chase, on the Upper Potomac, from a wound received at Edwards' Ferry Va., Oct. 22, 1861.

3. Brig.-Gens. S. B. Buckner and Lloyd Tilghman, rebel prisoners, arrived at Fort Warren, Boston, Mass.

3. U.S.Senate confirmed Gens. McDowell, Buell Burnside, McClernand, C. F. Smith, Lew. Wallace and Sigel as Maj.-Gens.; and Cols. Speed, of Tenn., Logan of Ill., McArthur of Iowa, Lauman of Iowa, Wallace of Ind., McCook of Ohio, Berry of Maine, and Terry of Conn., as Brigadiers.

4. Occupation of Fort Clinch and Fernandina, Fla., and St. Mary's and Brunswick, Ga., by Federal forces under Com. Dupont and Gen. Wright.

4. A squadron of 1st Michigan cavalry surprised and defeated a party of rebel cavalry at Berryville, Va., killing 3 and capturing 9 horses without loss.

4. Two bridges on the Nashville and Decatur railway, Tenn., destroyed by rebels.

5. Bunker Hill, Va., was occupied by rebel forces.

6. Two rebel officers were captured at Vienna, Va., by a detachment of Col. Averill's cavalry.

6 A rebel picket of 5 was captured by Van Alen's cavalry near Bunker Hill, Va.

7. Capt. Cole's Maryland cavalry encountered a few of Ashby's rebel cavalry, near Winchester, Va., 6 rebels were killed and 5 wounded. Capt. Cole had 3 men wounded.

6, 7, 8. Battle of Pea Ridge, Ark. The combined rebel forces under Gens. Van Dorn, Price, McCulloch and Pike, were defeated by the Federal army under Gens. Curtis, Sigel, Asboth and Davis. Federal loss in killed, wounded and missing, 1351. The rebel loss about 2000. Gens. McCulloch, McIntosh and Slack, were killed.

8. Destruction of the U. S. sloop-of-war Cumberland, and the frigate Congress, in action with the rebel iron battery Merrimac, in Hampton Roads, Va. 100 men were killed or drowned on the Cumberland.

8. By order of the President, Maj.-Gen. McClellan was directed to organize and command the army of the Potomac, divided into 5 army corps, under Maj.Gens. McDowell, Brig.-Gens. E. V. Sumner, S. P. Heintzelman, E. L. Keyes and N. P. Banks.

8. Col. Geary entered Leesburg, Va., capturing many prisoners, stores, &c.

8. Manassas, Va., was evacuated by the rebels.

9. Combat of the U. S. iron battery Monitor, and the rebel iron battery Merrimac, in Hampton Roads, Va. After a desperate combat of 3 hours, the Merrimac was compelled to retire, having received severe injuries.

9. The rebel battery at Cockpit Point, on the Potomac captured by Federal troops.

9. Brilliant charge of 14 of the Lincoln cavalry at Burk's station, near Fairfax

[illegible] Va. against [illegible] infantry [illegible] of [illegible] were killed [illegible] wounded and [illegible] captured. [illegible] was killed.

March 10. [illegible] was captured [illegible] Texan rangers.

[illegible]

[illegible] Mo. [illegible] miles below New Madrid.

[illegible] Gen. Banks' command.

[illegible] between the [illegible] and the [illegible] Mississippi [illegible] organized [illegible] Department [illegible]

[illegible] Department of the Miss. [illegible] assigned to Gen. Halleck [illegible] departments [illegible] Kansas [illegible] Tenn.

[illegible] Fla. [illegible] Winchester [illegible] was occupied [illegible]

[illegible] Jacksonville, Fla. [illegible] gunboats [illegible]

[illegible] New Madrid [illegible] killed and wounded.

[illegible] New Madrid [illegible] a mile [illegible] engagement. The [illegible] the Federals [illegible] heavy [illegible] wounded.

[illegible] Indians [illegible] Lieut. [illegible]

16. The Federal gunboats and mortars [illegible] Miss.

26. Two rebel captains and 17 privates were captured on Indian Creek, Missouri.

[illegible] Federal forces in Va. under Gen. Shields advanced from Winchester and drove the enemy towards Strasburg.

18. The naval force on the Mississippi at Island No. 10 attacked Gen. Foote's flotilla, but retired after slight loss on either side, the [illegible] two of the Federal gunboats with their guns.

[illegible] citizens of Loudon co. Va. were sent to Richmond on the Central cars and committed to one of the military prisons.

[illegible] Santa Fe, N. M. was [illegible] by rebel Texans under Major [illegible]

[illegible] Washington, N. C. occupied by Federal troops under [illegible] Stevenson.

22. Rebel forces under Gens. Jackson, Smith and Longstreet advanced upon Winchester, Va., where Gen. Shields' forces engaged them successfully until night.

[illegible] A skirmish occurred between a detachment of the [illegible] Kansas and Quantrell's band near Independence, Mo. The latter was routed with [illegible] killed. The Federals lost [illegible] killed and captured, [illegible] prisoners and [illegible] horses.

[illegible] Lieut. T. A. Budd and Acting Master Mather, attached to [illegible] squadron, having imprudently ventured on shore with a [illegible] men to examine a rebel earthwork over Mosquito Inlet, Fla., were fired upon by a party of rebels in ambush. [illegible] and [illegible] men were killed and several wounded.

[illegible] Morehead City, N. C. was occupied by Federal troops under Gen. Parke.

23. Battle of Winchester, Va. The fight of [illegible] was renewed, and after a desperate engagement the rebels were driven from the ground in disorder with a loss of [illegible] killed and wounded [illegible] prisoners. Federal loss [illegible] killed, [illegible] wounded.

26. Maj. Pyron's Texans were defeated at Apache Cañon, between Santa Fe and Fort Union, by Federal troops under Maj. Chivington.

[illegible] A band of rebels attacked [illegible] companies of State militia at Humansville, Polk co. Mo., and were defeated by them with a loss of 15 killed and many wounded.

27. [illegible] Va. was occupied by the Federal troops.

[illegible] The Federal gunboats and mortars under [illegible] Farragut and Porter attacked Forts Jackson and St. Philip, La.

[illegible] Gen. Beauregard [illegible] concentrated a large force at Corinth, Miss.

[illegible] Morgan's rebel cavalry captured a train on the Louisville and Nashville railway. The locomotive was run into a ditch and the cars destroyed. [illegible] Gen. Pope of Ky., and several other Federal officers were taken prisoners.

28. 1,200 U. S. troops, under Col. Slough, engaged the united rebel forces of Col. Scurry and Maj. Pyron at Valle's Ranch, N. M., from 10 A. M. to 5 P. M., when an armistice was agreed on. A flank movement the next day by Maj. Chivington, with 400 men, threw the rebels into confusion, and after burning their train, they sought safety in flight. Rebel loss, 80 killed, 100 wounded, 93 prisoners. Federal loss, 38 killed, 51 wounded, 17 prisoners. The Texans retired to Santa Fé and the Federals to Fort Union.

29. A detachment of the 1st Iowa cavalry, under Capt. Thompson, overtook the guerrilla band of Col. Parker, 10 miles west of Warrensburg, Mo. 15 rebels were killed and 25 taken prisoners, among the latter Col. Parker and Captain Walton. 2 Federals were killed and several wounded.

30. Maj.-Gen Hunter arrived at Hilton Head, S. C., and assumed command of the Department of the South, comprising South Carolina, Georgia and Florida.

31. 220 rebels, captured at Winchester, Va., arrived at Fort Delaware, Del. Bay.

Apr. 1. During a storm at night, Col. Roberts with 50 picked men of the 42d Illinois, and as many seamen under First Master Johnson, of the gunboat St. Louis, surprised the rebels at the upper battery of Island No. 10, and spiked 6 large guns.

1. Col. Carline, commanding the advance of Gen. Steele's brigade in Arkansas, had a skirmish at Putnam's Ferry, in which a rebel lieutenant and several privates were wounded, and 5 prisoners taken.

1. All of Maryland and Virginia lying between the Mountain Department and the Blue Ridge, was constituted the military Department of the Shenandoah, and assigned to Maj. Gen. Banks; and that portion of Virginia east of the Blue Ridge and west of the Potomac constituted the Department of the Rappahannock, and was assigned to Maj. Gen. McDowell.

1. Gen. Banks advanced from Strasburg, Va., to Woodstock, and thence to Edenburg, driving the enemy with slight skirmishing. The railway bridge at Edenburg was burnt by rebels under Gen. Jackson.

1. Heavy bombardment at Island No. 10.

2. Manassas Gap, Va., was occupied by Col. Geary's troops by strategy, frustrating a similar attempt by the rebels.

3. U. S. Senate passed a bill for the abolition of slavery in the District of Columbia, by a vote of 29 yeas, 14 nays.

3. Gen. Steele's forces in the advance of Gen. Curtis' army, reached Putnam, Ark.

4. A schooner containing 24 recruits *en route* for the rebel army, was captured on Black creek, near the Potomac river, Va.

4. The Federal gunboat Carondelet ran past the rebel batteries at Island No. 10, at night, without damage, and arrived at New Madrid.

5. Gen. McClellan's army advanced through a severe storm from Camp Misery, and after a tedious march arrived in front of the rebel works, and commenced the siege of Yorktown, Va. Heavy firing throughout the day resulted in a loss to the Federals of 3 killed, 22 wounded.

5. Federal transports and barges arrived at New Madrid, Mo., through the inland channel, cut by Col Bissel's engineer corps, thus avoiding the rebel batteries at No. 10.

6–7. Battle of Pittsburg Landing, Tenn. The combined rebel army, under Gens. Johnston and Beauregard, attacked Gen. Grant's army on the morning of the 6th. Federal loss, 1,614 killed, 7,721 wounded, 3,963 missing—total, 13,508; rebel loss, (Beauregard's report.) 1,728 killed, 8,012 wounded, 959 missing—total, 10,699.

7. Gen. Pope, with the assistance of the gunboats Pittsburg and Carondelet, landed his forces on the Tennessee shore, opposite New Madrid, and took position in rear of Island No. 10, at Tiptonville.

7. Island No. 10 on the Mississippi, and the adjacent works on the Tenn. shore, were abandoned by the rebels and taken possession of by Col Buford's brigade.

7. Apalachicola, Fla., was captured by the Federal gunboats Mercedita and Sagamore.

8. Surrender of the rebel army of 5,200 men and all their stores, under Gens. Mackall and Gantt, to the Federal forces under Gen. Paine, of Gen. Pope's division, at Tiptonville, Tenn.

8. Gen. W. T. Sherman was dispatched by Gen. Grant with a large reconnoitering force on the Corinth, Miss., road. A portion of his force was routed by a charge of rebel cavalry, and 15 killed and 25 wounded of the 77th Ohio regiment.

10. Huntsville, Ala., was occupied by Gen. Mitchel's forces. 200 prisoners, 15 locomotives, and many cars captured.

10. Batteries on Tybee Island commenced the attack of Fort Pulaski, Ga.

10. President Lincoln, by proclamation, recommended the people throughout the United States on the Sabbath succeeding the receipt of his Proclamation to return thanks to Almighty God for having vouchsafed signal victories over rebellious enemies, and also for having averted the dangers of foreign interference and invasion.

11. Surrender of Fort Pulaski, Ga., after

a bombardment of two days. Federal loss, 1 killed, 1 wounded; rebels, 3 wounded 360 prisoners, 47 guns, 40,000 lbs. powder.

April 11. The rebel steamers Merrimac, Jamestown and Yorktown, came down between Newport News and Sewall's Point, on the Chesapeake, and captured 3 vessels.

11. Severe skirmishing in front of Yorktown, Va., by General Jameson's brigade. 20 of the Federals were killed or wounded.

11. Gen. Halleck assumed command of the Federal army at Pittsburg, Tenn.

12. Gen. Milroy, at Monterey, Va., was attacked by a large force of rebels, whom he repulsed with slight loss.

12. The Charleston and Memphis railway at Chattanooga Junction was seized by Gen. Mitchel's forces, and 2,000 rebels and much property were captured.

12 4,000 men on five transports, accompanied by the gunboats Lexington and Tyler, left Pittsburg Landing, Tenn., and proceeded up the Tennessee river to Eastport, Miss., where they landed, and destroyed two bridges on the Ohio and Mobile railway, intercepting the rebel communication with Alabama. A body of Confederate cavalry were met on their return, who were routed, and four killed.

14. The U. S. forces were withdrawn from Jacksonville, Fla., and the rebels soon after returning the loyal inhabitants suffered severely, and many were driven away.

14. The Potomac flotilla ascended the Rappahannock river, Va., destroying several batteries. Three vessels were captured.

14. Com. Foote's mortar boats opened fire on Fort Wright, on the Mississippi.

15. M. Mercier, French Minister at Washington, paid an official visit to the rebel authorities at Richmond.

15. Ex-Sec. of War Cameron was arrested at Philadelphia, Pa., on the suit of Pierce Butler, for alleged illegal arrest.

16. Engagement at Lee's Mill, near Yorktown, Va. Federal loss, 32 killed and 100 wounded. Rebels, 25 killed, and 75 w.

17. Mount Jackson, in Shenandoah Co., Va., was occupied by Gen. Williams' troops, who captured 50 of Ashby's rebel cavalry.

17. A large boat was swamped at Castleman's Ferry, on the Shenandoah river, Va., by which between 40 and 50 of the 75th Penn. were drowned, among them Adj. Teatman, Capts. Wilson and Ward.

17. New Market, Va., occupied by Bank's army, and Fredericksburg by McDowell's.

17. Bombardment of Forts Wright, on the Mississippi, by the national flotilla.

17—24. Bombardment of Fort Jackson and St. Philip, on the Mississippi.

20. Battle of Camden or South Mills, N. C. Gen. Reno's forces drove the rebels from their batteries and entrenchments. Federal loss in killed and wounded, 90.

22. Rebel steamer J. Robb was captured on the Tenn. river by gunboat Tyler.

24. Yorktown, Va., was shelled by the Federal gunboats.

24. Federal fleet passed Forts Jackson and St. Philip, destroying 13 rebel gunboats, the ram Manassas, and 3 transports.

25. New Orleans captured. Rebel batteries on both sides of the river destroyed.

25. Maj.-Gen. C. F. Smith died at Savannah, Tenn.

26. Rebel schooner Arctic was captured by U. S. steamer Flambeau.

26. Rebel schooner Belle was captured by U. S. steamer Uncas.

26. Skirmish at Neosho, Mo., between 1st Missouri volunteers, under Major Hubbard, and rebels and Indians under Cols. Coffee and Sternwright. Rebels defeated.

26. An advance lunette of the rebels at Yorktown was carried by the 1st Mass.

26. Capture of Fort Macon, N. C., with its garrison of 450 men under Col. White, after a bombardment of 11 hours. Rebel loss, 7 killed, 18 wounded. Federal loss, 1 killed, 3 wounded.

28. Forts St. Philip and Jackson, La., surrendered; forts Livingston and Pike aband[illegible] and the rebel iron battery Louisiana blown up.

30. Skirmish of Gen. Mitchel's forces with the rebels near Bridgeport, Ala.

May 2. The U. S. steamer Brooklyn and several gunboats, left New Orleans, ascending the Mississippi, to open the river and connect with Commodore Davis' fleet.

3. A reconnoissance in force under Gen. Paine from Pope's division encountered rebel cavalry pickets near Farmington, Miss., in which 8 of the latter were killed.

4. Gen. Stoneman's advance of McClellan's army encountered a rebel force near Williamsburg, Va., seven of whom were killed and 25 captured. 2 Feds. killed, 20 w.

5. Battle of Williamsburg, Va. Gen. Kearney's and Hooker's divisions engaged the rebel army under Gen. Longstreet from dawn till dark, when the Federals were reinforced and rebels defeated. Fed. loss 2,073 in killed and wounded, and 623 prisoners. Reb. loss heavier, 500 prisoners.

6. Skirmish near Harrisonburg, Va., by Federal troops under Major Vought.

7. Westpoint, Va. Gen. Franklin's division of McClellan's army having been conveyed by transports to the head of York river, effected a landing, where he was attacked by a force of rebels, and with the aid of gunboats defeated the enemy.

CHRONOLOGY.

1862.

May 7. A detachment of the 13th Ind., Col. Foster, was led into an ambush at Somerville Heights, Va., by a superior force of rebels of the 7th Louisiana. After a severe skirmish, Col. Foster made an orderly retreat, with the loss of 29 men, inflicting equal loss to the enemy.

7. The 23d Ohio, Maj. Cauley, drove a rebel force from Giles's Court House, and the narrows of New river, W. Va., and captured 20 prisoners and some stores.

8. Skirmish near Corinth, Miss., by the 7th Ill. cavalry, Maj. Arlington, in which their commander was killed. 4 Federals wounded. Rebel loss 30.

8. The iron-clad steamer Galena, assisted by the gunboats Aroostook and Port Royal, attacked and silenced two rebel batteries a short distance from the mouth of the James river, Va., called the Upper and Lower shoal batteries. But trifling damage was experienced by the Federal vessels, and no casualties.

8. A reconnoissance in force was made by the united forces of Gens. Schenck and Milroy, near McDowell, W. Va., with 2,300 men, to check the advance of a superior force of rebels then threatening to attack them. An engagement of 5 hours' duration ensued, in which 30 of the Feds. were killed and 200 wounded. The loss of the enemy is computed to have been greater. The movement was successful in checking the advance of the rebs., and the Fed. force was safely withdrawn to Franklin, the rebels showing no disposition to renew the combat.

8. An address was issued to the democracy of the U. S. setting forth party organization as essential to the preservation of public liberty. It was signed by Messrs. Richardson, Knapp, and Robinson, of Ill.; Law and Voorhees of Ind.; White, Allen Noble, Morris, Pendleton, and Vallandigham, of Ohio; Ancona and Johnson, of Penn., and Shields, of Oregon.

8. A bill passed by the U. S. Senate, establishing Beaufort, S. C., as a port of entry.

9. Two guerrillas were hung at Chester, W. Va., in conformity with orders based on a proclamat'n of Gen. Fremont.

9. Gen. Hunter proclaimed the persons in the States of Ga., Fa., and S. C., heretofore held as slaves, "forever free."

9. Burning Springs, W. Va., was burned by rebel guerrillas.

9. Peasacola, Fla., evacuated by the rebs. after setting fire to forts, navy yard barracks and Marine hospital.

9. Capt. Connet and 48 men of the 27th Ind., were captured 12 miles from Athens Ala., by a superior cavalry force under Col. Woodward. 13 rebs. and 5 Feds. were killed.

9. At Farmington, 5 miles N. W. of Corinth, Miss., the rebs. in great force under Ruggles, Price and Van Dorn, attacked Plummer's and Palmer's brigades, attached to Maj-Gen. Pope's division, and compelled them to retreat. A brilliant cavalry charge was made by the 2d Iowa, who lost 90 horses, 2 men killed and 40 wounded. The entire Fed. loss was about 40 killed and 120 wounded. The reb. loss was much greater.

9. The prize steamer P. C. Wallis, while on the way from Ship Isl. to N. O., with a battery of artillery on board, sprung a leak and sunk. The crew were saved by the gunboat Saxon.

9. Two recruits for the Fed. army at Washington, N. C., assassinated by rebs.

9. A company of rebs. under Capt. Walker, attempted to surprise Fed. officers at Washington, N. C. Capt. Redding's company of 24th Mass., acting as pickets, killed Capt. Walker and 5 men. No Feds. were injured.

10. A spirited naval engagement occurred on the Miss. above Fort Wright. The Fed. gunboats besieging that place, under the command of Acting-Flag-Officer Davis, were attacked by the rebel gunboats and rams then stationed at that post, who after a half hour's contest were forced to retire. The Fed. gunboats Cincinnati and Mound City were badly injured in the contest, and the reb. vessels also were considerably cut up, though the casualties on either side were small.

10. White House, on the Pamunkey river Va., occupied by Federal cavalry, 7,000 bushels of wheat and 4,000 of corn captured.

10. $800,000 in specie seized by Gen.

Butler in New Orleans, at the office of the Consul for the Netherlands.

May 10. New Kent C. H., Va., occupied by Gen. Stoneman's Fed. cavalry.

10. The iron-clad steamer Ironsides was launched at Philadelphia.

10. The reb. schooner Maria Theresa, was captured by the U. S. gunboat Unadilla.

10. Norfolk, Va., was occupied by Fed. troops under Gen. Wool.

10. A plot discovered in Paducah, Ky. by which the town was to be handed over to the rebs. within a week. Information was given by one of the conspirators.

11. The fortifications of Craney I., Va., taken possession of by the Nat'l forces.

11. 48 freight and 4 passenger cars. and 2 locomotives were captured by 140 reb. cavalry under Col. Morgan, at Cave City, Ky.

11. Col. Phelan's reb. camp at Bloomfield, Mo., was broken up by the 1st Wis. cavalry.

11. A reb. lieutenant and 10 men were captured by Maj. Duffie's command, Harris' Light cavalry, near Fredericksburg, Va.

11. The reb. iron-plated steamer Merrimac was abandoned by her crew and blown up off Craney Island, Va., the retreat of the rebel forces from Yorktown and Norfolk isolating her from the Confederate forces.

12. The reb. steamer Governor Morton captured.

13. General Fremont, with his command, reached Franklin, W. Va., advancing by forced marches. Maj.-Gen. Halleck issued an order expelling newspaper correspondents from his lines.

13. Martial law enforced in Charleston, S. C.

13. Reb. Gen. Jackson made an unsuccessful attack on Gens. Milroy and Schenck's brigades near McDowell, Va., Fed. loss 20 killed and 177 wounded. Reb. loss 40 killed, 200 wounded. Feds. lost their camps, baggage, and stores.

13. Reb. armed steamer Planter, was run out of Charleston, S. C., by a negro crew, and surrendered to Commander Parrott, of the steamer Augusta.

13. Suffolk, Va., occupied by Federal troops under Maj. Dodge.

13. Gen. Butler forbid the opening of churches on the 15th inst. in N. O., for the purpose of observing a fast day prescribed by Jeff. Davis.

13. Attack on Fort Wright, Miss. river, by reb. mortar and gunboats.

13. Slight skirmish near Monterey, Tenn., by Gen. Smith's troops. Reb. loss 10; Union 2.

13. Natchez, Miss., surrendered to flag officer Farragut.

14. A skirmish near Trenton Bridge, N. C. Col. Amory with 17th and 25th Mass. defeated a reb. force, killing 10 of them.

14. Rebel steamer Alice captured in Roanoke river by U. S. steamers Ceres and Lockwood.

14. A party consisting of four officers' servants and several convalescent soldiers, in charge of Surgeon Charles Newham, 29th N. Y. V., when on the road to Moorfield, were attacked while passing through a gap on Lost river, near Wartonsville. With the exception of Dr. Newham, who, though severely wounded succeeded in cutting his way through, the whole party were either killed or taken prisoners.

15. The Fed. iron battery Monitor, together with the mailed gunboats Galena and E. A. Stevens, attacked Fort Darling, on Watches Bluff, 6 miles below Richmond, on the James river. The fight continued for four hours, when the ammunition of the Galena having become exhausted, the Fed. vessels retired. The Galena was badly damaged, and lost 17 men killed and about 20 wounded. The large rifled gun of the E. A. Stevens burst early in the action. All the vessels engaged under great disadvantage in not being able to obtain sufficient elevation of their guns to bear on the high bluffs occupied by the enemy.

15. A company of infantry from Gen. Geary's command were attacked by a body of rebel cavalry Fed. loss 17.

15. Slight skirmish near Batesville, Ark., by 5th Ill. cavalry, Lieut. Smith.

16. U. S. steamer Oriental wrecked near Cape Hatteras, N. C.

16. Reb. newspapers suppressed in N. Orleans by Gen. Butler, and the circulation of Confederate notes prohibited

16. Skirmish near Trenton, N. C. U. S. cavalry attacked a detachment of rebs. in ambush, and scattered them, killing 6 or 8, and wounding a larger number. Maj. Fitzsimmons of the cavalry wounded, and Lieut. Mayes and four men taken prisoners.

17. A successful movement was made by a portion of Gen. W. T. Sherman's division of the army investing Corinth, by which the rebs. were driven from their position at Russell's House, two miles from Corinth. 12 of the rebel dead

were left on the field, but all their wounded were removed. Gen M. L. Smith's brigade, of the Fed. army, lost 10 killed and 31 wounded.

17. Gen. Carleton's brigade entered Arizona; Col. West's regiment arrived at Luezon; and raised the National flag over the ruins of Fort Breckinridge.

17. The advance of the Army of the Potomac reached Bottom's Bridge on the Chickahominy river.

18. Engagement near Searcy, on Little Red river, Ark. 150 men of Gen. Osterhaus's troops engaged and defeated a superior force of the enemy, in which the latter lost about 100 men.

18. A fight near Princeton, Va., in which Gen. Cox's troops were defeated, with a loss of 30 killed and 70 wounded, by a rebel force under Humphrey Marshall.

18. Suffolk, Va., occupied by Feds.

19. The Army of the Potomac resumed its march from Cumberland across the Peninsula towards Richmond.

19. White House, on the Pamunkey, selected as the general depot of supplies for the Army of the Potomac.

19. Gens. Heintzelman and Keys, with 40,000 men, marched for Bottom's Bridge, on the Chickahominy.

19. Gen. McClellan, with his main army, reached Tunstall's Station.

19. A skirmish near Newbern, N. C. Fed. loss 5; reb. 11.

19. Lieut. Whitesides and 8 men of the 6th cavalry, captured a train of reb. Gen. Whiting's, with 100 mules and 8 negroes.

19. John T. Monroe, Mayor of N. Orleans, and other city officers, arrested by Gen. Butler and sent to Fort Jackson.

19. Pres. Lincoln, by proclamation, declared null and void general order No. 11 of Maj.-Gen. Hunter, commanding at Hilton Head, S. C., and dated May 9, in which he pronounced the slaves of the States of Georgia, Florida and South Carolina "forever free." The President asked the serious consideration of the States interested, to the resolution of Congress of May 6, 1862, offering to aid any State which should adopt a gradual abolition of slavery.

19. Typhoid and bilious fevers raging among the Fed. soldiers at Norfolk, Va. Deaths about 10 daily. The steamer Vanderbilt took 500 of the sick from Yorktown to Baltimore.

19. A boat from the Wachusett, manned by 6 officers and 12 men, with a flag of truce conveying a surgeon on shore, who had been sent a short distance above City Point, on the James river, Va., was fired on by a party of 20 or 30 rebs. while the surgeon and other officers were on shore. Three of the men in the boat were killed, and 2 wounded; while the party who had landed were made prisoners, and sent to Richmond.

20. Edward Stanley, of N. C., received a Fed. commission as Military Governor of that State.

20. Skirmish near Moorfield, Va. A party of soldiers under Lieut.-Col. Downey, captured 12 and killed 4 guerrillas.

20. 17 wagons and 86 mules with government stores were captured 20 miles from Rolla, Mo.

20. Reb. works on Cole's Island, S. C., burned.

20. The advance of Gen. McClellan's army under Gen. Stoneman, reached New Bridge, on the Chickahominy creek, 8 miles from Richmond, driving in the enemy's outposts. The enemy had then no forces south of the Chickahominy. Gen. Stoneman lost 1 killed and 3 wounded.

20. Lieut.-Cols. McIlhanny, Rawlings, Thursman, and Davis, four rebel officers, were captured by Brig.-Gen. Totten, while they were about to cross the Missouri river, above Jefferson City, on a mission to stir up rebellion in Missouri.

21. Skirmish near Corinth, Miss., by troops from the 1st and 20th Ky., under Fed. Col. Sedgewick. Union loss 25.

22. Lieut E. R Colburn of the Fed. gunboat Hunchback, commander of the U. S. Naval forces in North Carolina waters, in company with the gunboats Shansun and Whitehead, destroyed several rebel fortifications on the Mehirun and Chowan rivers, and captured 3 or 4 vessels laden with valuable cargoes.

23. The reb. steamer Daniel E. Miller, with military stores and 60 recruits, for Memphis, was captured on the St. Francis river, by the 1st Wis. cavalry, Capt. Daniels, he having a 6-pounder on shore.

23. Col. J. R. Kenly, with the 1st Md. regiment, part of the 29th Penn. reg't, and a small force of N. Y. cavalry, was attacked at Front Royal, Va., by a large force of rebs. under Gen. Jackson. After brave resistance the Feds. were defeated, and Col. Kenly, with the larger part of the Md. reg't taken prisoners.

23. Gen. Heath, with 3,000 men, attacked the Fed. force under Col. Crook, at Lewisburg, Va.: after a severe fight the rebs. were routed. Crook's force numbered 1,300. Fed. loss 10 killed, 40 wounded, and 8 missing. The loss of the

enemy much greater. 4 cannon, 200 stands of arms, and 100 prisoners were captured.

May 23. A portion of the 4th Mich. and 5th U. S. cavalry succeeded in crossing the Chickahominy, and getting, unperceived in the rear of four companies of the 5th Louisiana reg't, which had been drawn toward the creek by the sight of a portion of the Fed. forces on the opposite bank. Many of the rebs. were killed, 15 wounded, and 31 taken prisoners. One Union soldier killed, and 6 wounded.

23. Grand Gulf, Miss., shelled by Fed. gunboats in retaliation for the firing on Fed. transports by a masked battery near that place.

23. Gen. McClellan's army crossed Bottom's Bridge on the Chickahominy, and his advance was within 7 miles of Richmond.

24. Two Ga. reg'ts under Gen. Cobb, were attacked near Williamsville, by portions of 4 reg'ts belonging to Gen. Davidson's brigades, attached to Gen. McClellan's army before Richmond. The Fed. soldiers drove the rebs. from the town, with considerable loss. Fed. casualties 2 killed and 4 wounded.

24. The 4th Mich, encountered the 5th Louisiana a short distance above New Bridge, on the Chickahominy. 37 rebs. captured, and about 50 killed and wounded. Fed. loss 10.

24. All the railroads in the U. S. claimed by the government for military purposes.

24. The steamer Swan, with 1,000 bales of cotton and 800 bbls. rosin, captured off Cuba by U. S. brig Bainbridge and bark Amanda.

25. Gen. N. P. Banks, with 4,000 men, was attacked at Winchester, at daylight, by about 15,000 rebs. under Gens. Ewell and Johnson. After a spirited resistance Gen. Banks made good his retreat to Martinsburg.

25. A riot in Baltimore, created by the excitement caused on hearing of the defeat and capture of a large part of Col. Kenly's Md. regiment. Many secessionists who expressed joy at hearing of the misfortune, were roughly handled by the friends of the regiment.

26. After a five hours' chase the English iron steamer Cambria, with a cargo of stores for the rebs., was captured off Charleston, S. C., by the Fed. gunboat Huron.

26. Col. Cluseret, with the advance brigade of Gen. Fremont's army, overtook the rebel Gen. Jackson's forces, in full retreat, on the road from Winchester to Strasburg, Va. 25 of the rebs. were captured. Their killed and wounded unknown. 7 Fed. soldiers wounded.

26. British steamer Patras captured off Charleston, S. C., by U. S. gunboat Bienville.

26. N. Y. and Mass. militia left home for Washington at one day's notice.

27. The English steamer Gordon, captured off Wilmington, N. C., by the gunboats State of Georgia and Victoria.

27. Gens. Martindale and Butterfield's brigades engaged and defeated a rebel force of 8,000 near Hanover C. H., Va. Fed. loss 54 killed and 194 wounded and missing. Rebel loss between 2 and 300 killed and wounded, and 500 prisoners.

28. Engagement on the Corinth road, Miss. A reconnoissance by the 10th Iowa, Col. Purcell, of Gen. Halleck's forces, met and fought a rebel force. Federal loss 25 killed and wounded; 30 reb. dead left on the field.

28. Gens. Denver and Smith of Sherman's division, and Gen. Veatch, obtained possession of a strong position within 1,300 yards of the rebel lines at Corinth, Miss., giving the Federal army command of the enemy's lines. Union loss 6 killed, 12 wounded.

29. Capt. Frisbee, commanding a detachment of the 38th Ill. infantry, and the 1st Mo. cavalry, captured, near Neosho, Mo., 2 colonels, 1 lieutenant, a number of guns and revolvers, 15 horses, and a large train of forage and provisions.

29. English steamer Elizabeth, captured off Charleston, S. C., by U. S. gunboat Keystone State.

29. Ashland, Va., occupied by Federal troops, and a large number of cars with valuable rebel stores were captured.

29. Skirmish at Pocotaligo, S. C. Reb. loss about 20 killed and wounded; Union loss 11.

30. Booneville, 24 miles S. of Corinth, Miss., occupied by 2 regiments of Fed. cavalry under Col. Elliott, a large amount of stores destroyed, with depot, engines, and cars, and 200 rebel sick captured and paroled.

30. Capture of Corinth, Miss., by Gen. Halleck's army. 2,000 rebel prisoners, and large supplies taken.

30. Col. Elliott, with the 2nd Iowa cavalry, by forced marches from Corinth Miss., penetrated the enemy's lines to Booneville, on the Ohio and Mobile railway. They tore up the track in many places north and south of that point, destroyed the locomotives, and 26 cars la-

den with supplies for the rebel army. They also took 10,000 stand of arms, 3 pieces of artillery, large quantities of clothing and ammunition, and paroled 2,000 prisoners.

30. On the Winchester road, six miles from Front Royal, Va., a body of Fed. troops attacked a body of rebels, who fled at the first fire, leaving six of their number prisoners, but bearing away their killed and wounded. 1 English 12-pdr., and 12 wagons were captured; and 6 of the 1st Maryland regiment, who were captured in a previous battle at Front Royal, were released.

30. A brigade of National troops, with 4 companies of R. I. cavalry, entered Front Royal, Va., and surprised the 8th La., and 12th Ga. troops, capturing 6 officers and 150 men, killing and wounding 20, and securing 2 engines, 11 cars, and various stores. Fed. loss 8 killed 5 wounded.

30. 13 of the 11th Pa. cavalry captured near Zuni, Va.

31. Skirmish at Neosho, Mo. The 10th Ill. cavalry and 300 militia, under Capt. Richardson, were driven from the town by rebs. and Indians, under Maj. Wright, after a slight resistance, and a quantity of plunder obtained by the enemy.

31. Baton Rouge, La., occupied by Federal troops under Gen. Williams.

31. Skirmish near Washington, N. C., by a party of the 3rd N. Y. cavalry, in which reb. cavalry were defeated with a loss of 11. Federal loss, 2 wounded.

31. Six reb. prisoners ordered to be executed by Gen. Butler, at N. O., for violating their parole.

31. Battle of Fair Oaks, Va. General Casey's division, after a gallant resistance were overwhelmed by the reb. army. At night the rebs. occupied the camps of the 4th corps, but their advance was broken. Gens. Couch, Heintzelman, Kearney, Richardson, and Sedgwick, arrived on the field at night with reinforcements.

June 1. Col. Elliott with the 2d Ohio cavalry, returned to Corinth, Miss., from a successful raid on the Mobile and Ohio railroad. He burned 2 locomotives and 26 cars loaded with supplies, destroyed 10,000 muskets, and captured 2,000 prisoners.

1. Gen. Dix assigned to command Fortress Monroe and vicinity.

1. Rebel fortification at Pig Point, Va., destroyed.

1. Skirmish between Strasburg and Staunton, Va., between Gen. Fremont and Gen. Jackson's troops, with but slight results. Fed. loss about 12, mostly woun'd.

1. The reb. army renew the attack on the Fed. forces at Fair Oaks, Va., when the enemy were defeated and driven from the field, with a loss of 8,000 killed and wounded. Fed. loss 5,739.

1. Gen Wool promoted to a Maj. Generalship U. S. army.

1. Two boats' crews from the U. S. bark Kingfisher captured on the Ocilla river, Florida.

1. Skirmish near Strasburg, Va., by Col. Cluseret's Fed. troops and Ashby's cavalry.

3. Maj.-Gen. Robert E. Lee assigned to the command of the rebel army in front of Richmond.

4. Skirmish near Jasper, Tenn. Gen. Negley's troops routed a large force of reb. cavalry under Gen. Adams, capturing 25, with a large quantity of arms, and killing and wounding 12.

4. Sixteen hundred of Gen. Prentiss's troops captured at Pittsburg Landing, arrived at Nashville, on parole.

4. Forts Pillow and Randolph, on the Mississippi, were evacuated by the rebs. and occupied by Fed. forces on the ensuing day.

5. The 24th Mass. were attacked from an ambush, near Washington, N. C. 7 men were killed and several wounded.

5. Skirmish at New Bridge, on the Chickahominy, by Gen. McClellan's forces.

5. Sharp skirmish on James Island, S. C., by the "Roundhead" Pa. reg't and the 8th Michigan with rebels.

6. The 1st N. J. cavalry were caught in an ambush near Harrisonburg, Va., and sustained considerable loss. Col. Windham was captured. Gen. Bayard's brigade engaged the rebels at that point and defeated them.

6. Engagement between the Fed. gunboats and rams and a reb. fleet in front of Memphis, in which 4 of the latter were sunk or captured, and one escaped. 100 reb. prisoners taken. Fed. loss none. Memphis occupied by Federals.

7. Wm. Mumford, a citizen of New Orleans, was hung for pulling down the American flag from the mint.

7. Bombardment of rebel batteries at Chattanooga, Tenn., by Gen. Negley's command.

7. Schooner Rowena captured in Stono river by the Pawnee.

8. Lieut. John G. Sprotsden, executive officer of the U. S. gunboat Seneca, was killed by a reb. named George Huston, captain of a band of marauders near

Black Creek, Fla. The lieutenant had been despatched with a force of 70 men to arrest Huston and his gang, and had surrounded his house and demanded a surrender, when he was shot by Huston, who was in turn desperately wounded and captured.

June 8. Battle of Cross-Keys, Va., near Port Republic. Gen. Fremont drove Gen. Stonewall Jackson with considerable loss.

8. Skirmish on James Island, S. C., by Col. Morrow's Federal troops.

9. Battle of Port Republic, Va. Gen. Shields with 3,500 men was attacked by 12,000 rebs. under Jackson. Union troops retreated after severe loss on both sides.

10. Skirmish on James Island, S. C. About 500 rebs. advanced on the Federal lines for the purpose of captur'g pickets, when they encountered the 97th Pa. regiment, and 2 companies of the 45th Pa. The rebs were defeated, leaving 15 dead and 2 wounded on the field. Fed. loss, 4 killed and 13 wounded.

10. Fed. expedit'n up the White river, when near St. Charles was fired into from mask'd batteries, and the gunboat Mound City received a shot in her boiler which occasioned the destruction of 100 of her crew by scalding, 23 only escaping. The reb. works were captured by the land forces under Col. Fitch, who took 30 prisoners.

10 Baldwin and Guntown, Miss., 24 miles from Corinth, occupied by Federal forces under Gen. Granger, at which places the pursuit of Beauregard's army from Corinth terminated.

11. Skirmish near Montgomery, Ky. Feds. under Capts. Nicklin and Blood engaged a force of guerrillas, and captured 25 of them, several of their number being killed or wounded. 2 Feds. were killed.

11. A rebel battery of 4 guns captured at James Island, S. C.

12. A rebel cavalry force of 1,400 men, under Gen. J. E. B. Stuart, left Richmond before daylight, by the Charlottesville turnpike, and penetrated the Fed. lines to Hanover C. H., and the White House on the Pamunkey, and then by the way of New Kent C. H., crossed the Chickahominy near Blind Ford, returning to Richmond by the Charles City road. In their foray they were eminently successful. In an engagement with a small force of U. S. cavalry 3 or 4 of the Feds. were killed, and also 2 teamsters. The rebs. captured about 50 prisoners, burned 2 schooners and 40 wagons laden with supplies, destroyed the tents of the U. S. cavalry regiment, and also some hospital stores. The mules attached to the wagons were driven off by the rebs. in their retreat.

12. A fight near Village Creek, Ark. The 9th Ill. cavalry, Col. Brackett, engaged Hooker's reb. company, and defeated them with the loss of 28 killed, wounded and prisoners. Fed. loss 13 w.

12. A daring but unsuccessful attack was made on a reb fort on James Island, S. C., by the 79th N. Y., 8th Mich., and 28th Mass., in which the Feds. were defeated with considerable loss.

12. Forty farmers from Conway Co., Ark., came into the Fed. lines at Batesville, and enlisted in the army.

13. A negro settlement on Hutchinson's Island, S. C., was broken up by a raiding party of 300 rebs. from Fort Chapman.

13. Severe skirmishes in front of Gen. M'Clellan's lines, from Old Church to Fair Oaks.

13. The reb. transport Clara Dolsen captured on the White river, Ark., by the tug Spitfire.

13 Skirmish on James Isl., S. C. Reb. loss, 17 killed, 8 wounded. Union, 3 killed, 19 wounded.

14. Capt. Atkinson's company of 50th Ind. captured 6,200 pounds of powder at Sycamore mills, 30 miles below Nashville, Tenn.

15. The battle of Secessionville on James Isl., S. C. The Fed. forces under Gen. Benham, defeated with a loss of 685 men killed, wounded, and prisoners.

15. Skirmish near Fair Oaks, Va., in which an attempt of the rebs. to flank the Fed. lines during a thunderstorm was frustrated.

15. U. S gunboats Tahoma and Somerset, Lieuts. Howell and English, commanders, crossed the bar of St. Mark's river, Fla., and destroyed a reb. fort and barracks, driving out the reb. artillerists with 4 or 5 pieces.

17. The U. S. steamers Bienville, Somerset, and Montgomery, have captured several vessels recently on the Fla. coast, laden with stores and munitions for the rebs.

17. An act of Congress passed, forever prohibiting slavery in the territories of the U. S.

18. A reconnoissance of the 16th Mass. from the Potomac army, engaged the enemy in a severe fight with great credit, and a loss of about 25 men in killed and wounded.

18. Maj. Zeley's troops attacked a band of rebs. near Smithville, Ark., capturing

their leader, Capt. Jones, and 14 of his men. 4 rebs. wounded; Feds., 2 killed, 4 wounded.

18. Cumberland Gap, Tenn., occupied by Gen. Morgan's Fed. troops.

19. Skirmish by the 20th Ind. of the Army of the Potomac, in which great gallantry was shown, and slight loss suffered by the Fed. troops.

19. Reb. schooner Louisa, and two boats laden with rice captured on the Santee river, S. C., by U. S. steamer Albatross.

20. An attack was made by some of Com. Farragut's fleet on the reb. batteries at Ellis' Cliffs, on the Miss. river. The enemy's guns were silenced after a shot from one of them had severely wounded two of the crew of the Sarah Bruin.

20. Pres. Lincoln signed the bill prohibiting slavery forever in the U. S. territories.

21. A series of skirmishes took place at the mouth of Battle Creek, Tenn. Col. Lill's Fed. troops defeated a body of the enemy with slight loss.

21. Death of Col. Charles Ellet, of the Miss. ram squadron, at Cairo, Ill., of wounds.

21. Skirmish at Fair Oaks, Va.

22. Part of the 16th Ill. cavalry captured a train, 25 prisoners, and 10,000 lbs. bacon, near Coldwater, on the Miss. and Tenn R. R.

22. 3 men killed and 8 wounded of the 8th Vt., at Algiers, near N. O., by a party of guerrillas who surprised them.

23. Pres. Lincoln made a hurried visit to Gen. Scott, at West Point, N. Y., to confer with him in reference to some important changes in the military departments.

25. Battle of Oak Grove, Va. General Hooker's forces with a loss of 200 men, defeated the rebs., who suffered more severely.

25. Gen. Pope arrived in Washington, to take command of the Army of Va.

25. Gen. Fremont resigned his command in the U. S. Army.

25. A train of cars on the Memphis and Ohio railroad, with a company of Fed. troops, 80 mule teams, &c., was captured by the rebs. 10 Fed. soldiers were killed, and the cars and engine destroyed.

25. Col. George Crook, with 1,750 men from the 36th, 44th, and 47th Ohio, and the 2d Va. cavalry regiment, returned to his headquarters at Meadow Bluff, Greenbriar Co., Va., after driving 2,000 rebels under Gen. Heth, out of Monroe Co., retaking a large supply of provisions, grain, and forage, which had been seized by the rebs., capturing a number of the enemy, and restoring 100 refugees to their homes.

26. Skirmish on the Appomattox river, Va. 6 of Capt. Rogers' gunboat fleet engaged reb. batteries, 6 miles from the mouth of the river.

26. 3 reb. gunboats burned on the Yazoo river by their officers, to prevent their capture by the Union ram-flotilla, Lieut.-Col. Ellet, then in pursuit of them.

26. The great series of battles on the Chickahominy, before Richmond, commenced at 2 P. M. by the attack by a large force of rebels on McCall's division, on the extreme right of McClellan's army at Mechanicsville. After losing more than 1000 men, the rebels retreated. Fed. loss, 80 killed, 150 wounded.

26. Severe losses had occurred in picket skirmishing on the Chickahominy creek for two weeks previous. 9 Federals were killed on this day.

27. Skirmish on the Amite river, La. 21st Ind. Col. Keith, defeated 2 parties of rebels, after slight skirmishing.

27. Skirmish near Swift Creek bridge, N. C.

27. Battle of Gaines's Mill, near Richmond, Va. The Federals successfully resisted an attack by the rebel army and made good their retreat.

27. Severe fight near Village Creek, Ark. 9th Ill. cavalry, under Col. Brackett. Fed. loss 2 k. and 31 wounded.

27. The Vicksburg "canal" commenced, intended to isolate that place from the Mississippi river.

28. 5 clergymen imprisoned at Nashville, Tenn. by Gov. Johnson, for refusing to swear allegiance to the U. S. Government.

28. Battle of the Chickahominy, Va. Gen. Porter's troops bore the brunt of the fighting, the Feds. still successfully retreating.

28. 100 of the Maryland Home Guard were captured at Moorfield, Hardy Co., Va. by rebel troops under Col. Harness, formerly of Ashby's cavalry. The prisoners were paroled.

28. About $100,000 value of Government stores were destroyed by Federal troops at the White House landing on the Pamunkey river, Va., previous to evacuating that place, to prevent the rebels from seizing the same.

28. Flag-officer Farragut with nine vessels of his fleet ran by the rebel batteries at Vicksburg, through a severe fire, losing 4 men killed and 13 wounded.

June 29. The steamship Ann, of London, with a valuable cargo, was captured in the act of unloading by the U.S. steamer Kanawha, at the mouth of the Mobile Bay, under the guns of Fort Morgan.

29. Battle of Peach Orchard, Va., in which the rebels were repulsed.

29. Battle of Savage's Station, Va. The Union troops continuing their retreat were attacked. A sanguinary engagement ensued which resulted in heavy loss to both sides.

29. Fight at Henderson, Ky. Andrews' Mich. battery and Louisville Provost Guard routed a body of rebel guerrillas.

29. Heavy bombardment at Vicksburg, Miss.

30. Bridges at Harrodsburg and Nicholasville, Ky. burned by rebel guerrillas.

30. Battle of White Oak Swamp, Va. which lasted the entire day.

July 1. In response to a proposition from the loyal Governors of the States suggesting the employment of additional military force, President Lincoln called into service 300,000 men, to be apportioned from the several States.

1. Battle of Malvern Hills, the last of the 7 days' contests, lasting 2 hours. The rebels repulsed at all points. As the Fed. forces neared James river, the Fed. gunboats opened fire, and did great execution. The rebels were driven back discomfited.

1. Com. Porter's ram fleet skirmished with the rebel batteries at Vicksburg, Miss.

1. Col. Sheridan, of the 2d Michigan cavalry, commanding 728 men, was attacked by a force of over 4,000 rebs. near Booneville, Miss. An engagement of seven hours' duration ensued resulting in the total defeat of the rebels, leaving 65 dead on the field. The Federal loss was 41 in killed, wounded and missing.

2. Gen M'Clellan's army reached Harrison's Bar on the James river, Va.

2. Gen. Halleck left St Louis to take position as Gen.-in-chief at Washington.

2. Flag-officer Farragut, with nine vessels of his fleet, passed above the reb. batteries at Vicksburg, Miss., through a severe fire, thus forming a junction with the Fed. fleet of the Upper Mississippi. His loss in the engagement was 4 killed and 13 wounded.

3. The brig Delilah captured by U. S. steamer Quaker City off Hole-in-the-Wall

3. Skirmish on the James river, Va. Gen. Davidson's brigade captured 6 reb. guns and a number of prisoners.

3. Commencement of the bombardment of Vicksburgh, Miss. by the combined fleets of Coms. Farragut and Porter.

4. The United States flag waving in every State of the Union.

4. Successful skirmish near Little Red river, Ark. by Fed. troops under Lieut-Col. Wood.

4. Union pickets defeated in a skirmish at Port Royal Ferry, S. C.

4. The steamers State of Maine and Kennebec left Fortress Monroe with 559 wounded soldiers for New York.

4. 553 reb. prisoners, arrived at Fortress Monroe taken in the late battles near Richmond.

4. 4,600 Fed. prisoners were confined in Richmond, one fourth of whom were wounded or sick.

4. Skirmish near Grand Haze, on the White river, Ark. by 13th Ill.

4. Reb. gunboat Teazer captured on James river by U. S. steamer Maratanza.

6. A fight at Grand Prairie, near Aberdeen, Ark. Col. Spicely's infantry defeated reb. cavalry, routing them with great loss.

7. Steamer Emilie captured off Bull's Bay, S. C. by U. S. steamer Flag and bark Restless.

7. Col. Hovey, with 4 companies of his 33d Ill. regiment, 4 of the 11th Missouri, and a battalion of Ind. cavalry, attached to Gen. Curtis's army in Ark., routed 2 Texan regiments at a point between Cotton Plant and Bayou Coache. Rebel loss 110 killed, left on the field. Fed. 8 killed, 47 wounded.

8. Pres. Lincoln reviewed the army of the Potomac at Harrison's Landing, Va.

9. A detachment of 9th Pa. cavalry, 250 strong, under Maj. Jordan, were attacked at Tompkinsville, Monroe Co., Ky., by about 1,200 rebs. under Cols. John Morgan and Hunt. The Pennsylvanians were routed after a fight of 20 minutes, with a loss of 4 killed, 6 wounded and 20 prisoners, including Maj. Jordan. 10 rebs. were killed, and Col. Hunt mortally wounded.

9. Hamilton, N. C., captured by Fed. gunboats and 9th N. Y. volunteers.

9. Gold coin commanded a premium of 17 per cent. in New York, silver 10, and nickel 3 per cent.

10. Ninety rebs. while drilling in an old field between Gallatin and Heartsville, Tenn., were surprised and captured by Col. Boone's regiment, and taken to Nashville as prisoners.

11. Maj.-Gen. H. W. Halleck appoint'd commander-in-chief of the U. S. army.

11. Skirmish near New Hope, Ky. Fed. troops under Lieut.-Col. Moore, defeated rebel cavalry.

11. Capt. Cohl, with a company of Mo. State Militia, defeated a band of rebels commanded by Col. Quantrell, at Pleasant Hill, in which 6 rebs. were killed and 5 badly wounded. The Fed. loss was 9 killed and 15 wounded; Capt. Cohl being among the wounded.

12. Gen. Curtis' army arrived in safety at Helena, Ark., on the Mississippi river, having defeated the rebs. in every encounter during a five months' campaign, and frustrated their attempts to impede his march and cut off his supplies.

12. Fight at Lebanon, Ky. Union troops under Col. Johnson defeated by Morgan's cavalry, and the town captured by the rebels.

12. Fairmount, Mo., plundered by rebel guerrillas.

13. Skirmish at Rapidan Station, Va., by Fed. troops under Maj. Deems, who destroyed the bridge and defeated a party of rebels.

13. Memphis, Mo. robbed by rebel guerrillas.

13. A reb. force of 2,000 cavalry under Cols. Morgan and Forrest, attacked the 9th Mich. 3d Minn., and Hewitt's battery under Gen. T. A. Crittenden, at Murfreesborough, Tenn., capturing the entire force. Reb. loss, 30 killed and 100 wounded. Fed. loss, 33 killed, 62 wounded.

14. Cynthiana, Ky., captured by Morgan's rebel troops, and a small force of Feds., under Capt. Arthur, taken prisoners.

15. Maj. Miller, with 600 men from 10th Ill., 2d Wis., and 3d Mo., attacked a superior force of rebs. under Rains and Coffee, at Fayetteville, Ark., routing them with great loss.

15. Gen. David E. Twiggs died at Augusta, Ga.

15. The reb. iron-clad ram Arkansas, came down the Yazoo river and engaged the Fed. gunboats Carondelet and Tyler, and ram Lancaster. The ram succeeded in escaping to Vicksburg with a loss of 10 killed and 15 wounded, including the commander, Capt. Brown. 22 Federals were killed, and 55 wounded and missing.

15. A large and enthusiastic Union meeting was held in N. Y. city, in which all classes of citizens were fully represented, and a unanimity of purpose expressed to sustain the Government to the fullest extent in putting down the rebellion, and restoring the integrity of the Union.

16. Lieut. Rogers, of the U. S. steamer Huntsville, of the S. Atlantic blockading squadron, reported capturing the British schooner Agnes, with 60 bales cotton and 40 barrels rosin. Also the rebel steamer Reliance, from Dobay bar, Ga., bound for Nassau, with 243 bales Sea Island cotton.

17. Skirmish at Cynthiana, Ky., Capt. Glass' troops.

17. Gordonsville, Va., occupied by Gen. Pope's Fed. troops.

17. Adjournment of Congress.

17. Confiscation bill signed by the President.

17. Skirmish near Columbia, Tenn. Lieut. Roberts, of 1st Ky. Union cavalry, kept at bay a superior reb. force in a fight of 6 hours.

18. Twenty-eight men of company A., N. Y. cavalry, were captured at Orange C. H., on the Orange and Alexandria railway, by rebel cavalry under Gen. Ewell.

18. Severe fight near Memphis, Mo. 400 Feds. under Maj. Clopper, defeated a reb. force under Col. Porter. Fed. loss, 15 killed and 30 wounded. Reb. loss, 23 killed besides wounded.

18. The town of Newburg, Ind., robbed by reb. troops under Capt. Johnson.

19. Fifty-three men of 3d Mich. cavalry captured near Booneville, Miss.

19. The reb. Col. Morgan was attacked on Garret Davis' farm, near Paris, Ky., by Gen. Green Clay and Col. Metcalf, with 1,600 cavalry, and routed with loss.

19. A band of 32 reb. guerrillas crossed the Ohio river from Kentucky to Newburg, Ind., and plundered the hospital and other buildings, recrossing the river before the armed forces in the neighborhood could intercept them.

19. A down train on the Columbia railway, Tenn., when 12 miles below Reynolds Station, was thrown from the track, and Capt. J. Fatrem of the 6th Ohio, and four others killed, and about 30 wounded.

20. Skirmish on James river, Va., by 8th Pa. cavalry, Capt. Keenan.

20. One hundred and forty men of the Harris Light Cavalry, under Col. Davis, penetrated the reb. lines on the Virginia Central railway, 12 miles west of Hanover Junction, destroying the military stores and the railway at Beaver Dam Creek, and returned to Fredericksburg in safety, marching 80 miles in 30 hours.

21. All the militia in the State of Mo. were ordered to be enrolled by Gov.

Gamble, subject to the call of Gen. Schofield, for the purpose of destroying the guerrilla bands in the State.

July 21. A band of guerrillas under Capt. Reeves surprised a body of State militia commanded by Capt. Leeper, at Greenville, Wayne county, Mo., many of whom were killed and wounded and the remainder driven from the town.

22. A band of 40 rebels attacked a wagon train at Pittsburgh Landing, Tenn., and captured 60 wagons with army stores.

22. A Union cavalry company fired, by mistake, on a Confederate detachment with a flag of truce returning under a Union escort from Cumberland Gap, Tenn. A lieutenant was killed, and 6 privates wounded. Lieut.-Col. Kregan, commanding the Union escort, and Capt. Lyons, of Gen. Morgan's staff, were severely wounded. Several Union soldiers were killed and wounded.

22. Reb. steamer Reliance captured by U. S. steamer Huntsville.

22. Maj.-Gen. Sherman took command at Memphis, Tenn. 400 citizens took the oath, and 130 were sent south.

23. Florence, Ala. entered by rebel troops, who burned a large supply of Fed. stores.

23. 60 wagons, laden with commissary stores, were captured by rebels near Pittsburg Landing, Tenn.

23. An unsuccessful attempt was made to sink the reb. ram Arkansas, at Vicksburg, by Col. Ellet, with the Union ram Queen of the West.

23. Fight near Florida, Mo. Fed. cavalry under Maj. Caldwell attacked by rebs. under Col. Porter. Feds. defeated with a loss of 26.

23. An attempt was made by a portion of the rebel prisoners confined at Chicago, Ill., to escape from their guards, who rallied and drove them back, a few only escaping. Several of the prisoners were killed and wounded.

23. A detachment of four companies of Fed. troops, under Maj. Lippert, sent out from Rivas Station by Col. Boyd to intercept the guerrillas who made the raid on Greenville, Mo., met the enemy, and dispersed the band, taking 16 prisoners, and recovered the booty taken at Greenville.

23. Lieut.-Col. Kilpatrick, with part of the N. Y. Harris Light Cavalry, left Fredericksburg, Va., on the 22d, and encountered and defeated a body of rebel cavalry near Carmel Church, on the road to Richmond, whom they defeated, burned their camps and six cars loaded with corn, and broke up the telegraph to Gordonsville. An hour later they routed a large body of Stuart's cavalry, captured several prisoners and a large number of horses.

23. Gen. James H. Lane, of Kansas, was authorized by the Government to organize an independent brigade in Kansas.

24. Ex-President Martin Van Buren died at his residence at Lindenwold, N. Y., in the 80th year of his age.

24. Rebel raid into Gloucester Point, Va. Citizens impressed, and much property destroyed.

24. Steamer Tubal Cain captured by U. S. gunboat Octarora.

24. Skirmish at Malvern Hill, Va.

24. Skirmish at Coldwater, Miss.

24. Skirmish near Decatur, Ala. Part of 31st Ohio, under Capt. Harman, defeated a rebel force, who lost 10 killed and 30 wounded.

24. Lieut.-Col. Starr, with 80 of 9th Va. cavalry, surprised and captured at Summerville, Va., by rebel cavalry under Maj. Bailey.

25. The steamer S. R. Spaulding arrived at Philadelphia, Pa., with 240 wounded and sick soldiers released from Richmond.

25. 900 paroled wounded prisoners arrived at Fortress Monroe from Richmond.

25. Col. Magoffin, and 35 other rebel prisoners escaped from the military prison at Alton, Ill., by digging a tunnel under the wall. 3 or 4 gave themselves up next day, and several were recaptured.

25. A fight on the Hatchie river, near Brownsville, Tenn., between rebs. under Capt. Faulkner, and cavalry led by Maj. Wallace.

25. 2 companies of Fed. troops under Capt. Davidson, were surprised and captured at Courtland, Ala.

25. Skirmish near Orange C. H., Va. A skirmish party from Gen. Gibson's Fed. command defeated with a loss of 5 killed, and 12 wounded and prisoners.

26. Dispatch boat Sallie Wood captured by rebels 150 miles above Vicksburg.

26. Attack on Ft. James, on the Ogeeche river, Ga. by Fed. gunboats, repulsed.

27. Richmond, Ky., plundered by rebs. under Col. Morgan.

27. Battle near Bayou Bernard, Cherokee nation, between Col. Phillips' troops, and rebels under Col. Taylor. The latter defeated with the loss of 125 men and their commander

28. The office of *The St. Croix Herald* in St. Stephens, N. B., was visited by a mob and destroyed. It was the only newspaper in New Brunswick that advocated the Union cause.

28. Three rebel clergymen, Messrs. Elliot, Ford, and Baldwin, of Nashville, were committed to jail by order of Gov. Johnson.

28. Col. Guitar of the 9th Missouri Regiment, reinforced by Lieut.-Col. Shaffer and Maj. Clopper of Merrill's Horse, and Maj. Caldwell of the 3d Iowa cavalry, 650 strong, were attacked at Moore's Mills, seven miles east of Fulton, Mo., by Cols. Porter and Cobb, with 800 strong. Fed. loss 10 killed, and 30 wounded. The rebs. left 52 dead on the field, and had 100 wounded.

29. Russellville, Ky., attacked by rebs. under Col. Gano, and the Home Guards defeated.

29. Skirmish at Brownsville, Tenn. by Union cavalry under Capt. Dollin, and reb. troops. Feds. captured 11, and lost 4 killed, and 6 wounded. Rebs. lost 10 killed and wounded.

30. Between 400 and 500 rebel prisoners confined in Fort Delaware, Del., took the oath of allegi ance.

30. Hon. John S. Phelps, of Mo., the newly appointed military Governor of Arkansas, arrived at St. Louis.

30. Reb. raid into Paris, Ky., under Col. Jo. Thompson.

31. Steamer Memphis captured by U. S. gunboat Magnolia, off Charleston, S. C.

31. 5 men killed, and 4 wounded by shells thrown by the rebs. from the left bank of James river into the Fed. camp at Harrison's Landing.

31. Steamer Ocean Queen sailed from Fort Warren, Mass., for James river, with 200 released rebel prisoners.

31. A scouting party seven miles from Luray, in the direction of Shenandoah river, encountered a body of rebel horse, who fled, leaving 5 of their number prisoners, and 1 dead.

31. 250 citizens of Woodville, Rappahannock Co., Va., took the oath of allegiance before Capt. Baird, of Gen. Milroy's staff. Five refusing to affirm were arrested and sent to Gen. Sigel's headquarters.

Aug. 1. Artillery skirmishing on James river, Va., near Harrison's Landing, by reb. batteries and Union gunboat fleet.

1. All the buildings opposite Harrison's landing, Va., were destroyed by Union troops.

1. Skirmish at Newark, Mo. A company of State troops, under Capt. Lair, were captured by a superior force of rebs. under Col. Porter.

1. Skirmishing near Orange C. H., Va., by Fed. troops under Gen. Bayard.

2. Skirmish at Ozark, Mo. 75 Nationals under Capt. Birch engaged and defeated a rebel party.

2. Skirmish at Orange C. H., Va., by Gen. Crawford's Fed. troops, who lost 4 killed and 12 wounded.

3. The British propeller Columbia, with a cargo of 12 Armstrong guns, and several thousand Enfield rifles, was captured off the Bahamas by the U. S. gunboat Santiago de Cuba.

3. Alexandria, Mo., pillaged by rebel guerrillas.

3. Skirmish near Cox's river, Va. The 13th Va. cavalry were attacked by Col. Averill's Federal troops, and put to flight.

4. Col. Wynkoop's Fed. troops were defeated in a skirmish near Sparta, Tenn.

4. Skirmish on White river, 40 miles from Forsyth. Capt. Birch's company of 14th Mo. engaged Col. Lawther's reb. band. Fed. loss 3 killed 7 wounded.

4. An immediate draft of 300,000 men was ordered by Pres. Lincoln from the militia of the States, for nine months. Also an additional quota by special draft to fill up the ranks of the 300,000 volunteers previously called for, should the same not be enlisted by the 15th of August.

5. Reb. Gen. J. C. Breckinridge, with 5,000 men, attacked Gen. Williams, with 2,500 men at Baton Rouge, La. Rebels defeated. Gen. Williams killed. Fed. loss 250 killed, wounded, and missing. Reb. loss 600.

5. Skirmish at Malvern Hills, Va. Gen. Hooker's Fed. troops engaged.

5. Skirmish at Point Pleasant, Mo.

6. Skirmish at Monteralla, Mo. Maj. Montgomery's troops defeated guerrillas.

6. Destruction of rebel ram Arkansas by U. S. gunboat Essex, Capt. Porter, near Vicksburg, Miss.

6. Brig.-Gen. R. L. McCook died in the Fed. camp near Deckard, Tenn., from wounds received from guerrillas while in an ambulance.

6. Fed. troops under Gens. Gibbon and Cutler encountered Stuart's reb. cavalry 7 miles beyond Mattapony river, Va. 72 Feds. taken prisoners. The Union forces destroyed several bridges and considerable reb. stores.

Aug. 6. Skirmishes near Tazewell, Tenn. Col. De Courcey's Union troops repulsed a reb. force.

7. Battle near Fort Fillmore, N. Mex. Col. Sibley's reb. troops were defeated by Unionists under Col. Canby.

7. Reb. cavalry under Capt. Faulkner, surprised near Trenton, Tenn., by 2d Ill. cavalry. Reb. loss 20 killed and 30 wounded.

7. Reb. Col. Porter defeated near Kirkville, Mo., by 1,000 Feds. under Col. McNeill.

7. Fight in Dodd Co., Mo. Maj. Montgomery's Feds. defeated rebs. under Col. Collin. Reb. loss. 11 killed, 4 wounded, and 17 prisoners.

7. Skirmish at Wolftown, near Madison C. H., Va.

7. Malvern Hills, Va., abandoned by Gen. Hooker's Fed. troops.

9. 26 reb. prisoners shot at Macon City, Mo., for violating their parole.

9. Porter's guerrillas routed by Col. McNeill's Fed. troops at Stockton, Macon Co., Mo.

9. Battle of Cedar Mountain, Va. Gen. Banks' corps attacked near the Rapidan river by reb. Gen. Jackson, with superior force. Rebs. repulsed. Fed. loss, 1500, k. w. and pris.

9. U. S. steam frigate Lackawanna launched at Brooklyn, L. I.

9-10. Recruiting very brisk throughout the country. Many fled to Canada and other remote places to avoid being drafted. Traveling restricted, by order of Government, to prevent fugitives from escaping.

10. U. S. steamer Freeborn brought 25 prisoners and 5 sailboats to Washington, D. C. captured while engaged in contraband trade on the Chesapeake.

10. Donaldsonville, La., partially destroyed by men from U. S. sloop Brooklyn.

11. Bayou Sara, La., seized by national troops.

11. Col. Buell, with 7th Mo. cavalry, was defeated at Independence, Mo., by rebels under Col. Hughes, who captured the town.

11. Skirmish 11 miles E. of Helena, Ark. 3d Wis. defeated reb. cavalry under Jeff. Thompson.

11. Part of 11th Ill. cavalry defeated rebs. at Salisbury, 5 miles E. of Grand Junction, Tenn. capturing a captain and 27 horses.

11. Skirmishes near Williamsport, Tenn. Maj. Kennedy's Fed. troops defeated rebels.

11. Fight near Compton's Ferry, on Grand river, Mo. Col. Guitar's Union cavalry defeated rebs. under Col. Poindexter, who lost 100 k. and w. and 200 pris.

11. A skirmish near Reelsville, Calloway Co., Mo. Col. Smart's Mo. State cavalry routed Cobb's guerrillas.

11. Skirmish near Kinderhook, Tenn. Col. McGowan's Union troops defeated Anderson's rebels, who lost 7 k. and 27 prisoners.

11. Battle at Clarendon, Monroe Co., Ark. Gen. Hovey's Fed. troops defeated rebels, and took 600 prisoners.

12. The Fed. garrison at Gallatin, Tenn. captured by, Col. J. H. Morgan's cavalry, who in turn were driven out by Col. Miller's Fed. troops, who killed 6 rebs. and wounded a number in the charge.

13. Collision on the Potomac river, Va. by steamers Peabody and West Point. 73 lives were lost.

13. Col. Guitar overtook Poindexter's reb. troops at Yellow Creek, Clinton Co. Mo. and scattered them, taking 60 prisoners.

13. 24th Mass., Gen. Stevenson, with gunboats Wilson and Ellis proceeded from Newbern, N. C., to Swansboro', and destroyed rebel salt works.

14. Slight skirmish near Helena, Ark.

15. 10 rebel recruits captured in St. Mary's Co., Md, by Fed. cavalry.

15. Skirmish on the Obion river, Tenn., at Merriwether's Landing, Col. T. W. Harris's Fed. troops routed rebs. under Capt. Binfield, who lost 20 k. and 9 prisoners.

16. Cols. Corcoran and Wilcox, Lieut.-Col. Brown and Maj. Rogers, late prisoners, reached Fort Monroe, having been exchanged by the rebels.

16. Lieut. Black and 5 men captured by the rebs. on the Rapidan river, Va.

16. 8 gunboats and rams, under Col. Ellet, with the 57th Ohio and 33d Ind., in transports, left Helena, Ark., this day, sailed down the Mississppi to Milliken's Bend, where they captured the steamer Fairplay, with arms, &c. for 6000 men. Further captures were made at Haines' Bluff and at Richmond, La., and property destroyed.

16. Gen. McClellan's army evacuated Harrison's Landing, Va., and removed to Williamsburg.

16. Fight at Lone Jack, Mo. 800 State militia under Maj. Foster, engaged a superior rebel force under Col. Coffee. Feds. defeated with loss of 60 k. and 100 wounded. Reb. loss 110 k. and w.

18. The steamers Skylark and Sallie were burned by rebels, and their crews captured, at the mouth of Duck creek, 50 miles above Fort Henry, Tenn. river.

19. Union garrison at Clarksville, Tenn., the 71st Ohio, under Col. Mason, surrendered to a rebel force, under Col. Woodward.

19. Steamer Swallow burned by rebels, 25 miles below Memphis, Tenn.

19. Skirmish near Rienzi, Miss.

19. Maj.-Gen. Wright assigned to command Department of Ohio.

19. Skirmish near Hickman, Mo. Rebs. defeated by cavalry under Capt. Moore. Fed. loss 2 w. Reb. loss 4 k. 19 prisoners.

19. Sioux Indians destroyed U. S. agencies at Yellow Medicine, and Red Wood, and partly destroyed New Ulm, Minn., killing and wounding more than 100 persons.

20. Skirmish at Brandy station, Va. Gen. Pope's army, retreating to the Rappahannock river, were overtaken by Lee's forces, and a fight ensued, chiefly an artillery duel.

20. Skirmish at Edgefield Junction, Tenn. Part of 50th Ind. and Col. J. H. Morgan's reb. cavalry. The latter retreated with a loss of 7 killed and 20 wounded.

20. Skirmish near Union Mills, Mo. A small force of Feds. under Maj. Price were ambushed by rebs. but defeated them, capturing 4 men and 16 horses, and killing one man. Fed. loss 4 killed and 3 wounded.

21. Gen. Pope and Gen. Lee's armies facing each other on the Rappahannock river. An attempt by the rebs. to cross at Kelly's Ford was foiled by Gen. Reno's troops, who attacked them with artillery and cavalry.

21. Reb. schooner Eliza captured off Charleston, S. C., by U. S steamer Bienville.

21. Union pickets on Pinckney Island, Hilton Head, S. C., were attacked by rebs. who captured 32, killed 3 and wounded 3

22. Defeat of Gen. Johnson near Gallatin, Tenn. by Morgan's Confed. cavalry. Fed. loss, 64 killed, 100 wounded, and 200 prisoners, including Gen. Johnson and his staff.

22. Death of Rear-Adm. George Campbell Read, at Philadelphia.

22. Skirmishes near Crab Orchard, Ky. 9th Pa. cavalry, under Gen. G. C. Smith defeated reb. cavalry under Col. Scott.

22. Gen. Stuart's reb. cavalry penetrated in the rear of Gen. Pope's army, at Catlett's Station, Va., destroyed sutler's stores, sacked the hospital, and captured the wagons and papers of Gen Pope.

22. Fort Ridgely, Minn. was attacked by a large body of Indians, who were repulsed with great loss. Fed. loss, 3 killed and 30 wounded.

22. Artillery skirmishing along the Rappahannock river, Va., by the armies of Pope and Lee. Gen. Sigel's corps engaged the enemy with spirit, and inflicted severe loss on the rebs. before they were permitted to cross the river.

23. The U. S. sloop-of-war Adirondack was wrecked on a coral reef near Little Abaco, W. I. The crew saved.

23. The schooner Louisa was captured by the U. S. steamer Bienville, at Charleston, S. C.

23. A train of cars on the Memphis and Charleston railroad attacked by 400 guerrillas 3 miles from Courtland, Tenn., who destroyed the cars. Part of the 42d Ill. was on board. 8 rebs. killed. Fed. loss 2 wounded and 2 missing.

23. Mutiny in Spinola's Empire Brigade at E. New York. 1 man killed and several wounded.

23. A passenger train was destroyed on the Winchester Va. railroad near Harper's Ferry 4 of the 1st Mich. captured.

24. Continuation of artillery battle on the banks of the Rappahannock river, Va., between Pope's and Lee's armies Gen. Milroy's Fed. brigade suffered severe loss.

24. Skirmish near Lamar, Kansas. Quantrell and Hays' reb. troops attacked Kansas troops under Maj. Campbell and Capt. Grund. Fed. loss 2 killed and 21 wounded.

24 Reb. schooner Water-witch, captured off Aransas, Texas, by U. S. schooner Corypheus.

24. Skirmish near Dallas, Mo. 12th Mo. cavalry, Maj. B. F. Lazear, defeated Col. Jeffries' reb. troops with loss.

25. 18 rebs. captured near Mount Sterling, Ky. by Capt. Warren's Bath County Guards.

25. Maj. Lippert, with 3 companies of 13th Ill. cavalry was attacked by 300 reb. cavalry under Col. Hicks, 36 miles beyond Bloomfield, Mo. Rebs. defeated, 20 killed and many wounded and taken prisoners.

25. Col. Woodward, with a strong force of rebs. attacked Fort Donelson, Tenn. and was repulsed with heavy loss.

25. New Ulm, Minn. was evacuated by the entire population and garrison under Capt. Flaudrau, after fighting the Sioux Indians for two days.

Aug. 25. Skirmish with guerrillas near Danville, Ky., by Danville and Harrodsburgh Home Guards.

26. Skirmish near Madisonville, Ky. A Union force under Col. Foster defeated reb. guerrillas.

26. Fifth Iowa cavalry, Col. Lowe, defeated rebs. under Col. Woodward near Fort Donelson, Tenn. Fed. loss 2 killed and 18 wounded.

26. A large quantity of Government stores were destroyed at Manassas, Va., by reb. cavalry under Fitz-Hugh Lee, who drove the Fed. forces towards Alexandria.

26. Gen. Burnside relinquished command of Department of N. Carolina He was succeeded by Gen. Foster.

27. Schooner Anna Sophia captured by the gunboat R. R. Cuyler off Wilmington, N. C.

27. Rebs. under Col. Coffee defeated on the Osage river, near Lone Jack, Mo., by Gen. Blunt's troops.

27. At Waterford, Va., part of Capt Means' company of Fed. cavalry was captured by rebs. under Capt. White.

27. Gen Hooker's division engaged rebs. under Gen. Ewell at Kettle Run, Va., near Bristow's station, and drove them from the field; loss about 300 on each side.

28. Fight at Readyville, Tenn. The 23d Ky., Col. Murphy, defeated reb. cavalry under Gen. Forrest.

28. $500,000 was assessed on wealthy secessionists at St. Louis, Mo., by Gen. Schofield, for the relief of destitute Unionists.

28. Severe fight six miles west of Centreville, Va. Gens. M'Dowell and Sigel' troops defeated rebs. under Gen. Jackson, who was driven back with loss, including many prisoners.

28. City Point on the James river, Va., destroyed by Fed. gunboats under Com. Wilkes.

28 Skirmish at Shady Springs, 10 miles from Raleigh C. H., Va. 2d Va. Fed. cavalry, Lieut Montgomery, defeated reb. cavalry, taking 5 prisoners.

29. Battle at Groveton, Va. The troops of Gens. Hooker, Sigel, Kearney, Reno, and King defeated rebs. under Jackson and Longstreet, with great loss. The fight lasted from dawn till dark.

29. Twelve officers of 71st Ohio dismissed the service for publishing a card stating they had advised Col. Mason to surrender Clarksville, Tenn., to the rebs.

29. Eighteen guerrillas captured 12 miles S. E. of Memphis, Tenn.

29. Skirmish near Manchester, Tenn. 18th Ohio, Capt. Miller, defeated rebel cavalry with loss.

29. Skirmish at Bonnet Carré, La. 8th Vt., Col. Thomas, defeated guerrillas and captured army stores.

29-30. Battles at Richmond, Ky. Feds. under Gens Manson and Cruft compelled to retreat before rebs. under Gen. E. Kirby Smith, after losing 200 killed, 700 wounded and 2,000 prisoners.

30. Fight at Bolivar, Tenn. 78th Ohio, Col. Leggett, routed a superior force of rebs. under Gen. Armstrong. Fed. loss, 5 killed, 18 wounded, 64 missing.

30. Buckhannon, Va., captured by rebs., and Government military stores seized.

30. Fight at M'Minnville, Tenn. 26th Ohio, Col. Fyffe, defeated Gen. Forrest's rebel cavalry.

30. Gen. Pope's forces, consisting of the corps of Gen. Heintzelman, Porter, M'Dowell and Banks, engaged Lee's army at the old battle ground of Bull Run, Va. After severe loss the Federals fell back to Centreville, where they were supported by Sumner's and Franklin's corps.

31. Fredericksburg, Va., evacuated by Gen. Burnside. The three bridges, foundry and military storehouses burned.

31. Huntsville, Ala., evacuated by Gen. Buell.

31. Great excitement in the north, on hearing of the disaster to Gen. Pope's army. Immense quantities of hospital and other stores, contributed and forwarded this day.

31. Skirmish at Medor Station on Mississippi Central R.R., Tenn. Armstrong's reb. cavalry attacked the place, but were driven off with loss.

31. Stevenson, Ala., captured by rebel troops under Col. McKinstry, and a large amount of ammunition and stores seized.

31. Reb. steamer Emma, with 740 bales of cotton, grounded and burned on the Savannah river.

31. Bayou Sara, La., burned by the crew of U. S. gunboat Essex.

Sep. 1. Battle at Britton's Lane, near Denmark, Tenn. 30th Illinois, Col. Dennis, defeated a superior force of rebs. under Gen. Armstrong. Reb. loss, 180 killed, 220 wounded. Fed. loss, 200 killed and wounded.

1. Lexington, Ky., occupied by Gen. E. K. Smith's rebel troops.

1. Natchez, Miss., shelled by Federal gunboats.

1. Severe fight at Stevenson, Ala.

Rebs. retire with great loss. Feds. engaged: Simonton's Ohio, and Loomis' Mich. batteries, and 10th Wis. and 13th Mich. regiments.

1. Severe engagement at Chantilly, near Fairfax C. H., Va. Gen. Pope's army defeated Jackson, Ewell, and Hill. Heavy loss on both sides. Death of Gens. Kearney and Stevens.

1. The spirit ration in the U. S. navy discontinued on this day by act of Congress.

2. Great excitement in Cincinnati, O., and Covington and Newport, Ky., in consequence of the approach of Kirby Smith's reb. army. Business suspended, and citizens of all classes in the field drilling.

2. A train of 100 wagons, with army stores, captured by rebs. between Fairfax and Centreville, Va., which necessitated the retreat of the Union army to Munson's Hill.

2. Versailles, Ky., occupied by rebel cavalry under Gen. Scott.

2. Fight at Morgansfield, Ky. 8th Ky. cavalry, Col. Shackleford, defeated guerrillas under Col. A. R. Johnson.

2. Fight near Plymouth, N.C. A party of loyal inhabitants led by Serg't Green, of Hawkins' Zouaves, and some of his men defeated Col. Garret's rebel force, who lost 30 killed and 40 taken prisoners.

2. Hutchinson and Forest City, Minn., attacked by hostile Indians, who were defeated at both places.

2. Winchester, Va., evacuated by Gen. Pope's army, who retreated to Harper's Ferry.

2. The U. S. steamer W. B. Terry captured by rebs on the Tenn. river, while aground at Duck Shoals.

2. Skirmish near Slaughterville, Ky. Fed. troops, under Lieut.-Col. Foster, defeated reb. cavalry, the latter losing 3 killed, 2 wounded and 25 prisoners.

2. Fight near Grieger's Lake, Ky. Col. Shackelford's Fed. troops defeated Col. Johnson with 600 rebels.

3. Gen. Pope asked to be relieved from command of the army of the Potomac, and was transferred to the North-west.

4. Gov. Curtin, of Pa., called out the whole of the State militia to repel an expected invasion.

4. Fed. troops, near Fort Ridgely, Minn., attacked by Indians, 13 soldiers killed and 47 wounded.

4. The Confed. army crossed the Potomac near Poolesville, Md., and invaded that State.

4. Maj. Wheeler with a detachment of Dodge's N. Y. Mounted Rifles, returned to Suffolk, Va., from a scout 12 miles west of South Mills, where they captured 113 rebs. and 38 negroes, who were prisoners.

4. Three bridges burnt by rebels on Benson Creek, 60 miles east of Louisville, Ky.

4. Jeff. Davis appointed the 18th inst. as a day of thanksgiving for Confederate victories.

4. Skirmish near Cumberland Gap, Tenn., in which rebs. were defeated with loss.

4. Frederick City, Md., evacuated by Feds. after burning hospital and commissary stores.

4. Joseph Holt, of Ky., appointed Judge Advocate General of the U. S. army.

4. Ravenswood, Va., sacked by rebels.

4. The ship Ocmulgee burned at sea by rebel privateer "290."

5. The Fed. army under M'Clellan had advanced from the Capital to the upper Potomac, Md. side.

6. Washington, N. C., attacked by rebs., who were repulsed with loss of 33 killed and 100 wounded. Fed. loss 8 killed, 36 wounded.

6. Col. W. W. Lowe re-took Clarkesville, Tenn., driving out the reb. garrison.

6. The town of Platte, Johnson Co., Kansas, was sacked by rebel guerrillas, under Quantrell, and several of the inhabitants murdered.

6. Skirmish near Cacapon Bridge, 17 miles from Winchester, Va. Union troops under Col. M'Reynolds defeated Imboden's rebel cavalry.

6. Four hundred reb. cavalry attacked an outpost of Gen. Julius White's troops near Martinsburg, Va. Reb. loss 50 prisoners, besides killed and wounded. Fed. loss, 2 killed and 10 wounded.

6. Frederick, Md., occupied by Gen. Lee's troops.

6. Three hundred Indians attacked Fort Abercrombie, Minn., and were driven off with loss. Fed. loss, 1 killed and 3 wounded.

6. Washington, N. C., attacked by rebs., who were repulsed with a loss of 30 killed and 36 taken prisoners. The Fed. gunboat Picket exploded her magazine during the engagement, killing and wounding 18 men.

6. Forty of the Fed. 4th Va., Maj. Hall, surprised near Chapmansville, Va., by 300 rebs. under Col. Stratton. Maj Hall wounded, and Col. Stratton killed, when Feds. escape with slight loss.

Sept. 6. Pikeville, Va., captured and sacked by rebel cavalry.

7. Gen. Banks assigned to command fortifications around Washington.

7. Great excitement on the Pa. border towns by the influx of refugees from Maryland, and the dread of reb. invasion.

7. Shepherdsville, Ky., captured, and 85 Fed. soldiers taken prisoners.

8. Gens. Lee and Johnson issued proclamations to the people of Md., endeavoring to incite them to rebellion. The inhabitants received them coldly.

8. Skirmish near Poolesville, Md. Maj. Chapman, with 3d Ind. and 8th Ill. cavalry, defeated rebels, who lost 7 killed. Federal loss 1 killed 8 wounded.

8. Fight on the Miss. river, 25 miles above N. Orleans. 25th Ind. dispersed 500 Texans, with slight loss.

9. Schr. Rambler captured by U. S. steamer Connecticut, in lat. 28°, long. 94° 10′.

9. Skirmish 5 miles N. of Pleasant Hill, Mo. Col. Burris defeated Quantrell's reb. troops, with slight loss, capturing most of their plunder and stores.

9. Middletown, Md., occupied by rebs.

9. Skirmish at Williamsburg, Va. Rebs. under Col. Shingles surprise 5th Pa. cavalry, Col. Campbell, and capture the town. Col. Campbell, 5 captains, 4 lieutenants, and a few privates taken prisoners. Col. Shingles and 8 rebs. killed.

9. Gen. Stuart's reb. cavalry repulsed in an attempt to cross the Potomac at Edward's Ferry, with a loss of 90 men, by Gen. Keyes.

9. Gen. O. M. Mitchell appointed to command the Department of the South, relieving Gen. Hunter.

9. The Fed. garrison at Fayette C. H., Va., surrounded by a large rebel force. They cut their way out, losing 100 in killed and wounded.

10. Col. Grierson with 300 men defeated rebs. near Coldwater, Miss. Reb. loss, 4 killed and 30 wounded.

10 The 34th and 37th Ohio Col. Siber, were defeated at Fayette, Va., by 5,000 rebs. under Gen Loring. Fed. loss over 100 in killed and wounded.

10. 6th U. S. cavalry, under Captain Saunders, defeated at Sugar Loaf Mountain, near Barnesville, Md., with slight loss.

11. Hagerstown, Md., occupied by rebs. who seized 1200 bbls. of flour.

11. The Gov. of Pa. called for 50,000 men to repel rebel invasion.

11. Westminster, Md., occupied by reb. cavalry, who robbed all the stores in the place.

11. Fed. forces under Col. Lightburn retreated from Gauley, Va., after destroying government stores.

11. Reb. troops under E. K. Smith, advanced within 7 miles of Cincinnati, O., and skirmished with the Fed. pickets.

11. Bloomfield, Mo., defended by 1,500 State militia, captured by rebs. after a fight of 2 hours.

12. The reb. army retreated from before Cincinnati, pursued by Gen. Wallace as far as Florence, Ky.

12. Gen. McClellan's army entered Frederick, Md.

12. Fight on the Elk river, near Charleston, Va., by Feds. under Col. Lightburn, and a reb. force, without result.

12. Capt. Harry Gilmore, and 7 other rebs. arrested near Baltimore, Md., and sent to Fort McHenry.

12. Frankfort, Ky., occupied by rebel cavalry, under Gen. E. K. Smith.

12. Fight at Middletown, Md. Fed. loss, 80 killed and wounded.

13. 500 rebs. under Col. Porter, released 40 reb. prisoners at Palmyra, Mo.

14. A fort at Bacon creek, Ky., with 30 men of the 54th Ind., captured by rebs. under Col. J. J. Morrison.

14. Battle of South Mountain, Md. Fed. troops under Gens. Hooker and Reno, defeated Lee's army. Fed. loss 443 killed, 1,806 wounded and 76 missing. Gen. Reno killed.

14. Fight at Munfordsville, Ky. 17th Ind., Col. Wilder, defeated rebs., under Gen. Duncan, with severe loss.

14. 2,000 Fed. cavalry, cut their way out of Harper's Ferry, Va., which was besieged by rebs., and captured Gen. Longstreet's train and 100 prisoners.

15. Surrender of Harper's Ferry, Va., with a large supply of military stores, and 11,000 men to the rebs. after 3 days' siege. Col. Miles, the Fed. commander, killed.

15. Col. M'Neill defeated reb. guerrillas under Col. Porter, near Shelburne, Mo., taking 20 wagons and other spoils, with slight loss.

15. Fight at Green river, Ky., on the line of the Louisville and Nashville railroad. Rebs. defeated.

16. Capture of the Fed. garrison at Munfordsville, Ky., under Col. Dunham, 4,000 strong, with 10 pieces of artillery, by rebs. under Gen. Bragg. 50 Feds. killed and wounded.

17. Fight near Durhamville, Tenn. 150 of 52nd Ind., Lt. R. Griffin, defeated

rebs. under Lieut.-Col. Faulkner. Reb. loss, 8 killed and 20 wounded. Fed. loss, 2 killed and 10 wounded.

17. Fight at Falmouth, on Kentucky Central R. R. Col. Berry with 10 men defeated a larger force of Texan rangers, of whom 2 were killed, 4 wounded and 1 prisoner. 1 Fed. wounded.

17. Ship Virginia, of Mass., burned by Alabama, Capt. Semmes.

17. Skirmish near Florence, Ky. 53 of 10th Ky. cavalry, Maj. Foley, defeated 100 rebs., who lost 5 killed and 7 wounded. Fed. loss, 1 killed and 1 wounded.

17. Battle of Antietam, Md. The entire Fed. army of Gen. McClellan, and reb. army of Gen. Lee engaged. Defeat of rebs. with loss of 15,000 men. Fed. loss, 12,500.

17. Fight at Leesburg, Va. The Ira Harris cavalry, Col. Kilpatrick, defeated a reb. infantry regiment, capturing several guns and a number of prisoners.

17. The U. S. gunboats Paul Jones, Cimerone, and 3 other vessels attacked reb. batteries on St. John's river, Florida.

17. Cumberland Gap, Tenn., evacuated by Gen. Morgan's Fed. troops.

18. Ship Elisha Dunbar, of Mass., burned by the Alabama.

18. Rebs. evacuated Harper's Ferry, Va.

19. Gen. Lee's army crossed the Potomac river to Va., pursued by Gen. Pleasanton's cavalry.

19-20. Battle of Iuka, Miss. General Rosecrans' army defeated rebs., who lost 253 killed, 400 wounded, and 600 prisoners. Fed. loss, 135 killed, and 527 wounded.

19-20. Skirmishes at Owensboro', Ky. Fed. Col. Netter killed. 1st Ind. cavalry, Lieut-Col. Wood, routed rebs. with severe loss. Fed. loss, 2 killed, 18 wounded.

20. Fight near Shirley's Ford, Spring river, Mo. 3rd Ind., Col. Ritchie, defeated 600 rebs. and Indians, who lost 60 or 70 killed and wounded.

21. Col. Barnes, with a Fed. cavalry brigade, defeated in an attempt to cross the Potomac from Md., losing 150 men, in killed, wounded and prisoners.

21. The town of Prentiss, Miss., burned by Col. Lippincott of the ram Queen of the West, in retaliation for reb. batteries there firing on transports.

21. Skirmish at Munfordsville, Ky. Reb. cavalry defeated with loss by Feds. under Col. E. McCook.

21. 100 reb. troops routed at Cassville, Mo., by part of 1st Ark. cavalry, Captain Gilstray, who captured 19 rebs.

21. Citizens of San Francisco, Cal. contributed $100,000 in gold to the U. S Sanitary Commission.

21. Rebs. defeated at Shepherdsville, Ky., by Feds. under Col. Granger. Reb. loss 5 killed and 28 prisoners.

22. Skirmish near Sturgeon, Mo. Rebs. under Capt. Cunningham defeated by Maj. Hunt's force.

22. Fight at Ashby's Gap, Va. Col R. B. Price with 2d Pa. cavalry, defeated rebs. under Lieut-Col. Green, capturing the latter officer and 2 lieuts.

22. Pres. Lincoln proclaimed, that on the 1st day of Jan. 1863 "all slaves in States or parts of States in rebellion" should be forever free.

23. Col. Sibley defeated a band of 300 Sioux Indians who attacked his encampment on Yellow Medicine river, Minn. 30 Indians killed and many wounded. 4 whites killed and 30 wounded.

23. Fight at Sutton, Va. Maj. Withers, with 10th Va., (Fed.) driven from Sutton to Bulltown, after a gallant resistance.

23. A large quantity of English arms captured at Reynolds' Ford, Va., by 62d Pa Col. Switzer.

23. Randolph, Tenn, on the Miss. river, burned by steamers Ohio Belle and Eugene, in retaliation for firing on transports from that place.

24. Proclamation of Pres. Lincoln ordering the enforcement of martial law, against all persons discouraging enlistments or giving aid to the rebellion, and suspending the habeas corpus with reference to all persons arrested by military authority.

24. The office of the "American Volunteer," at Carlisle, Pa. was destroyed by citizens and soldiers for severe reflections on the Government.

24. A Convention of Governors from 14 loyal States, and 3 proxies from others met at Altoona, Pa, who endorsed the Emancipation Proclamation, and advised the Pres. to organize a reserve force of 100,000 men.

24. Gen. Beauregard appointed to command reb. forces in S. C. and Georgia.

24. Gen. Butler at New Orleans, ordered all Americans in his Department to renew their oath of allegiance to the Government, and to furnish returns of their real and personal property, under penalty of fine and imprisonment.

25. Sabine Pass, Texas, captured by U. S. steamers Kensington, and Henry Crocker, and schr. Rachel Seaman.

26. Skirmish near Warrenton Junction, Va. Reb. cavalry defeated by Col.

McClean's troops, who captured rebel commissary stores.

Sept. 26. An unsuccessful attempt to capture steamer Forest Queen at Ashport, Tenn., by rebs. under Capt. Faulkner.

26. Prentiss, Miss., burned by U. S. ram Queen of the West, in retaliation for firing on that vessel and transports.

27. 34th Ohio, Col. Toland, attacked Col. Jenkins's reb. cavalry at Buffalo, on the Kanawha river, Va., but were driven off, after killing 7, capturing 9, and destroying the camp, without loss to themselves.

27. Home Guards at Augusta, Ky., captured by rebs. under Basil Duke, after a brave resistance, with loss to the enemy.

27. 91 women and children rescued from Indians by Col. Sibley on Chippeway river, Minn.; 16 Indians captured.

28. Reb. steamer Sunbeam captured by U. S. gunboats State of Georgia and Mystic, off Wilmington, N. C.

28. Skirmish on Blackwater river, 25 miles from Suffolk, Va. Col. C. C. Dodge, with Fed. cavalry and artillery, defeated reb. infantry.

28. Augusta, Georgia, captured by 600 reb. cavalry.

29. Gen. Jeff. C. Davis shot Gen. Wm. Nelson, at the Galt House, in Louisville, Ky., killing him almost instantly.

29. A brigade of Fed. cavalry, under Lieut.-Col. Karge, on a reconnoissance from Centreville, Va., to Warrenton, captured and paroled 1,650 rebels.

29. Brig.-Gen. Rodman died near Hagerstown, Md., of a wound received at the battle of Antietam.

29. A spirited cavalry skirmish near Sharpsburgh, Md. Rebs. dispersed, and a squad of them captured.

29. 363 disloyal citizens of Carroll Co., Mo., were assessed by the Federal authorities in aid of loyal citizens and soldiers who had been robbed in that Co.

30. Fight at Newtonia, Mo. A Fed. brigade under Gen. Salomon, attacked a body of rebs. under Col. Cooper, and were defeated by them, losing 50 in killed and wounded, and 100 prisoners.

30. Reb. bomb-proof magazines at Lower Shipping Point, Va., destroyed by sailors under Lieut.-Com. M'Graw.

30. Fight at Russelville, Ky. 17th Ky., Col. Harrison, defeated 350 rebs., who lost 35 killed, and 10 prisoners.

30. Grayson, Ky., occupied by rebel troops.

30. Salt works at Bluffton, S. C., destroyed by 48th N. Y., Col. Barton.

Oct. 1. The U. S. gunboat fleet on the western waters turned over from the War to the Navy Department.

1. Fight on Floyd's Fork, Ky. A Fed. brigade under Col. E. N. Kirk, encountered and overcame a rebel force after a slight engagement.

1. Shelbyville, Ky., evacuated by the rebels.

1. Fight near Gallatin, Tenn. 1st Tenn. cavalry, Col. Stokes, defeated rebs. under Col. Bennett, who lost 40 killed, many wounded, and 39 prisoners.

1. 9 National pickets dispersed some rebs. at Newbern, N. C.

1. Gen. Pleasanton's cavalry engaged reb. forces under Gen. Hampton at Martinsburg and at Shepherdstown, Va. Reb. loss 60 killed and wounded, and 9 prisoners. Fed. loss 12 wounded and 3 prisoners.

2. Fight near Olive Hill, Ky. Carter Co. Home Guards repulsed a portion of reb. Gen. Morgan's command. Morgan retreated to the Licking river, destroying 35 houses on his route.

2. Gen. Foster's Union troops accompanied by gunboats, left Washington, N. C., taking possession of Hamilton, and driving the rebels towards Tarboro'.

2. Skirmishing near Mount Washington, Ky., on the Bardstown turnpike, by Gen. Buell's army and rebels under Gen. E. Kirby Smith.

3. Rebel fortifications at St. John's Bluff, on St. John's river, Fla., captured by 1500 Feds. under Gen. Brannan, assisted by 7 gunb's from Hilton Head, S. C.

3. Fight on the Blackwater river, near Franklin, Va. 3 Fed. gunboats, Commodore Perry, Hunchback, and Whitehead, under Capt. Flusser, engaged a large force of rebs. 6 hours. Fed. loss 19 k. and wounded.

3. 11th Pa. cavalry, Col. Spears, engaged reb. forces at Franklin, on Blackwater river, Va. Rebs. retreated with loss of 30 or 40 killed and wounded.

3–5. A series of battles near Corinth, Miss. A reb. army of 38,000 men under Price, Van Dorn, and Lovell, attacked Rosecrans' army, under Gens. Ord, Hurlbut, and Veatch. Rebs. routed with heavy loss of k. and w., and 1,000 pris. National loss also heavy.

4. Richard Howes, inaugurated rebel governor of Kentucky, at Frankfort.

4. A fight near Bardstown, Ky. Fed. advance guard under Maj. Foster, defeated by rear-guard of Polk's army.

4. A company of the 54th Pa. captured

at Paw-Paw, on the Ball. and Ohio railroad.

4. Fed. cavalry under Col. M'Reynolds, captured a rebel camp near the above place, with 2 guns, 10 wagons and 60 horses.

5. Gen. Price's rebel army, retreating from Corinth, Miss, were overtaken by Gens. Ord and Hurlbut at the Hatchie river, where, after 6 hours' fighting, the rebels broke in disorder, leaving their dead and wounded, 400 prisoners, and 2 batteries.

5. Skirmish 6 miles north of Glasgow, Ky. Feds. under Col. Bruce, routed a rebel force, taking a number of horses and cattle.

5. Jacksonville, Fla., occupied by Union forces under Gen. Brannon.

6. A mob in Blackford Co., Ind., destroyed the enrolling papers and draft boxes.

6. A rebel battery at Cockpit Point, Va., on the Potomac, destroyed by a Fed. gunboat.

6. Skirmish near Charlestown, Va. 6th U. S. cavalry and Robertson's battery engaged a rebel force with slight results.

6. Fight at Lavergne, near Nashville, Tenn. Gen. Palmer's Union brigade, 2,500 men, were attacked by rebels under Gen. Anderson, who were defeated with a loss of 10 killed and wounded. Fed. loss, 18 in killed and wounded.

7. Lexington, Ky., evacuated by rebels under E. Kirby Smith, who retreated towards Cumberland Gap.

7. The monitor Nahant launched at Boston.

7. Skirmish near Sibley's Landing, Mo. 5th Mo. cavalry defeated rebels under Quantrell and Childs.

7. Gen. Morgan's Union troops reached Frankfort, Ky.

7. The bark Wave, and brig Dunkirk, were destroyed by the rebel privateer, Alabama.

8. Battle at Chaplin Hills, Perryville, Ky., by the armies of Gens. Buell and Bragg. Rebs. retreated across Chaplin river. Fed. loss, 3,200 in killed, wounded and missing. Rebel loss fully as great.

8. 550 Feds. under Major Bradford, 17 government wagons, and a number of sutler's wagons, were captured by rebels under E. Kirby Smith, near Frankfort, Ky.

9. Galveston, Texas, occupied by Feds. under Commander Renshaw.

9. Skirmish near Laurenceburg, Ky. 1st Ohio, Col. Parrott, defeated part of Gen. Smith's troops with considerable loss. Union loss, 6 killed, 8 wounded.

9. Gen. Sigel's cavalry captured 40 rebs. and several wagons at Aldie, Va.

9. The monitor Montauk launched at Greenpoint, L. I.

9. The rebel steamer Gov. Milton captured on St. John's river, Fla., by gunboat Darlington.

10. 1,800 reb. cavalry, under J. E. B. Stuart, crossed the Potomac at McCoy's creek, and penetrated to Mercersburg and Chambersburg, Pa., and after capturing and destroying much property, made good their retreat with slight loss.

10. Gen. Schofield drove the Confederate forces across the Mo. line into Ark.

10. 1,600 rebs. the rear-guard of Bragg's army, captured at Harrodsburg, Ky., by Lieut-Col. Boyle, with 9th Ky. cavalry.

10. 100 reb. guerrillas entered Hawesville, Ind., but were driven out by the Conuelton Home Guard.

11. Skirmish near Helena, Ark. 4th Iowa cavalry, Major Rector, defeated Texan rangers under Col. Giddings, capturing 9 of them. 3 Feds. killed and 9 wounded.

11. Ship Manchester, of N. Y., captured and burned by the Alabama.

11. 27 rebs. of Col. Imboden's command, with all their camp equipage, captured by 200 of Col. McReynolds' cavalry 17 miles from Winchester, Va.

11. The U. S. gunboat Maratanza lying off Cape Fear river, N. C., had 2 men killed and 5 wounded by a reb. battery.

11 Gen. Dumont's Fed. troops captured 350 rebs., a wagon train, and 2 pieces of artillery at Versailles, Ky.

12. Skirmishing on the Potomac river, at the mouth of the Monocacy, near White's Ford, by Gen. Pleasanton's cavalry with rebs. under Gen. Stuart.

12. 29 persons arrested and 2 hung at Gainesville, Texas, who were accused of Union sentiments.

13. More than 100 prisoners taken by Union troops under Gen. Stahel, in the vicinity of Paris, Snicker's Gap, and Leesburg, Va.

13. The 6th Mo., Col. Catherwood, returned to camp at Sedalia, Mo., after a successful scout, in which several bands of guerrillas were broken up, and 50 of them killed and wounded.

14. The English propeller Ouachita, captured in the Gulf Stream by U. S. gunboat Memphis.

14. Skirmish at Stanford, Ky., by scouts of Gens Buell's and Bragg's armies. 14 rebs. captured, and several killed.

Oct. 15. The bark Lamplighter, of Boston, captured by the Alabama.

15. Drafting in Boston and Baltimore.

15. Steamer Hazel Dell captured at Caseyville, Ky., by rebs. under Cols. Anderson and Johnson.

15. Skirmish near Carsville, Va. Part of 7th Pa. cavalry, Lieut. Williams, defeated by rebs., losing several of their number.

15. U. S. Steamer Kensington, Master Crocker, destroyed a railroad bridge and burned 2 vessels at Taylor's Bayou, Tex.

16. The sloop-of-war Ticonderoga was launched at Brooklyn, N. Y.

16. Gen. Humphrey's troops driven from Shepherdstown, Va., by rebs., with slight loss.

16. Skirmish near Charlestown, Va. Gen. Hancock's troops successfully engaged rebs. Union loss, 1 killed and 8 wounded. Reb. loss, 9 wounded and taken prisoners.

17. The Fed. garrison on the Tenn. shore, opposite Island No. 10 attacked by reb. forces, who were defeated with loss.

17. Morgan's Confed. cavalry dashed into Lexington, Ky., and attacked 350 Fed. cavalry, under Major Seidel, 3rd O. Fed loss, 4 killed, 24 wounded, and 120 prisoners.

17. Quantrell's guerrillas entered Shawnee, Kansas, sacked the town, burned 13 houses and killed 4 men.

17. Skirmish at Thoroughfare Gap, Va. Gen. Stahel's troops drove rebs. toward Haymarket, and captured 100 prisoners.

17. The draft resisted in Berkley, Luzerne co., Pa. 4 insurgents killed. Resistance also in Carbondale, Scranton, and other towns in the mining district.

18. Pickets of the 43rd Ind. dispersed by rebs. at Helena, Ark., losing several of their number.

18. 350 of the 4th Ohio cavalry, Capt. Robey, captured at Lexington, Ky., by reb. cavalry under Gen. Morgan.

18. 10 guerrillas were shot at Palmyra, Mo., by order of Gen. McNeill, in retaliation for the murder of Andrew Allsman, an aged Union citizen.

18. Nine Union pickets were shot on the Mississippi, opposite Helena, Ark.

18. A lieut. with 26 men and a supply train for Gen. Stahel were captured by rebs. at Haymarket, and taken to Warrenton, Va.

19. A train of 82 wagons was captured by Morgan's reb. cavalry at Bardstown, Ky.

19. Fight on the Cumberland river 7 miles from Nashville, Tenn. Col. Miller's brigade of Fed. troops routed a force of Confederate cavalry, and captured a large store of army supplies.

20. 500 cases of yellow fever reported at Wilmington, N. C., 30 or 40 dying daily.

20. Skirmish on the Auxvois river, Mo. Major Woodson, with 10th Mo. militia dispersed rebel guerrillas with slight loss, capturing their camp stores and horses.

20. The 10th Illinois cavalry, Lieut-Col. Stuart, defeated 250 reb. cavalry, near Marshfield, Mo., taking 27 prisoners.

21. Skirmishing in Loudon co., Va., by Gen. Geary's Union troops, who took 75 prisoners.

21. Skirmish at Woodville, Tenn. 2nd Illinois cavalry, Major J. J. Mudd, defeated guerrillas under Haywood, capturing 40 with their arms, and 100 horses and mules.

21. Fight at Fort Cobb, Indian Terr. Loyal Indians from 6 tribes defeated rebs of the Tongkawa tribe, under Col. Leper, with great slaughter. Col. Leper killed.

22. Gen. Blunt's army defeated 5,000 rebs. at old Fort Wayne, Marysville, N. W. Ark., capturing all their artillery and transportation equipage.

22. Rebs. under Gen. Hindman driven from Huntsville, Ark., by Gen. Schofield.

22. Battle at Pocotaligo, S. C. Gen. Brannon's Fed. troops defeated with a loss of 30 killed and 180 wounded, by rebels under Gen. Beauregard.

22. Skirmish near Van Buren, Ark. Union cavalry under Major Lazear defeated 450 rebels under Col. Boone, with considerable loss.

22. 30 wagons of the 5th and 9th Ill. cavalry captured by Texan troops near Helena, Ark.

22. Union pickets defeated in a skirmish near Nashville, Tenn.

22. Brig Robert Bruce, captured off Shallotte inlet, N. C., by U. S. gunboat Penobscot.

22. Skirmish near Hedgesville, Va. 4th Pa. cavalry, Capt. Duncan, defeated rebels, capturing 19 prisoners.

23. 200 of the 83d Ill., Major Blott, defeated rebels at Waverly, Tenn. Rebel loss, 40 killed and wounded, and 30 prisoners. Union loss, 1 killed, 5 wounded.

23. Skirmish near Shelby Depot, Tenn. 55th Illinois, Col. Stuart, defeated rebels, who lost 8 or 10 men.

23. 500 Fed. cavalry, Col. E. M'Cook, defeated Morgan's cavalry at Point Lick, Big Hill, and Richmond, Ky., taking 33 wagons and 200 prisoners.

23. Ship Lafayette, of Conn., burned by the Alabama.

24. A Fed. force of 80 was defeated at Manassas Junction, Va., losing 17 prisoners.

24. Skirmish at Grand Prairie, Mo. Maj. F. G. White's cavalry defeated a reb. force, who lost 8 killed and 20 wounded. Fed. loss, 3 wounded.

24. Skirmish on the Blackwater, near Suffolk, Va. Gen. Perry's troops defeated rebs. who lost 6 men. One Unionist killed.

24. Sixteen of Gen. Morgan's men captured by a Federal force at Morgantown, Ky.

24. Steamer Scotia capt'ed off Charleston, S C., by U. S. bark Restless.

25. Gen. Buell removed from the Department of Ky., and Gen. Rosecrans appointed command r.

25. Part of 43d Ind., on a scout near Helena, Ark., 3 of them killed and 2 wounded by guerrillas in ambush.

27. Steamer Anglia capt'd off Charleston, S. C., by U. S. bark Restless and steamer Flag.

27. Skirmish near Fayetteville, Ark. Gen. Herron's Fed. troops defeated guerrillas, killing 8, and capturing their wagons.

27. Skirmish at Putnam's Ferry, Mo. 23d Iowa, Col. Lewis, defeated a large force of rebs., who lost several killed and 40 prisoners.

27. Fight near Donaldsonville, La. Gen. Weitzel's troops defeated rebs., who lost 6 killed, 15 wounded and 208 prisoners. Fed. loss, 18 killed, 74 wounded.

27. Gen. Pleasanton's cavalry drove the rebs. from Snicker's Gap, Va.

28. Capt. Partridge's Fed. pickets were captured near Pensacola, Fla.

28. The steamer Caroline captured off Mobile, Ala., by U. S. steamer Montgomery.

28. Gen. Herron, with 1,000 men attacked a Confederate camp near Fayetteville, Ark., under Col. Craven, routing them with a loss of 8 killed and their camp equipage.

28. A company of reb. cavalry captured near Cotton Creek, Fla., by Union troops.

28. The bark Lauretta, of N. Y., captured and burned by the Alabama.

29. Skirmish 5 miles from Petersburg, Va. Lieut.-Col. Quirk routed a detachment of Stuart's reb. cavalry, capturing 16 men and 200 cattle.

29. Fight near Butler, Bates Co., Mo. 1st Kansas (colored), Col. Seaman, defeated reb. guerrillas under Cockerill, with a loss of 30 killed and wounded. Union loss, 8 killed, 10 wounded.

29. Maj. Keenan, 8th Pa. cavalry captured 100 rebs. while on a scout in the Shenandoah valley, Va.

29. Ship Alleghanian, of New York, burned on the Rappahannock river, Va., by rebels.

30. Maj.-Gen. O. M. Mitchell, Commander of Department of the South, died at Beaufort, S. C.

30. Skirmish at Thoroughfare Gap, Va. 1st N. J. cavalry, Col. Wyndham, engaged a rebel force with slight loss.

31. The town of Franklin, on the Blackwater river, Va., partially destroyed by Union batteries, a reb. force stationed there being driven out with loss.

31. The Wilmington, N. C. saltworks destroyed by Capt. Cushing, gunboat Ellis.

Nov. 1. The U. S. steamer Northerner, and gunboat States of the North, with a detachment of 3d N. Y. cavalry and 2 pieces of Allen's artillery, under Maj. Garrard, captured 2 rebel schooners on Pango Creek, N. C. Disembarking at Montgomery, the troops marched to Germantown, Swanquarter, and Middletown, captur ng in those places 25 prisoners and 130 horses and mules.

1. The town of Lavacca, on Matagorda Bay, Texas, bombarded by U. S. gunboats Clifton and Westfield.

1. Skirmish at Franklin, Va. Gen. Wessell's brigade, 11th Pa. cavalry, and other troops, drove the rebels from the town with some loss.

2. Skirmishes near Philomont, Va. by Gen. Pleasanton's cavalry with Stuart's rebel forces.

2. Snicker's Gap. Va. occupied by Gen. Hancock's troops after a slight skirmish with the enemy.

2. Col. Dewey's troops returned to Patterson, Wayne Co., Mo., from an expedition to Pittman's ferry, Currant river, where they captured 13 rebels.

2. A skirmish near Williamstown, N. C. between part of the 20th N. C. rebels under Col. Burgwyn, and some Federal troops.

2. Col. Lee, of Hamilton's National cavalry, returned to Grand Junction, Miss. after a three days' expedition towards Ripley and 10 miles south, having captured 65 of the enemy with slight resistance.

2. The ship Levi Starbuck captured and burned by the Alabama.

3. A fight in Bayou Teche, La., 5 Union

gunboats engaged a large rebel force and the gunboat Cotton. The rebels retreated after burning 75 cars and engines, and 1000 hogsheads of sugar. Fed. loss about 14 killed and wounded.

Nov. 3. Tampa, Fla. was bombarded by the Union forces.

3. 300 rebs. under Quantrell attacked a wagon train of 13 wagons, escorted by 22 of the 6th Mo. cavalry, Lieut. Newby, near Harrisonville, Mo., killing 8 of the escort, wounding 4 and taking 5 prisoners, and burning the wagons. The rebel troops were shortly after overtaken by the 5th and 6th Mo. cavalry and defeated with severe loss.

3. The steamer Darlington, with col'd troops under Col. O. T. Beard, proceeded up Bell river, Fla., to Cooper's, where they destroyed the salt works, and all stores that could not be carried off. From thence they went up Jolly river, destroying salt works, with a large amount of corn and salt.

3. Skirmish near New Baltimore, Va. Capt. Flint, with pickets from 1st Vt. cavalry, defeated a reb. party.

3. Piedmont, Va., occupied by Union cavalry under Pleasanton and Averill.

3. Fight in Webster Co., Ky. Col. Foster captured 3 lieutenants, 22 men, 40 horses, &c.

3. Horatio Seymour elected Governor of New York.

4. 3 Union pickets captured near Bolivar Heights, Va.

4. La Grange, Miss. occupied by Gen. Grant's forces.

4. Bark Sophia captured off N. C. coast by U. S. steamers Daylight and Mount Vernon.

4. The U. S. steamer Darlington, with Col. O. T. Beard's colored troops destroyed rebel salt works at King's Bay, Ga., after slight skirmishing with the enemy.

5. Skirmish at Lamar, Mo. 80 State militia driven from the place by Quantrell's rebel troop.

5. Skirmish at Barber's Cross-Roads, Va. Gen. Pleasanton's cavalry defeated a detachment of Gen. Stuart's reb. troops.

5. Maj. Holloway's Federal cavalry defeated a party of guerrillas under Col. Fowler, between Henderson and Bowling Green, Ky. Reb. loss 8 killed, including the commander, besides a large number of wounded prisoners.

5. Skirmish at New Baltimore, Va. Col. Wyndham's Fed. cavalry defeated rebels.

5. Skirmish near Nashville, Tenn. Gen. Negley's Fed. troops defeated Gen. J. H. Morgan's forces, capturing 23 Union loss 5 killed, 19 wounded.

5. Gen. McClellan relieved from command of the Army of the Potomac, and Gen. Burnside appointed his successor.

6. Warrenton, Va., captured by Gen. Reynolds, who took 7 Confed. prisoners.

6. Fight at Piketon, Ky. Col. Dills routed Confederates, capturing 80, and securing 150 muskets, 40 horses, wagons, &c.

6. Skirmish near Leatherwood, Ky. Capt. Powell's Fed. company routed guerrillas, who fled, leaving 6 of their number dead, and their captain mortally wounded.

7. At Beaver Creek, Mo., Capt. Barstow's company of 10th Ill. cavalry, and 2 militia companies, defended a block house for 5 hours against a superior force, when he surrendered.

7. Expedition up the Sapelo river, Ga., by U. S. steamers Potomska and Darlington, and 48th N. Y., Col. O. T. Beard. A valuable salt work destroyed, and a number of rebs. and slaves captured.

7. Skirmish at Lamar, Mo. State militia successfully resist an attack from Quantrell's band.

7. 300 Indians, who were engaged in the massacres in Minnesota, were sentenced to be hung—most of whom were afterwards pardoned.

8. Skirmish at Rappahannock bridge, Va. Gen. Bayard's troops captured 12 of Longstreet's rebels.

8. Skirmish at Hudsonville, Miss. 7th Kansas, Col. Lee, defeated rebels, who lost 16 killed, and 175 captured.

8. Ship T. B. Wales burned by the Alabama.

8. Skirmish near Marianna, Ark. Part of 3d and 4th Iowa cavalry, Capt M. L. Perkins, defeated rebels, who lost 5 killed and several wounded. 1 Fed. wounded.

9. Skirmish at Fredericksburg, Va. Capt. Dahlgren's troops drove off a Confed. party, after a sharp skirmish, capturing 39 prisoners and stores.

9. Gen. Kelley's Fed. cavalry defeated Imboden's troops 18 miles S.W. of Moorefield, Va.

9 St. Mary's, Fla., burned by U. S. gunboat Mohawk, in retaliation for the treachery of the inhabitants.

9. Skirmish in Perry Co., Ky., on the Kentucky river. Capts. Morgan and Eversoll's troops defeated guerrillas.

10. Lieut. Ash, 2d U. S. dragoons, defeated part of 5th Va. cavalry, 10 miles south of Warrenton, Va.

10. Capt. G. W. Gilmore captured two

wagons and several rebels near Williamsburg, Greenbrier Co., Va.

11. Skirmish near Huntsville, Tenn. Capt. Duncan's Home Guards routed a small band of rebs. who lost 6 killed and several wounded.

11. A fight near Lebanon, Tenn. National cavalry under Capts. Kennett and Wolford defeated Morgan's men, who lost 7 killed and 125 prisoners.

11. National pickets driven in with slight loss at Newbern, N. C.

11. 134 prisoners taken and 16 rebs. killed by Col. Lee's Kansas cavalry near La Grange, Tenn.

11. Gen. Ransom defeated Confederate forces near Garretsburg, Ky.

12. Gen. Hooker appointed to relieve Gen. Fitz-John Porter in command of the 5th Army Corps.

12. Cavalry engagement near Lamar, Miss. Detachments of 2nd Ill. and 27th Kansas, Maj. J. J. Mudd, routed a force of rebs. with severe loss.

13. Slight skirmish at Holly Springs, Miss. Col. Lee's cavalry killed 4 rebs. and captured several.

13. Expedition to the Doboy river, Ga., by U. S. steamers Ben Deford and Darlington, with Col. Beard's colored troops, who seized a large quantity of reb. property.

13. A reb. camp near Calhoun, Green river, Ky. was surprised by Col. Shanks, with 400 men, who captured their arms and camp equipage.

15. Fight near Fayetteville, Va., by Fed. troops under Gen. Sturgis and a large body of rebs., who were defeated.

16. The remaining corps of the army of the Potomac, excepting the 5th and Gen. Pleasanton's cavalry, left Warrenton, and proceeded towards Fredericksburg.

17. Pickets of the 104th Pa. surprised at Gloucester Point, Pa. and 1 killed, 3 wounded, and 2 captured.

18. Skirmish at Rural Hills, Tenn. Col. Hawkins' troops defeated reb. cavalry, who left 16 of their number dead on the field.

18. At Cove Creek, near Kinston, N. C. Lieut.-Col. Mix with part of 3d N. Y. cavalry and Allis's artillery, defeated the 10th N. C. infantry and some of the 2d N. C. cavalry, who retreated with the loss of arms and equipments.

18. Falmouth, Va. occupied by Gen. Sumner's Fed. troops.

18. The English schooners Ariel and Ann Marie captured off Little Run, S. C. by U. S. gunboat Monticello.

19. James A Seddons appointed reb. Sec.-of-War, in place of G. W. Randolph, resigned.

19. The 1st Gen. Council of the Epis Church in the reb. States met at Augusta, Ga.

20. Col. Carlin's expedition returned to Nashville, Tenn., from Clarksville, having captured 43 rebs., 40 horses, &c.

20. Fed. pickets surprised at Bull Run bridge, Va., and 3 captured.

20. Warrenton and Leesburg, Va., occupied by reb. cavalry.

21. Gen. Sumner, commanding right wing of army of the Potomac, in front of Fredericksburg, Va.

21. Skirmish at Bayou Bontouca, near Fort Pike, La. Capt. Darling's company of 31st Mass. defeated rebs. under Capt. Evans, who lost 4 killed and several wounded. Union loss 1 wounded.

22. All political State prisoners held by military authority in the U. S. released by order of the Sec. of War.

22. Part of 1st N. Y. cavalry, Capt. Harkins, defeated rebs. near Winchester, Va., who lost 4 men and 30 horses.

22. An expedition into Matthew Co., Va., by steamer Mahaska, Capt. F. A. Parker, with land forces under Gen. Naglee, destroyed 12 salt works, and 20 or 30 vessels and other reb. property.

22. Skirmish near Halltown, Va., by Gen. Geary's troops.

23. Lieut. Cushing, U. S. steamer Ellis, captured 2 schrs. on New river, N. C., but lost his own vessel on the shoals in returning.

24. A reb. picket of 12 men captured by Gen. Kelley's cavalry 4 miles from Winchester, Va.

24. A Fed. supply-train of 47 wagons, escorted by 50 3d Mo. cavalry, was attacked by rebs. about 30 miles south of Lebanon, Texas Co., Mo. 5 of the escort were killed and 20 wagons captured.

25. The U. S. gunboat Lexington, J. W. Shirk, attacked 20 miles below Helena, Ark. The enemy were repelled, leaving several of their number killed. Capt. Shirk landed a party of sailors, who carried off 20 negroes and 16 bales of cotton.

25. A slight skirmish at Zuni, on the Blackwater river, Va., by mounted rifles under Col. Dodge, and a reb. force.

25. A company of Fed. troops captured at Henderson, Tenn., by reb. cavalry.

25. In Crawford Co., Mo., a company of reb. guerrillas carried off horses, firearms, clothing, &c., from farmers. Re-

turning, near Huzza river, Iron Co., they were overtaken by Capt. N. B. Reeve's company, who killed 2 of their party and recovered the plunder.

Nov. 25. Col. Paxton's loyal Va. cavalry captured 118 prisoners, 300 stand of arms, 100 horses, and other property, near Sinking Creek, W. Va.

26. Fight at Cold Knob Mountain, Va. 2d Va. cavalry, Col. J. C. Paxton, defeated reb. troops, of whom over 100 were taken prisoners.

25. 25 guerrillas, under Evan Dorsey, crossed the Potomac, and robbed the stores and stables in Urbanna, 7 miles above Frederic, Md. killing a man named Harris.

26. 7th Ill. cavalry attacked rebs. near Summerville, Miss., and captured 28 of their number.

27. Indiana troops, under Cols. Hurd and Dodge, defeated rebels near La Vergne, Tenn., several of whom were killed. National loss 10 wounded.

28. Gen. Blunt defeated Gen. Marmaduke's Confederate forces *en route* for Missouri, at Kane Hill, Ark. The battle raged over 12 miles. The rebels retreated to Van Buren, Ark.

28. At Hartwood Church, 15 miles from Falmouth, Va., 2 squadrons of 3d Pa. cavalry, Gen. Averill's brigade, captured by the enemy, after a brief resistance, in which they lost 4 killed and 9 wounded.

28. A large Fed. expedition, under Gen. A. P. Hovey, left Helena, Ark., and arrived at Delta, Miss., cutting the Tenn. and Mississippi railroad, and destroying 2 engines and 30 cars. Gen. Washburne's cavalry encountered the rear of Price's rebel army, and captured 50 men, near the Big Black river.

29. The U. S. steamer Star was burned by rebs. 2 miles below Plaquemine, La.

29. Gen. Stahl, with 300 cavalry, attacked rebs. at Snicker's Gap, Va., killing 45, capturing 40.

30. A skirmish near Abbeville, Miss., by Col. Lee's troops with a rebel force.

30. The schooner Levi Rowe captured off N. Carolina by U. S. steamer Mount Vernon.

30. The bark Parker Cook destroyed by reb. steamer Alabama in the Mona Passage.

Dec. 1. U. S. Congress convened at Washington.

1. Col. Lee's cavalry took possession of rebel forts on the Tallahatchie river. He also captured a battery of 6 guns on the north side of the river.

1. Skirmish near Horse Creek, Dade Co., Mo. Maj. Kelley's 4th Mo. cavalry routed a band of rebs., capturing 5.

1. Skirmish near Charlestown, Va. Gen. Slocum's Fed. troops defeated rebel cavalry under White and Henderson, killing 5, and wounding 18.

1. At Franklin, Va., Gen. Peck recaptured the Pittsburg battery, taken from the Fed. forces on the Peninsula.

2. A fight near Franklin, Va. 11th Pa. cavalry, Col. Spear, with artillery supports, defeated reb. cavalry with severe loss.

2. Lieut. Hoffman and 6 men of 1st N. J. cavalry, captured while on picket duty 3 miles from Dumfries, Va.

2. Two companies of 8th Pa. cavalry, Capt. Wilson, defeated with severe loss at King George Court House, Va.

2. Part of Gen. Banks' expedition to New Orleans sailed from New York.

2. Gen. Geary defeated rebels near Charlestown, Va., killing and wounding 70, and capturing 145.

3. Princeton, Ky., occupied by Federal troops, 91st Ind. and 15th Ky., under Maj. A. P. Henry, who captured a number of rebels.

3. Skirmishes near Oxford, Miss. Col. Hatch's brigade captured 92 rebs. Fed. loss in killed and wounded, 20.

4. Skirmish near Tuscumbia, Ala. Rebs. abandoned their camps, losing 70 men prisoners, and their horses.

4. Winchester, Va., occupied by Gen. Geary's troops, the rebel garrison leaving on his approach.

4. A sharp fight at Watervalley, Miss. Col. Hatch and Lee's Fed. brigades defeated a rebel force, capturing 300 men and 50 horses.

5. Fed. cavalry under Cols. Dickey and Lee defeated by rebel infantry after two hours' fight. Union loss, 100 killed, wounded, and missing.

5. The 30th Iowa and 29th Wis. attacked by rebs. at Helena, Ark., whom they repulsed, killing 8, and capturing 30.

6. The schr. Medora, with rebel army stores, was captured at Hackett's Point Md., by Capt. Kearney's company.

6. A forage train, in charge of 93d Ohio, Col. Anderson, was attacked by rebs near Lebanon, Tenn., who were driven off.

6. Gen. Banks' expedition sailed from New York to New Orleans.

7. U. S. mail steamer Ariel captured off Cuba by rebel steamer Alabama, but released on bond for $228,000.

7. Gens. Blunt and Herron defeated

15,000 rebels under Gens. Hindman, Marmaduke, Parsons, and Frost, at Prairie Grove, N.W. Ark. Federal loss, 495 killed, 600 wounded. Confed. loss, 1,500 killed and wounded.

7. The 106th and 108th Ohio, and 104th Ill., under Col. A. B. Moore, were attacked by a rebel force under Gen. J. H. Morgan, at Hartsville, Tenn. After a fight in which 55 of the Feds. were killed, and over 100 wounded, the entire force surrendered to the rebels, who lost about the same number in killed and wounded.

7. 60 of the 8th Pa. cavalry defeated at King George's C. H., Va. Loss 20.

9. A body of rebels attacked a forage train, under escort, near LaVergne, Tenn., but were repulsed with considerable loss.

9. U. S. steamer Lake City was burned by rebels at Concordia, Ark. In retaliation, the steamer De Soto went to Concordia, and burned 42 houses.

9. Skirmish near Brentville, Tenn. Federals under Col. John A. Martin, defeated a rebel force.

10. Congress passed a bill admitting to the Union the State of Western Va.

10. Plymouth, N. C., captured and burned by the Confederates.

11. The U. S. gunboat Cairo sunk in the Yazoo river by a torpedo. The crew saved.

11. The city of Fredericksburg, Va., bombarded and occupied by Fed. troops.

12. Skirmish near Corinth, Miss. 52d Ill., Col. Sweeney, engaged a rebel force led by Col. Roddy. Rebel loss, 11 killed, 30 wounded; Union loss, 1 killed, and 2 prisoners.

12. 1,750 paroled Union prisoners, who had been captured by Gen. Morgan, arrived at Nashville.

12. Artillery skirmish by Gen. Terry's Federal troops, near Zuni, on the Blackwater river, Va.

12. At Dumfries, Va., 37 National pickets and sutlers were captured by Gen. Stuart's cavalry.

12. Gen. Foster engaged and defeated Confederates near Kingston, N. C., capturing 400 prisoners, 13 pieces of artillery, &c.

12. Rebel salt works at Yellville, Ark., destroyed by Federal troops under Capt. M. Birch.

12. Rebs. attacked at Franklin, Tenn., by cavalry under Gen. D. S. Stanley, who drove them from the town, and destroyed mills and other property. Reb. loss, 5 killed, 10 wounded. One Fed. killed.

13. Battle of Fredericksburg, Va. The reb. works were attacked by the National army under Gen. Burnside. It consisted of three grand divisions led by Gens. Sumner, Hooker and Franklin. The Fed. army was repulsed, losing 1,512 killed, 6,000 wounded, and 460 prisoners. The rebels lost 1,800 men.

13. Jeff. Davis reviewed the reb. forces under Bragg at Murfreesboro'.

13. Two regiments of Union infantry and one of cavalry surprised a rebel force at Tuscumbia, Ala., completely routing them and capturing 70 prisoners, their horses and baggage. Federal loss, 1 killed, 14 wounded.

13. Gov. Johnson, of Tenn., assessed disloyal citizens of Nashville in various amounts to be paid in 5 monthly instalments, in behalf of widows and orphans of that city who had been reduced to want in consequence of their husbands and fathers being forced into the rebel armies.

13. Skirmish at South-west Creek, N. C. Gen. Foster's troops routed rebels, who lost a number of prisoners and guns.

13. Unsuccessful attack on reb. works on the river at Kinston, N. C., by small boats under Capt. Murray.

14. Two hundred Feds. under Capt. Thornberry, of 39th Ky., were defeated by 800 rebels at Wireman's Shoals, 5 miles below Prestonsburg, Ky. Rebs. captured 700 muskets, as many uniforms, and 40,000 rounds of cartridges.

14. The *True Presbyterian* and the *Baptist Recorder*, of Louisville, Ky., were suppressed, and the editor of the *Recorder* sent to prison.

14. Coffeeville, Miss., occupied by Fed. forces under Cols. Mizner and Lee.

14. Gen. Foster's troops engaged and defeated the Confeds. near Kingston, N. C., capturing 400 prisoners, 13 pieces of artillery, &c. Reb. loss, 71 killed, 268 wounded. Fed. loss, 90 killed, 478 w.

14. A Confed. cavalry force crossed the Potomac at Poolesville, Md., and captured 13 Fed. soldiers of the Scott cavalry, killing or wounding about 20 more.

14. Gen. Banks' expedition arrived at New Orleans.

14. A picket guard of 21 men of the 6th Mo., were captured by rebs. at Helena, Ark.

14. Slight skirmish at Woodsonville, Tenn.

14. A wagon train laden with provisions and clothing for Fed. troops at Ringgold Barracks, Texas, on its way from Fort Brown, under escort, was attacked

by Mexicans and captured, and the escort killed, excepting one man.

Dec. 15. Gen. Hovey's expedition returned to Helena, Ark.

15. Gen. Butler superseded in command of the Department of the Gulf by Gen. Banks.

16. Rebs. under Gen. Evans defeated in an artillery duel on the banks of the river Neuse, near Whitehall, N. C., by Gen. Foster's troops.

16. Three hundred Ga., Texas and Ky. cavalry captured near New Haven, Ky., by a detachment of Walford's cavalry, under Capt. Adams.

16. The army of the Potomac withdrawn to the north side of the Rappahannock, from Fredericksburg, Va.

17. Baton Rouge, La., occupied by Fed. troops under Gen. Grover.

17. Fight at Goldsboro', N.C. Gen. Foster's troops destroyed a valuable bridge, and defeated rebels under Gen. Evans.

18. Lexington, Ky., occupied by rebs. under Gen. Forrest, after defeating the 11th Ill. cavalry, Col. R. G. Ingersoll, who fought 2 hours, and lost 40 men and 2 cannon.

18 The steamer Mill Boy, at Commerce, Miss., was fired on by reb. cavalry and 3 men killed. The U. S. gunboat Juliet and City Belle with 11th and 47th Ind. were dispatched to Commerce and burnt the town and plantations in the neighborhood

19. Holly Springs, Miss., surrendered to rebs. with 1,800 men and 150 officers. $1,000,000 worth of commissary stores, &c., destroyed.

19. A lieutenant and 30 men of 10th N. Y. cavalry, with 14 wagons, captured at Occoquan, Va., by reb. cavalry, who were overtaken by Col. Rush's cavalry and compelled to destroy their plunder.

19. Col. Dickey's Fed. cavalry returned to camp, near Oxford, Miss., from a 6 days' scout, with 150 prisoners. 34 miles of the Ohio and Mobile railroad were destroyed, with a large amount of rebel stores.

20. Skirmish near Halltown, Va. Capt. Vernon's Fed. cavalry defeated rebs., capturing 3.

19–20. A body of reb. cavalry under Col. Forrest attacked a Fed. force at Davis's Mills, Tenn., and were repulsed by them. On the succeeding day, Humboldt, Trenton, Dyers, Rutherton, and Kenton were visited by them, and telegraph lines and railroad bridges destroyed, thus severing Gen. Grant's communication between Columbus and Corinth.

20. Gen. W. T. Sherman's expeditionary army against Vicksburg embarked at Memphis, Tenn., in over 100 transports.

21. Gen. Carter, with 1000 cavalry, entered E. Tenn., and captured 550 rebels and 700 stand of arms.

21. Skirmish near Nashville, Tenn. Gen. Van Cleve's troops with reb. artil'y.

21. Secretaries Seward and Chase tendered their resignation to Pres. Lincoln, who informed them that the acceptance of them would be incompatible with the public welfare; when the resignations were withdrawn.

21. The 25th Ind., Col. W. H. Morgan, in garrison at Davis's Mills, Wolf river, Miss., were attacked by a large cavalry force of rebs. under Gen. Van. After 3 hours' contest the rebels withdrew, leaving 22 dead, 30 wounded, 20 prisoners, and 100 stand of arms.

22. Skirmish at Isle of Wight Court House, Va. Lieut. Underdonk's N. Y. mounted rifles defeated by Gen. Pryor's troops. Rebs. lost 2 men.

22. Maj.-Gen. R. C. Schenck assumed command of the Middle Department and 8th Army corps, headquarters at Baltimore, Md.

23. A proclamation from Jeff. Davis, threatening to hang Gen. Butler, or any of his officers who should be captured, in retaliation for the hanging of W. B. Mumford at N. Orleans.

23. Gen. Sigel's troops attacked at Dumfries, Va. by reb. cavalry, who were repulsed.

24. Skirmish near Munfordsville, Ky. Capt. Dickey's company of 2d Mich. were defeated by rebs. of Gen. Morgan's army, losing 23 men prisoners.

24. Skirmish on the Blackwater river, Va., 4 miles above Franklin. 11th Pa. cavalry, Col. Spears, dispersed rebel troops, capturing 4.

24. Gen. M. L. Smith's Fed. troops destroyed Vicksburg and Texas railroad 10 miles W. of Vicksburg, and burned stations at Delhi and Dallas.

25. Skirmish at Green's Chapel, near Munfordville, Ky. Col. Gray's Fed. troops defeated rebs. of Morgan's army, who lost 9 killed, 22 wounded and 5 prisoners.

25. Col. Shanks with 12th Ky. cavalry attacked rebs. near Bear Wallow, Ky. killing 1, wounding 2 and capturing 10.

26. 38 Indians hung at Mankato, Minn. for participating in the late massacres in that State.

26. Maj. Stevens, with 150 of 4th Ky. attacked a reb. camp in Powell Co., Ky.

capturing 12 men, with most of the camp equipage.

27. A company of Pa. cavalry, under Capt. Johnson, captured at Occoquan, Va.

27. Elizabethtown, Ky. with a garrison of nearly 500 men under Col. H. S. Smith, was captured by Gen. Morgan's reb. army, after a short resistance. An immense amount of public and private stores were carried off by the rebs.

27. Fight at Dumfries, Va. Col. C. Candy's troops were attacked by rebs. under Gens. Stuart and Fitz Hugh Lee, who were driven off with the loss of 30 or 40 men in killed and wounded. Fed. loss about 10 killed and wounded.

27—29. Attack on Vicksburg, Miss. by Gen. Sherman's army and Fed. gunboats. Gen. Sherman's army ascended the Yazoo river on transports, landed and attacked the reb. works in the rear of Vicksburg, while the gunboats assailed the batteries at Haines' Bluff. The Feds., after sanguinary conflicts, carried the first and second lines of defence and advanced within 2 1-2 miles of the city, where they were defeated and compelled to withdraw, with a loss of 600 killed, 1,500 wounded and 1,000 missing.

28. The trestle-work at Muldraugh's Hill, defended by the 71st Ind., captured and destroyed by rebels under Gen. Morgan after 6 hours' fight.

28. New Madrid, Mo., evacuated by Unionists, after destroying the barracks and magazine.

28. Skirmish near Suffolk, Va. Col. Gibbs' troops routed rebel cavalry.

28. Van Buren, Ark., with a rebel garrison of 120 men, 6 steamboats, and a large amount of ammunition and stores was captured by Gen. Blunt's army, with slight loss.

28. Major Foley with 250 of the 6th and 10th Ky. cavalry, surprised a rebel camp at Elkford, Campbell Co., Ky. 30 rebels killed, 176 wounded, 51 prisoners, and 80 horses taken.

28. Skirmish near Clinton, La. Stuart's reb. cavalry defeated by a National force.

30. The Union and Watanga bridges on the E. Tenn. and Va. railroad destroyed by Gen. Carter's Fed. troops, who defeated a rebel force, of whom 400 were taken prisoners, and 150 k. and w. with slight loss to the Unionists.

30. The iron-clad steamer Monitor, Commander Bankhead, foundered near Cape Hatteras, N. C. 4 officers and 12 of the crew, and also 8 R. I. soldiers were lost with her.

30. Battle at Parker's Cross Roads, Tenn. A desperate conflict of several hours' duration between Gen. Sullivan's troops, and Gen. Forrest's rebel cavalry, in which the latter were defeated with a loss of 600 in killed, wounded and prisoners. Fed. loss, about 200.

31. Beginning of the Battle of Stone river, or Murfreesboro'. 10 hours continuous fighting without result.

31. Gen. McClernand succeeded Gen. Sherman at Vicksburg and the Fed. army retired to Milliken's Bend.

1863.

Jan. 1. Pres. Lincoln issued his Emancipation Proclamation, declaring all the slaves then held in rebellious territory to be forever free.

1. Galveston, Tex., recaptured by rebs. under Gen. Magruder, with its garrison of 300 men. 6 Fed. gunboats were in the harbor. The Harriet Lane was captured after a severe fight, in which Capt. Wainwright was killed, and many of his crew. The Fed. flag-ship Westfield was blown up by Commander Renshaw, to avoid capture, by which he lost his life, with many of the crew.

2. The battle of Stone river, or Murfreesboro', Tenn., between Gen. Rosecrans' army and Gen. Bragg's rebel troops, which commenced two days before, was resumed, and after an obstinate and bloody contest, which lasted all day, the rebels were defeated with great slaughter. Fed. loss, 1,533 killed, 6,000 wounded, 2,000 prisoners; rebel loss, over 10,000, of whom 9,000 were killed and wounded.

2. Reb. cavalry under Major Herring, captured 10 sutlers' wagons and their attendants at Dumfries, Va., belonging to Maine and New York regiments.

3. A rebel camp near La Grange, Ark., was surprised by Gen. Washburne's cavalry. 10 of the rebels were captured, and 10 killed or wounded.

3. Rebs. under Gen. Jones attacked Col. Washburne's troops at Moorfield, near New Creek, Va., and captured 65 of them.

5. Fed. troops in Hardy Co., Va., attacked by rebels under Capt. J. H. McNeill, who captured 33 men, 61 horses and camp stores.

5. The Fed. schr. Home, Capt. Cushing, destroyed a small rebel fort on Little river, N. C.

6. The iron steamer Antona, laden with arms and medicine, was captured off Mobile, by U. S. steamer Pocahontas.

7. 450 women and children left Wash-

ington, D. C., for Richmond and other points south, by special permit.

Jan. 8. A rebel force of 5,000, under Gens. Marmaduke and Burbridge, attacked the garrison at Springfield, Mo. They were repulsed by the Feds. under Gen. Brown and Col. Crabb. Fed. loss 17 killed and 50 wounded. Reb. loss 200.

8. Union force from Yorktown, Va., under Major W. P. Hall, made a raid to the Pamunkey river, and destroyed a ferryboat, steamers, sloops, railroad and depots, and large warehouses containing rebel stores.

8. The 20th Ill. cavalry, Capt. Moore, attacked a rebel camp near Ripley, Tenn., held by Lieut.-Col. Dawson, killing 8, wounding 20, and capturing 46 prisoners. Fed. loss, 3 wounded.

9. Reb. troops under Gen. Pryor crossed the Blackwater, near Suffolk, Va., and attacked Gen. Corcoran's brigade of Gen. Peck's troops. Enemy defeated. Fed. loss, 104.

9. Col. Ludlow effected an exchange of prisoners at City Point, Va., by which 20,000 men were restored to the National army.

10. Skirmish at Catlett's Station, Va. Col. Schimmelfennig's troops, and Hampton's rebel cavalry.

10. 21st Iowa, Col. Merritt, attacked by Marmaduke's troops at Hartsville, Mo. Rebs. defeated. Fed. loss, 35 killed and wounded. Reb. loss, 150 killed and wounded, and 150 prisoners.

11. U. S. steamer Hatteras, Lieut. R. G. Blake, sunk off Texas, by rebel steamer Alabama. 100 of the Fed. crew captured.

11. Steamer Grampus, No. 2, at the mouth of Wolf river, Tenn., captured and burned by 13 rebels.

11. Arkansas Post, Fort Hindman, on the Ark. river, captured by Admiral Porter's squadron and Gen. McClernand's army. Fed loss, nearly 1,000 in killed, wounded and missing. Reb. loss, 550 killed and wounded, and 5,000 prisoners

12. The brig J. P. Ellicott captured by rebel privateer Retribution, and put in charge of a prize crew. The wife of the mate of the Ellicott succeeded in getting the rebels intoxicated, put them in irons, piloted the vessel to St. Thomas, and delivered her and the prisoners to the U. S. Consul.

12. A rebel raid upon Holly Springs, Miss.

13. Gunboat Major Slidell and 3 boats with wounded troops captured by guerrillas on the Cumberland river, the wounded robbed, and all but one of the boats burned.

14. Four Union gunboats under Com. Buchanan, assisted by Gen. Weitzel's troops, engaged the rebel iron clad gunboat Cotton, aided by Col. Gray's soldiers, on the Bayou Teche, La. The Cotton was destroyed after several hours' combat. Commodore Buchanan was killed.

14. The steamer Forest Queen was burned by guerrillas at Commerce, Miss.

14. The Fed. gunboat Queen of the West, Col. Charles E. Ellet, was captured on the Red river near Gordon's Landing.

15. Mound City, Ark., burned by Fed. troops.

15. 17 of the 22d Wis. captured near Clarendon, Ark. 7 rebels killed and wounded.

16. U. S. steamer Columbia stranded at Masonboro' Inlet, N. C. Her officers surrendered to the rebels, under Col. Lamb.

16. Duvall's Bluff, Ark., captured by Fed. gunboat Baron de Kalb, and others of Porter's flotilla, and Gen. Gorman's troops. 100 prisoners taken. Lieut. J. G. Walker, 7 prisoners and a large supply of arms taken.

16. Reb. privateer Oreto escaped from Mobile.

16. U. S. transport ship Planter, with troops, wrecked near Stranger's Key, Bahama.

17. Des Arc, Ark., captured by Fed. troops, without opposition.

17. Skirmish at Pollocksville, N. C., the rebels fleeing from the town.

19. Skirmish near Barnesville, Va. Lieut. Vezin and 112 men charged a large party of reb. cavalry, rescuing 6 of their company who were prisoners and capturing 4 rebels.

19. The brig Estelle captured by the reb. privateer Oreto, or Florida, Capt. Maffit.

19. The army of the Potomac, Gen. Burnside, moved down the Rappahannock.

21. The National ship Morning Light and the schooner Velocity were captured by reb. steamers Josiah Bell and Uncle Ben, near Sabine Pass, Texas.

21. Reb. camp broken up near Columbia, Mo., by 61st Mo., Col. Douglass, and 6 prisoners taken. 2 Feds. wounded.

21. Gen. Fitz John Porter dismissed from the U. S. service.

21. Col. Hutchinson, with 100 rebel cavalry, captured a company of U. S. troops and 30 wagons, at Murfreesboro', Tenn.

22. Gen. Burnside's second attempt to cross the Rappahannock foiled by a rain storm, which made the roads impassable.

22. The brig Windward captured by the reb. privateer Florida, off Cuba.

23. A company of Feds., under Capt. Taylor, was attacked in Johnson Co., E. Tenn., by rebs., under Col. Folk. 4 Feds. killed and several wounded and captured, some of whom were hung.

23. Arkansas Post, Ark., evacuated by Fed. troops, and the fort blown up.

24. Maj.-Gen. Burnside transferred the command of the army of the Potomac to Gen. Jos. Hooker. Maj.-Gens. Sumner and Franklin commanding right and left wings, relieved from their commands.

25. Attack by rebs. on the railroad near Nashville, Tenn. They were repulsed.

25. Reb. pickets near Kinston, N. C., captured.

26. The bark Golden Rule was captured and burnt by the Alabama, 50 miles south of St. Domingo.

26. A fight near Woodbury, Tenn. Gen. Palmer's Fed. troops defeated a reb. force, who lost 35 killed and over 100 prisoners. Fed. loss 2 killed and 9 wounded.

27. Attack on rebs. at Bloomfield, Mo., by 68th Mo. militia, Col. Lindsay, who drove the enemy from the town, capturing 52 prisoners, 70 horses and 100 stand of arms.

27. Bombardment of Fort McAllister, Ga., by monitor Montauk, Capt. Worden, and 3 gunboats.

27. Skirmish at Indian Village, on Bayou Plaquemine, La., by Gen. Weitzel's Fed. brigade, who defeated a rebel force.

27. Col. Wyndham's Fed. troops attacked Stuart's cavalry near Middleburg, Va., defeating them, and capturing 26 men and 40 head of cattle.

28. The reb. steamer Julia Roan, with 300 men, was captured by Col. Harrison's Fed. troops, 130 of 1st Ark. cavalry, near Van Buren, Mo.

29. The British iron steamer Princess Royal, laden with arms, was captured off Charleston, S. C.

29. A fight near Bear river, Washington Territory. Union troops under Col. Connor defeated Indians with severe loss, after 4 hours' battle.

29. Gen. McClernand's troops landed 5 miles from the mouth of the Yazoo river, in view of Vicksburg.

30. U. S. gunboat Isaac Smith captured in Stono river, S. C.

30. A reb. camp at Trenton, Tenn., in charge of Capt. Dawson, was attacked by 22d Ohio, Col. Wood, and 34 rebels captured, or killed.

30. 300 rebel conscript soldiers surrendered at Murfreesboro', Tenn., and took the oath of allegiance to the U. S. government.

30. A fight at Deserted House, 9 miles from Suffolk, Va., between Feds. under Gen. Corcoran, and Gen. Pryor's troops. Loss in killed and wounded about 60 on each side.

31. Two rebel gunboats and rams, and 3 steamers, under Com. Ingraham, came down the Charleston, S. C., harbor, and attacked 3 vessels of the blockading squadron, the Mercedita, the Keystone State, and the Quaker City, damaging them severely, and capturing and paroling the crew of the Mercedita. 30 Feds. killed and 50 wounded.

31. Kennett's National cavalry attacked Wheeler's brigade, near Nashville, Tenn. Reb. loss 12 killed and 12 wounded, and 300 prisoners. 5 Feds. wounded.

31. Attack on Fed. soldiers by deserters and mob in Morgan Co., Ind. The mob dispersed, and 8 of them captured.

31. Shelybville, Ky., entered by Fed. troops under Gen. J. C. Davis.

Feb. 1. Second attack on Fort McAllister, Ga. Reb. commander Maj. Galbè, killed. Fed. vessels retire without loss.

1. Franklin, Tenn., occupied by Fed. forces under Col. R. Johnson, with slight loss.

1. Unsuccessful attack on Island No. 10, in the Miss. river, by a large force of rebs., with slight loss.

1. Col. Stokes, with loyal Tenn. and Ky. troops, attacked a reb. camp at Middleton, Tenn., capturing Maj. Douglass and 100 of his men.

2. The Union ram Queen of the West ran by the rebel batteries at Vicksburg, Miss.

3. Skirmish at Mingo Swamp, Mo. Fed. troops under Maj. Reeder defeated rebs. under D. McGee, who was killed, with 8 of his men, and 20 wounded.

3. Fort Donelson, Tenn., garrisoned by 83 Ill., Col. Harding, was attacked by a large force under Wheeler and Forrest. Rebs. repulsed with a loss of 100 killed, 400 wounded and 300 prisoners. Fed. loss 12 killed and 30 wounded.

4. Skirmish near Lake Providence, La., in which 30 rebs. were killed and wounded, and 90 horses taken.

4. Cavalry dash upon Batesville. Ark.,

under Col. G. E. Waring, driving rebels under Marmaduke out of the town, with severe loss, and capturing Col. Adams and other rebels.

Feb. 5. Skirmish on Bear Creek, Johnson Co., Mo. Capt. Ranney, of 40th Mo. militia drove a small rebel force.

5. Skirmish near Stafford's, Va.

6. Union raid upon Middleburgh, by 5th N. Y. cavalry. Several rebs. captured.

6. Skirmish between Winchester and Martinsburg, Va. 1st N. Y. cavalry, Capt. Jones, defeated a small reb. force.

7. A squadron of the 5th Pa. cavalry were led into ambush 9 miles from Williamsburg, Va., and 35 of their number killed, wounded, or captured.

7. Reb Capt. Dawson and several of his men were captured by Col. Wood, 22d Ohio, near Dyersburg, Va

7. Reb. Sec. of State declared Galveston and Sabine Pass, Texas, open to commerce.

8. A reb. camp attacked near Independence, Mo., by Lieut. Coburn, 5th Mo. cavalry. 8 rebs. killed, 2 wounded, and all their arms captured.

8. Ram Queen of the West returned from an expedition down the Mississippi, near Port Hudson, having sunk 3 steamers loaded with provisions for rebs, and captured 56 prisoners.

8. Gens. Davis' and Morgan's troops returned to Nashville, Tenn., from the pursuit of Forrest. They captured 50 rebs. 7 miles E. of Charlotte, including Col. Carroll.

8. Lebanon, Tenn., occupied by Fed. troops, who captured 600 rebels.

9. Skirmish near Summerville, Va Maj. Knox's Fed. cavalry defeated rebs.

9. Gen. Rosecrans, in Tenn., ordered the execution of all rebs. caught in Fed. uniform or carrying the national flag.

10. Fight at Old river, La. Capt. Tucker, 1st Kansas, defeated 3d La. reb cavalry, who lost 25 prisoners, and 11 killed or wounded. Union loss, 8.

10. The 11th Wis. and 11th Ill. attacked near Lake Providence, on the Miss., by rebs., who were repulsed. 32 taken prisoners

12. N. Y. ship Jacob Bell burnt by the Florida.

12. Skirmish near Smithfield, Va. 12th Pa cavalry engaged Capt. Baylor's reb. troops.

12. Skirmish near Bolivar, Tenn. 4 rebs. killed, 5 wounded, by Fed. cavalry, who were defeated.

14. Barge New Era, No. 5, captured by Fed. ram Queen of the West, near Fort Taylor, Red river. The ram was then run ashore by a treacherous pilot, and captured by the rebels.

14. 5th Mich. cavalry surprised near Annandale, Va., with loss of 15 men.

15. Fight near Canesville, Tenn. The 123d Ill., Col. Monroe, defeated some of Gen. Morgan's cavalry, of whom 20 were killed, many wounded, and 6 captured. Also 50 horses and 300 stand of arms. 3 Federals wounded.

15. Serg't Holmes, with 14 of 2d Minn., escorting a wagon train near Nolensville, Tenn., repulsed a superior force of rebel cavalry, of whom 8 were killed, 20 wounded, and 4 prisoners.

15. Fight near Arkadelphia, Ark. Feds. under Capt. Brown defeated the enemy, who lost 14 killed and 12 wounded. Fed. loss, 2 killed, 12 wounded.

17. A forage train in charge of some of 116th and 123d Ohio captured by rebs. near Romney, Va.

17. U. S. steamer Hercules burnt by rebels near Memphis, Tenn.

18. Mortar boats opened fire on Vicksburg.

18. Clifton, Tenn., burnt by 3d Mich. cavalry.

18. Disloyal State Convent. at Frankfort, Ky., dispersed by military.

19. A party of 1st Ind. cavalry, Lt.-Col. Wood, routed by reb. cavalry near Coldwater, Miss. Federal loss, 6 killed, 3 wounded, and 15 captured.

19. Hopefield, Ark., opposite Memphis, Tenn., burnt by order of Gen. Hurlbut.

20. Skirmish near the Yazoo Pass. 5th Ill. cavalry dispersed rebel troops, killing 6 and capturing 26. Fed. loss 5 wounded.

21. The ship Golden Eagle and bark Olive Jane burnt by rebel steamer Alabama.

21. Union gunboats Freeborn and Dragon engaged a rebel battery on the Rappahannock river, Va. Three Feds. wounded.

21. A guerrilla raid upon Shakertown, Ky. Government property and cars destroyed. 4 rebels captured by Col. Briston.

22. Capt. Cornyn, 10th Mo. cavalry, visited Florence and Tuscumbia, Ala., and captured horses, mules, negroes, and 100 rebs.

22. At Gatesville, Va., 9 of the 57th rebel Va. were captured by Federal troops.

22. The Yazoo Pass exped'n reached Moon Lake.

23. Fight near Greenville, Miss. Gen Ferguson's rebel troops engaged Nationals under Gen. Burbridge. Maj. Mudd, 2d Ill., killed.

23. Skirmish near Athens, Ky., with Morgan's guerrillas.

23. Rebel force of 700 devastating E Kentucky. A large amount of government property destroyed at Paris, Ky.

23. An attempt by rebels to capture the steamer Belle at Cottonwood Landing, Tenn., was repulsed. 1 killed on each side.

24. Gunboat Indianola captured near Grand Gulf, Miss., by 4 rebel steamers.

25. Skirmish at Hartwood Church, Va., near Kelly's Ford. Gen. Averill's troops defeated Stuart's rebel cavalry.

25. Rebel troops under Clarke dispersed at Lickiowa, Ky.

25. The steamer Peterhoff captured off St. Thomas by U. S. gunboat Vanderbilt.

25. Skirmish 5 miles from Falmouth, Va. 6th U. S. cavalry defeated Stuart's cavalry, of whom 10 were captured.

26. Cavalry fight near Woodstock, Va. The 13th Pa. and 1st N.Y. were defeated by the enemy, who killed and captured 200.

26. Cherokee National Council repealed the ordinance of secession, and abolished slavery.

26. A government freight train captured by rebels near Woodburn, Tenn.

27. Destruction of rebel steamer Nashville in Ogeechee river, near Fort McAllister, Fla., by gunboat Montauk, Capt. Worden.

27. Skirmish 15 miles from Newbern, N. C. Capt. Jacobs' N. Y. cavalry defeated rebels, who lost 3 killed and 48 prisoners. 1 Fed. wounded.

March 1. Union dash into Bloomfield, Mo. Provost-marshal and 20 prisoners taken.

1. Fight at Bradyville, Tenn. 2,500 of Rosecrans' army drove Morgan's reb. division from the town, killing 8, wounding 30, and capturing 89. Fed loss, 15 in killed and wounded.

1. English steamer Queen of the Wave captured near Georgetown, S. C., by U. S. gunboat Connemaugh.

1. Rebs. captured 50 of 1st Vt. cavalry, Capts. Wood and Huntoon, at Aldie, Va.

2. Sharp contest on the Salem pike, 16 miles from Murfreesboro', between the regulars of Rosecrans' army and a large force from Bragg's. The rebs. defeated.

2. Four guerrillas captured 3 miles from Russelville, Ky.

2. Slight cavalry fight near Petersburg, Tenn. Rebels routed with 12 killed and 20 wounded.

2. Capt. Schultze's Fed. cavalry defeated Mosby's troops near Aldie, Va., capturing 30.

3. Fort McAllister, Ga., bombarded without success.

3. The Enrolment and Conscription act passed by Congress, approved. All arms-bearing men with certain exceptions were to be enrolled by April 1st ensuing, and the President was authorized to call for quotas from the enrolled names.

4. Fight on Harpeth river, near Chapel Hill, Tenn. Col. Johnson's Tenn. Fed. cavalry engaged Col. Roger's troops, killing 12 and capturing 72.

4. Adjournment of 37th Congress.

4. Skirmishes at Skeet and Swan Quarter, N. C. Rebels beaten, 28 killed and wounded. Unionists, 3 killed and 15 wounded

5. U. S. Senate met in extra session.

5. Fight at Thompson's Station, near Franklin, Tenn. A Fed. force under Col. Colburn was attacked by a large army under Van Dorn, and defeated in battle, after which the entire Union brigade was captured, excepting 150 men. Fed loss, 100 killed, 300 wounded, and 1,200 prisoners. Rebel loss, 120 killed and 300 wounded.

5. The *Crisis* newspaper office, at Columbus, O., was destroyed by soldiers.

6. Successful foray of Fed. troops under Col. Phelps in Northumberland Co., Va.

6. Ship Star of Peace captured and burnt by rebel privateer Florida.

6. Gen. Hunter ordered the drafting of negroes in the Department of the South.

7. A scouting expedition from Belle Plain, Va., returned with several prisoners and much property.

7. A brigade of cavalry under Gen. Manly attacked rebel cavalry of Gen. Russell at Unionville, Tenn. Rebel loss, 50 killed, 180 wounded, and all their stores.

8. Mosby (reb.) dashed into Fairfax, Va., and captured Brig.-Gen. Stoughton and 30 men and 58 horses.

8. 43d Mass., Col. Holbrook, captured a rebel cavalry company near Newbern, N. C.

9. A small rebel force captured, six miles below Port Hudson, on the Mississippi.

9. The screw-steamer Douro captured by U. S. gunboat Quaker City.

March 9. Guerrillas defeated near Bolivar, Tenn., with the loss of 18 captured.

9. Skirmish at Blackwater Bridge, Va., by Feds. under Col. Chickering.

9. Skirmish on Amite river, La. Rebs. dispersed.

10. Rebel steamer Parallel burnt on the Mississippi with 3,000 bales of cotton.

10 Several rebels captured at Rutherford's creek, Tenn., by Gen. Granger's troops.

10. Jacksonville, Fla., captured by 1st S. C. (colored) regiment.

10. Skirmish near Covington, Tenn. Col. Grierson's cavalry attacked Col. Richardson's rebel camp, killing 25 and capturing a large number.

11. A skirmish 12 miles E. of Paris, Ky. Guerrillas attacked a Fed. forage train, and were repulsed.

12. Gen. Gordon's troops returned to Franklin, Tenn., from pursuing Van Dorn's troops beyond Duck river. Fed. loss in skirmishes, 9.

13. Unsuccessful assault on Fort Greenwood, on the Tallahatchie, Miss., by Union gunboats Chillicothe and DeKalb, and a land battery.

13. Skirmish at Berwick City, La.

13. The signal station at Spanish Wells, S. C., burnt by a party of rebels. A lieut. and 8 men captured.

13. Rebel troops under Gen. Pettigrew attacked Gen. Foster's troops at Newbern, N. C., but were repulsed.

14. Admiral Farragut, with 7 of his fleet, attacked the rebel batteries at Vicksburg, Miss. The Hartford (flagship) and the Albatross passed the batteries and went up the river. The Mississippi was destroyed, and part of her crew captured.

14. Col. Minty's Fed. cavalry returned to Murfreesboro', Tenn., after 11 days' absence, with 50 rebel prisoners and a large amount of stores.

15. Schooner Chapman, fitted out and manned as a rebel privateer in San Francisco, was captured while attempting to leave that port. 20 rebels and 6 brass Dahlgren guns were taken

15. The *Jeffersonian* newspaper office at Richmond, Ind., was destroyed by Union soldiers.

17. A sharp conflict at Kelly's Ford, Va., between a body of Gen. Averill's Fed. cavalry and a rebel force. Gen. Averill's troops were defeated, but 80 of the enemy were captured.

17. Attack on rebel works near Franklin, Va. Fed. troops under Col. Spear driven off, with 1 man killed and 16 wounded.

17. Col. J. B. Fry detailed as Provost-Marshal-General of the U. S.

18. Skirmishing at Berwick Bay, La. Capt. Perkins, 1st Louisiana cavalry, defeated rebs., who lost 10 killed and 20 wounded.

19. Steamer Georgiana, with arms for the rebels, destroyed off Charleston.

19. Skirmish on Duck river, near Franklin, Tenn.

20. Col. Hall's brigade, of Rosecrans's army, attacked at Vaught's Hill, near Milton, Tenn., by Morgan's and Breckinridge's cavalry. The rebels defeated, losing 40 killed, 140 wounded, and 12 prisoners. Fed. loss 7 killed and 31 wounded.

21. Fight at Cottage Grove, Tenn. Rebels defeated with severe loss.

21. Capture of British steamer Nicholas I. while attempting to enter Wilmington harbor, N. C., by U. S. steamship Victoria. She had 16 tons of powder and 50,000 Enfield rifles.

21. Skirmish near Seneca, Pendleton Co, Va. A party of loyal men called "swampers" defeated by rebels.

21. An expedition up the bayous returned to the Yazoo river, after defeating the rebels at Deer Creek, and destroying 2,000 bales of cotton, 50,000 bushels of corn, and all the houses on the route.

22. 50 of the 5th Mo. cavalry defeated by Quantrell's guerrillas, near Blue Spring, Mo. Fed. loss, 9 killed, 5 missing, and several wounded.

22. Mount Sterling, Ky., attacked by rebels under Col Cluke. The Fed. garrison of 200, under Capt. Radcliff, captured, and the town burned.

22. Steamer Granite City captured by U. S. gunboat Tioga, off the Bahamas.

16 24. Bread, riots at Atlanta, Ga., Salisbury, N. C., Richmond, Va., Raleigh, N. C., and Petersburg, Va.

24. Pontchatoula, La., captured by Fed troops under Col. Clark.

24. The schooners Mary Jane and Rising Dawn captured by U. S. gunboats State of Georgia and Mount Vernon, off Wilmington, N. C.

25. The Fed. gunboats Lancaster and Switzerland attempted to pass the rebel batteries at Vicksburg. The Lancaster was sunk, and the Switzerland escaped, much damaged.

25. At Brentwood, Tenn., 300 Federal troops, under Lieut.-Col. Bloodgood, were captured by rebel forces under Wheeler

and Forrest, and the town sacked. A Federal cavalry force, under Gen. Smith, overtook the rebels in their retreat, and defeated them, capturing 42 prisoners, and recovering part of their booty. Loss, about 15 on each side in k. and w.

25. Steamer Dolphin captu'd off Porto Rico by U. S. gunboat Wachusett.

26. Expedition returned to Carthage, Tenn., with 28 rebel prisoners.

26. Gen. Burnside took command of the Department of the Ohio.

27. Fast day in the rebel States.

27. Jacksonville, Fla., burned by Fed. troops.

27. U. S. steamer Hartford passed below the rebel batteries at Warrenton, Miss.

28. Gunboat Diana captured by rebels at Pattersonville, La. 31 of the crew killed or wounded, and 170 prisoners.

28. Coles Island, S. C., occupied by N. Y. troops, under Col. G. F. B. Dandy.

28. Steamer Sam. Gaty plundered by rebels at Sibley, Mo.

28. The rebels attacked Williamsburg, Va., and were repulsed by the 5th Pa. cavalry, Col. Lewis.

29. A party of blockade runners taken at Poplar creek, Md.

29. Sixth Ill. cavalry, Col. Loomis, surprised by rebs. under Col. Richardson, near Somerville, Tenn. Fed. loss 40 in k. or w. Rebs. driven off.

30. Battle near Somerset, Ky. Fed. troops under Gen. Gillmore defeated Pegram's army of 2600, after a battle of 4 hours. Reb. loss 350. 400 cattle taken.

30. Washington, N. C., was attacked by rebels under Hill and Pettigrew. The Fed. pickets and skirmishers driven in with loss, and the rebels driven out of range afterwards by Fed. gunboats.

30. 700 rebels, under Gen. Jenkins, captured Point Pleasant, W. Va., but were subsequently driven out, losing 12 killed and 14 prisoners. Fed. loss 1 killed and 1 wounded.

30. Richmond, Miss., occupied by Gen. McClernand's Fed. troops, after sharp skirmishing.

31. Gen. Herron appointed to command the army of the frontier.

April 1. Admiral Farragut, with the National gunboats Hartford, Switzerland and Albatross, engaged the rebel batteries at Grand Gulf, Miss., and passed them without serious loss.

1. Severe fight at Dranesville, Va., between 1st Vt. cavalry, and Capt. Mosby's rebel troops. Feds. defeated with a loss of 60 in killed, wounded, and pris.

1. The town of Palmyra, Tenn., burned by a Fed. gunboat, Capt. Fitz.

2. Women's bread riot at Richmond, Va.

2. Skirmish at Woodbury, Tenn. Gen. Hazen's Fed. troops engaged and defeated rebels, killing 12 and capturing and wounding 30.

2. Admiral Farragut's vessels proceeded to the mouth of the Red river, destroying rebel boats.

2. Gunboat St. Clair disabled by rebs. above Fort Donelson, on the Cumberland river. She was rescued by the steamer Luminous.

2. Hicks' rebel guerrillas, in Jackson Co., Mo., were attacked by Maj. Ransom with the 6th Ks. 17 rebels killed, and considerable property captured.

2. Fight at Snow Hill, Tenn. Gen. Stanley engaged Morton and Wharton's rebel regiments, who were defeated, and 15 or 20 killed, and 50 captured.

3. Arrests of Knights of the Golden Circle, at Reading, Pa.

3. Steamer Tampico captured off Sabine Pass, Texas, by U. S. gunboat New London.

3. Capt. Worthington's loyal Ark. cavalry returned to Fayetteville, Ark., after four skirmishes, in which two rebel captains were k., 1 w., 22 men k. and 7 taken.

4. Unionists under Gen. Potter repulsed with loss of 5 men in attempt to capture rebel battery on Pamlico river, N. C.

4. Palmyra, Tenn., burned by the gunboat Lexington.

4. U. S. steamer Sylvan Shore fired on near Washington, N. C., and several of her crew killed or wounded.

5. Ship Louisa Hatch captured by the Alabama.

5. Troops sent from Newbern to rescue Gen. Foster, besieged in Washington, N.C.

5. Skirmish in Black Bayou, La.

6. Col. Wilder's Fed. command on an expedition within the rebel lines in Tenn. destroyed much provision, and brought in 350 negroes.

6. Rebel camp at Green Hill, Tenn., broken up; 5 killed and 15 taken.

7. Bombardment of Fort Sumter by Admiral Dupont; the fleet driven off; fort little injured.

7. U. S. gunboat Barataria lost in Amite river, La.

7. Successful foray into Gloucester Co., Va.

8. Gunboat George Washington, stranded in Broad river, S. C., attacked by rebs. and blown up.

April 8. The Tallahatchie fleet returned to Helena, Ark., after an absence of 43 days, with the divisions of Gens. Ross and Quimby. 30 soldiers were killed and a number wounded.

8. 60 rebels captured in Loudon Co., Va., by Gen. Copeland's brigade.

8. U. S. steamer Lovell and propeller Saxonia captured 15 miles below Clarkesville, Tenn.

9. Pascagoula, Miss., taken by a Union force from Ship Island, but abandoned the same day.

9. Fight at Blount's Mills, N. C. Unionists driven off with small loss.

10. Battle at Franklin, Tenn. Van Dorn's attack repulsed. Union loss about 100. Rebel, 300 k. and w.

10. Rebels routed near Germantown, Ky.

10. Skirmish near Waverly, Tenn. 21 Unionists taken prisoners.

11. Col. Streight's raiding force left Nashville for Georgia.

11. Union cavalry camp near Williamsburg, Va., broken up by rebel attack.

12. Ironclad fleet leaves Charleston harbor.

12. Skirmish near Gloucester Point, Va.

12. Lieut.-Col. Kimball killed by Gen. Corcoran.

13. Transport Escort ran the batteries below Washington, N. C., bringing aid for Gen. Foster.

13. Skirmish near Suffolk, Va.

13. Gen. Stoneman's cavalry advanced in detachments to Warrenton, Bealton, Rappahannock bridge, Liberty, and all the fords of the Rapidan, Va., preparatory to a general advance of the army of the Potomac against General Lee.

14. Battle at Bayou Teche, La. Rebs. defeated and their three gunboats, Diana, Hart, and Queen of the West, destroyed. Union loss about 350. Reb. much larger.

14. Gen. Foster escaped from Washington, N. C., by running the rebel blockade in the steamer Escort.

14. Rebel battery on Nansemond river silenced by gunboats.

14. U. S. gunboat West End attacked by a reb. battery near Suffolk, Va., and considerably damaged. 5 of her crew killed and 18 wounded.

15. Col. Evans routed 200 Indians, 75 miles south of Daybreak, in Utah, killing 30. Fed. loss, 8.

15. Franklin, La., occupied by Union troops.

15. Rebs. raise the siege of Washington, N. C.

15. Fighting continued on the Nansemond river.

15. Dash upon Pikeville, Ky., by 39th Ky., Col. Dills. 17 reb. officers and 61 privates captured.

15. Destruction of reb. steamer Queen of the West, in Berwick's Bay, La., by U. S gunboat Estella. 90 rebs. captured, and 30 lost.

16. Admiral Porter's fleet of 8 gunboats and several transports ran pass the Vicksburg batteries, losing only 1 transport and no men.

16. Fight with Indians at Medalia, Minn.

16. Steamer Gertrude captured off Harbor Islands, W. I., by U. S. steamer Vanderbilt.

17. The 99th and 130th N. Y. engaged reb. troops near Suffolk, Va. 2 Feds. killed and 3 wounded.

17. Gen. Donelson (reb.), nephew of Andrew Jackson, died at Knoxville.

17. Col. Grierson's famous cavalry raiding force started from La Grange, Tenn.

17. Skirmish at Bear Creek. Rebs. defeated by Gen. Dodge's troops.

17. Skirmish at Vermillion Bayou, La. Rebs. driven off by Gen. Grover's troops, who took 1,000 prisoners.

18. Gen. Getty's troops, in conjunction with gunboats on Nansemond river, N. C., under Lieut. Lamson, captured a reb. battery of 8 pieces and 200 prisoners, at the West Branch.

18. The siege of Washington, N. C., raised, after an investment of 3 weeks by a large Confederate force.

18. Fayetteville, Ark., attacked by a reb. army under Gen. Cabell, who were repulsed by 2,000 Feds. under Col. Harrison.

18 Reconnoitering party at Sabine Pass captured by concealed rebs. Capt. McDermott, of gunboat Cayuga, killed.

18 19. Cols. Graham and Riley defeated reb. forces in several skirmishes on Cumberland river, Tenn., killing and wounding 40.

19. Cavalry skirmishing near Hernando, Miss., with varying success.

19. Severe fight on the Coldwater, near Hernando, Tenn. A Fed. brigade under Col. Bryant defeated rebel troops in a series of skirmishes. Reb. loss, 20 killed, 40 wounded. Fed. 10 killed, 20 w.

20. Opelousas, La., occupied by Union forces.

20. Cavalry skirmish near Helena, Arkansas.

20. Fight at Patterson, Mo. Feds. un-

der Col. Smart defeated with loss of 50 in killed and wounded.

20. Bute a la Rose, La., captured by Union gunboats. 60 prisoners taken.

21. Skirmish and capture of a few rebs. near Berryville, Va., by Capt. Laypole, of 6th Va.

21. An expedition under Gen. Graham returned to Louisville, Ky., after proceeding to Celina on the Cumberland, and destroying a large amount of rebel stores and 40 boats. 60 rebs. killed and wounded.

22. Reb. raid on Tompkinsville, Ky. The Court house burned, and 5 Union men killed.

22. Reb. steamer Ellen captured near Courtableau, La.

22. Seven of the 8th Mo. cavalry, and a Baptist minister shot by guerrillas in Cedar Co., Mo.

22. Occupation of McMinnville, Tenn., by Union troops under Gen. Reynolds and Col. Wilder.

22. Majs. McGee and White's troops encountered 300 rebs. near Strasburg, Va., and defeated them. Rebel loss 5 killed, 9 wounded, and 25 prisoners. Union loss, 2.

22. Six gunboats and 12 barges passed the rebel batteries at Vicksburg.

23. Lieut. Cushing, with a party of men from the gunboat Commodore Barney, had a skirmish with rebel cavalry near Chuckatuck, Va., with small loss.

23. Skirmish at Beverly, Va. Loyalists under Col. Latham.

24. Tuscumbia, Ala., occupied by Federal forces under Col. Dodge.

24. 4 rebel schooners captured off Mobile, Ala., by gunboat De Soto.

24. Two rebel schooners captured near New Inlet, N. C., by U. S. steamer State of Georgia.

24. Rebels defeated at Weber Falls, Ark., by Col. Phillips' troops.

23-27. Gen. Ellet's Maine Brigade made a successful expedition up the Tennessee river, destroying the towns of Hamburg and Eastport, and a large store of war material. The rebels were defeated in an attack on the vessels while returning, losing 10 killed and 20 wounded. Federal loss, 2 killed, 4 wounded.

24. Skirmishing near Suffolk, Va.

24. Unionists defeated at Beverly, Va.

25. Rebel shore batteries at Duck river shoals, Tenn. river, silenced by gunboats. 25 rebels killed and wounded.

25. Fight at Greenland Gap, Va. Rebels severely punished by 23d Illinois, Capt. Wallace.

26. 30 rebel cotton-gins and mills and 350,000 bushels of corn destroyed by a raid to Deer Creek, Miss.

26. Cape Girardeau, Mo., attacked by Marmaduke's rebels, who were defeated with heavy loss by Gen. McNeil's troops. Rebel loss 40 killed and 200 wounded.

26. Gen. Burnside assumed command of the Department of Ohio.

27. A body of Texan Rangers were attacked 8 miles from Franklin Tenn., by 700 Federal cavalry under Col. Watkins, of the 6th Kentucky, who defeated them, capturing 200 prisoners.

27. The steamship Anglo Saxon, from Liverpool, wrecked 4 miles off Cape Race, with 360 passengers, and a crew of 84. Only 190 persons saved.

27. Fight at Philippi, West Virginia, by Col. Mulligan's Federal troops.

27. Gen. Hooker's army began its march towards Fredericksburg, Va.

28. Hooker's army crossed the Rappahannock.

28. Capture of 4 companies of Federals at Morgantown, West Virginia.

28. A rebel regiment surprised and captured near Jackson, Missouri, by artillery and 1st Iowa cavalry.

28. Skirmish near Mill Spring, Kentucky, by Col. Adams' Federal cavalry.

29. Two companies of the 106th New York, in garrison at Fairmount, W. Va., were captured by rebels under Jackson and Imboden, after a brave resistance in which the rebels suffered severely.

29. Gen. Jackson destroyed the railroad bridges on the Monongahela river.

29. Bombardment of Grand Gulf, Miss., by Porter's fleet. Rebel works greatly damaged. Fleet considerably injured. 20 killed and many wounded.

30. Gen. Grant's army lands near Port Gibson, Miss.

30. Rebel battery on the Nansemond river silenced.

30. 52 Union cavalry, the 6th N. Y., Lieut.-Col. McVicar, captured near Spotsylvania, Va. 58 others cut their way out. Col. McVicar was killed.

30. Skirmish near Williamsburg, Va. Rebels defeated by Col. R. M. West's troops.

30. A portion of Gen. Hooker's army crossed the Rappahannock at Fredericksburg, Va., and after slight resistance took possession of the rifle-pits below the city and captured 500 prisoners.

May 1. Attack on Van Dorn's rebel pickets by Fed. cavalry under Col. Campbell, near Franklin, Tenn. 30 of the enemy killed and wounded, and 11 captured.

May 1. Skirmish on the Nansemond river, near Suffolk, Va. The 99th N. Y., Col. Nixon, defeated rebs. with severe loss. Union loss 41 in killed and wounded.

1. Battle of Port Gibson, Miss. Gen. Grant's army defeated the troops of Gen. J. S. Bowen. Reb. loss 1,500 in killed, wounded and prisoners.

1. Fight at Monticello, Ky. 5,000 Feds. under Gen. Carter defeated Col. Morrison's troops, with small loss on either side.

1. Heavy artillery skirmishing between the armies of Gen. Hooker and Gen. Lee, at Chancellorsville, Va.

1. Skirmish near La Grange, Ark. 3rd Iowa cavalry, Capt. De Huff, defeated, with loss of 41 killed, wounded, and missing.

2. Gen. Sedgwick's corps of the Army of Va. attacked the reb. works on the heights, in the rear of Fredericksburg, and carried them after a desperate struggle, in which the Fed. loss was over 2,000 in killed and wounded.

2. Marmaduke's reb. army overtaken by Gen. McNeill at Chalk Bluff, on the Ark., and driven into Ark.

2 Col. Grierson's cavalry arrived at Baton Rouge, La., after a raid of 15 days through Miss., defeating the rebs. in several encounters.

2. Artillery skirmish on the Nansemond river, Va., by Gen. Getty's troops and reb. forces.

2-3. Battle of Chancellorsville, Va. The army of Gen. Lee attacked the Fed. forces under Gen. Hooker, and after a series of sanguinary contests, the Union army was compelled to retire, and recrossed the Rappahannock. Very heavy loss on both sides.

2-7. Great Fed. cavalry raid within the rebel lines, from Gloucester Point, Va., on the south, and the Alleghany ridge on the west. Many bridges, and an immense quantity of telegraph lines throughout the route, were destroyed, and many prisoners, and 1,000 horses taken.

3. Col. Streight, with 1,500 Fed. troops, after inflicting serious loss to the enemy, by a raid of 20 days through Georgia, and [illegible]bama, was captured near Gadsde[illegible], Ala.

3. [illegible]rmish near Suffolk, Va. 13th N. H., and 89th N. Y., captured reb. rifle pits.

3. Gen. Mosby's reb. cavalry attacked Col. de Forest's cavalry at Warrentown Junction, and were defeated by the latter with heavy loss.

3. Fed. gunboats repulsed in an attack on Haines's Bluff, on the Miss. Several of the vessels badly damaged, and 80 of their men killed and wounded.

3. Reb. batteries at Grand Gulf, Miss., evacuated by the enemy, and taken possession of by Admiral Porter.

3. The ship Sea Lark burned by the Alabama.

3. Col. Montgomery's colored troops returned to Beaufort, S. C., from a raid up the Combahee river, having captured 800 slaves, and destroyed $1,500,000 of property.

4. Capt. H. Dwight killed by rebels after surrendering, near Washington, La.

4. The battle near Fredericksburg, Va., continued, the rebs. recovering nearly all the defences back of the town.

5. Riot at Dayton, Ohio, consequent on the arrest of C. L. Vallandigham, by military authority.

5. A rebel company captured at Pettie's Mills, N. C., by 3d N. Y. cavalry.

5. Fort de Russy, on the Red river, captured by Admiral Porter.

6. All of Gen. Hooker's army retreated to the north bank of the Rappahannock river.

6. Alexandria, Miss., occupied by National forces under Admiral Porter.

6. Fight near Tupelo, Miss., between Gen. Ruggles' reb. cavalry, and Col. Cornyn's troops. Rebs. defeated, losing 90 prisoners.

6. Steamer Eugenia captured by Fed. gunboat Cuyler, off Mobile, Ala.

7. Steamer Cherokee captured off Charleston, S. C., by U. S. gunboat Canandaigua.

7. Col. Kilpatrick's cavalry, after marching around Lee's army, arrived at Gloucester Point, Va.

7. Reconnoissance from the Peninsula to White House; some prisoners retaken from the rebs.

8. The ship Crazy Jane captured in Tampa Bay, Fla., by U. S. gunboat Tahoma.

8. Rebel Gen. Earl Van Dorn was killed by Dr. Peters, of Maury Co., Tenn.

8. An attack on Port Hudson commenced by Fed. fleet.

9. Col. McCook's 2d Ind. cavalry captured 8 rebels scouting near Stone river, Tenn.

10. Death of rebel Gen. "Stonewall" Jackson, from wounds received at the battle of Chancellorsville.

10. Port Hudson assault renewed; rebel batteries silenced.

11. Fight at Greasy Creek, Ky. Col.

Jacobs' Fed. troops defeated by Morgan's cavalry. Union loss, 25 killed and wounded. Rebel loss greater.

11. Crystal Springs, Miss., burned by Fed cavalry.

12. Raymond, Miss., captured by Gen. McPherson's Fed. troops. Union loss, 51 killed, 181 wounded. Rebel loss, 75 killed, 250 wounded, 185 prisoners.

12. Skirmish near Franklin, Ky. Rebs. defeated.

12. Col. Breckinridge's Fed. Tenn. cavalry defeated rebels at Linden, on Tenn. river, capturing 40 and killing 3.

13. Rebel guerrillas and Indians attacked at Pontchatoula, La., by Col. Davis, who destroyed their camp, and took 17 prisoners.

13. Skirmish at South Union, Ky. Rebels attack a train, and are worsted.

13. Yazoo City, Miss., was captured by Fed. gunboats under Lieut. Walker, and $2,000,000 of property destroyed.

14. Gen. Johnston's army defeated near Jackson, Miss., by Gen. Grant's Fed. army. Rebel loss, 400 men, 17 pieces of artillery.

14. Skirmish at Fairfax Court House, Va., by Fed. troops with Black Horse cavalry.

14. Hammond Station, La., destroyed by Fed. troops.

15. Jackson, Miss., occupied by Fed. troops.

15. Rebels defeated at Camp Moore, La., by Col. Davis's Fed. troops.

15 Wm. Corbin and T. P. Graw hung at Johnson's Island, O.; found guilty of recruiting for the rebel service within the Union lines.

15. Fed. dispatch boats Emily and Arrow captured by rebels on the Albemarle and Chesapeake canal.

15. The ship Crown Point burnt by the privateer Florida.

15. Several severe cavalry skirmishes near Carrsville and Suffolk, Va., by Gen. Peck's troops with rebels.

15. A detachment of U. S. cavalry captured at Charleston, Va., who were afterwards rescued by a force from Gen. Milroy's command, who also took 40 rebel prisoners.

16. A skirmish at Bradyville Pike, near Cripple creek, Tenn. Gen. Palmer's Union Tenn. cavalry attacked part of 3d Georgia, under Col. Thompson, killing several, and taking 18 prisoners.

16. Skirmish at Berry's Ferry, Va. 16 of 1st N. Y. cavalry, Lieut. Vermillion, defeated 23 rebels, killing 2, wounding 5, and capturing 10.

16. The 1st N.Y. mounted rifles routed with considerable loss near Suffolk, Va.

16. Rebel steamer Cuba destroyed by gunboat De Soto in the Gulf of Mexico.

16. The battle of Champion Hill, or Baker's creek, Miss. Gen. Grant's troops defeated rebel army under Gen. Pemberton, who lost 4,000 men and 29 cannon, and retreated behind Big Black river.

16. Battle at Big Black river, Miss. Gen. Pemberton's army defeated with loss of 2,600 men and 17 cannon, and driven within the intrenchments at Vicksburg, by Gen. Grant's army.

16. Jackson, Miss., evacuated by Fed. troops.

16. Rebel schooner Isabel seized off Mobile, and 16 men captured, by U. S. steamer R. R. Cuyler.

16. Rebel guerrillas destroyed oil springs and other property at Burning Springs, Wirt Co., Va

16. Col. Breckinridge, with 55 loyal W. Tenn. cavalry, attacked a rebel force at Linden, on the Tenn. river, capturing 35 prisoners, and destroying their camp and stores.

17. Richmond, Clay Co., Mo., was attacked by rebel troops, who captured 2 companies of the 25th Mo.

18. Vicksburg invested by the Union army.

18. Two companies of 2d Kansas artillery, Maj. Ward, defeated by rebels near Sherwood, Mo., and 26 of the soldiers killed, wounded, or taken prisoners.

18. Haines' Bluff, on the Yazoo river, captured by Admiral Porter.

18. National troops fired into each other by mistake near Deserted House, Va. 3 killed and 4 wounded of the 170th N. Y.

19. Skirmish near Winchester, Va. Gen. Milroy's Fed. cavalry killed 6 and captured 7 of the enemy.

19. Spanish steamer Union captured by U. S. gunboat Nashville.

20. Rebel riflepits on the north side of Vicksburg captured by Gen. Steele.

20. Skirmish by pickets between Fayetteville and Raleigh, Va.

20. Skirmish near Fort Gibson, Ark. Price's troops defeated by Feds. under Col. Phillips.

20. Steamer Eagle captured near Nassau, N. P., by gunboat Octorora.

20. Two rebel regiments attacked at Middletown, Tenn., by Fed cavalry under Gen. Stanley. The enemy routed, losing 8 killed, 90 pris. and 200 horses.

21. Richmond and Plattsburg, Mo., plundered by rebels.

May 21. Vicksburg fully invested by Union troops.

21. A rebel camp broken up near Middletown, Tenn., by 103d Ill. 11 rebels captured.

21. Port Hudson, Miss., besieged by Fed. troops under Gen. Banks, after sharp skirmishing with the enemy while marching from Baton Rouge.

22. Gen. Grant's army repulsed with heavy loss in an attempt to storm the fortifications at Vicksburg.

22. Col. Kilpatrick's Fed. cavalry returned to Gloucester Point, after a successful raid into Gloucester and Matthew counties, Va., destroying much property.

22–23. Col. Jones, 58th Pa., engaged and defeated the rebels at Gum Swamp, N. C., capturing 165 prisoners with military stores. Fed. loss, 2 killed, 6 wounded.

24. Austin, Miss., burned by Union forces under Gen. Ellet.

24. A Fed. wagon train with 30 colored troops was captured near Shawnee creek, Kansas.

24. Gen. Schofield appointed to supercede Gen. Curtis in command of the Department of the West.

24. Skirmish on the Mississippi river, 6 miles above Austria. Gen. Ellet's marine brigade defeated a rebel force, who lost 5 killed, 3 prisoners. Union loss 2 killed, 19 wounded.

25. Skirmish near Hartford, Ky.

25. Skirmish at Senatobia, Miss. Col. McCrellis defeated a rebel force, who lost 6 killed and 3 wounded.

26. Col. Wilder's Fed. regiment defeated Breckinridge's cavalry near McMinnville, Tenn., and captured a number of prisoners.

25–27. Fed. gunboats under Lt. Walker, after capturing Haines' Bluff, ascended to Yazoo City, Miss., and destroyed 3 rebel steamers and a large ram, not finished. Also the navy yard and naval stores.

26. Destruction of the U. S. gunboat Cincinnati by rebel batteries at Vicksburg. 35 of her crew killed and w.

27. Gen. Banks' army defeated in an assault on the reb. works at Port Hudson.

27. Col. Cornyn's Fed. command defeated Gen. Roddy's troops at Florence, Ala., capturing 100 soldiers, 300 negroes, 400 mules, and destroying reb. property.

28. First colored regiment from the North left Boston.

28. The 8th Ill., Col. Clendenin, returned to the army of the Potomac from an expedition on the banks of the Rappahannock and Potomac rivers, below Fredericksburg, Va., having destroyed one million dollars of property, and brought into camp 810 negroes.

28. Wolford's Fed. cavalry defeated near Somerset, Ky.

28. Skirmish near Doniphan, Mo. 13th Ill. cavalry, Major Lippert, defeated with loss of 80 of their number in killed, wounded, and missing.

29. Skirmish by 1st Vt. cavalry with Stuart's cavalry, near Thoroughfare Gap, Va.

30. Rebel Col. Mosby, with 200 cavalry, after destroying a Government train at Catlett's Station, Va., was overtaken near Greenwich by Col. Maur, of the 7th Mich. cavalry with N. Y. and Vt. troops, and dispersed with the loss of their cannon. Fed. loss, 17 killed and wounded.

30. A train of 16 cars from Alexandria, Va., was destroyed by rebel guerrillas near Warrenton Junction.

30. A rebel camp near Carthage, Tenn., surprised by the 26th Ohio, who captured 22 prisoners and 35 horses.

30. The town of Tappahannock, Va., captured by Fed. gunboats, who destroyed rebel stores.

31. Guerrillas defeated with the loss of 10 men by militia in Lincoln Co., Mo.

31. Fed. gunboat Alert exploded and sunk at Norfolk, Va.

31. Cavalry expedition captured 16 rebels near Monticello, Ky.

31. Successful raid of Col. Kilpatrick's Fed. cavalry from Yorktown to Urbana, Va., bringing in 1000 negroes and 300 horses.

June 1. Blair's reconnoisance in search of Joe Johnston returns, having been unsuccessful.

1. Skirmishing in Howard Co., Mo.

2. 3,000 rebel prisoners arrive at Indianapolis, Ind.

2. Gen. Burnside prohibited the circulation in his Department of the *N. Y. World* and the *Chicago Times*.

2. West Point, Va., evacuated by the Union troops.

3. Indian (rebel) prisoners arrive in New York.

3. New York Supreme Court decide against legal tender notes.

3. Mass convention of Peace Democrats at New York.

3. Admiral Foote ordered to relieve Admiral Dupont at Charleston.

3. Skirmish near Manchester, Tenn.

3. Bombardment of Port Hudson continued.

4. Rebel guerrillas defeated near Fairfax, Va.

4. Bluffton, S.C., burned by Union troops.

4. Fight at Satartia, Miss. 100 rebels taken by Gen. Kimball.

4. Simmonsport, La., destroyed by Federal gunboats.

4. Simultaneous attacks on the Federal garrisons at Franklin and Triune, Tenn., which were repulsed in both instances with severe loss to the rebels.

4. Col. Wilder's mounted infantry broke up a rebel camp at Liberty, Tenn., capturing 62 men and their horses.

5. A division of Hooker's army cross the Rappahannock and captured 96 prisoners. Fed. loss 35 in k. and w.

5. Raid to Warwick river, Va. Rebel boats destroyed.

6. Fight at Milliken's Bend, Miss. Reb. Gen. McCullough, with 2,500 men, attacked 3 negro regiments and 23d Iowa. Heavy loss on both sides. Rebs. defeated.

8. District of the Frontier set off and given to Gen. Blunt.

8. 2 reb. spies shot at Franklin, Tenn.

8. Reconnoissance on the Chickahominy.

9 Explosion in Fort Lyon, near Alexandria, Va. 30 men killed.

9. Skirmish at Triune, Tenn. Rebels repulsed.

9. Severe cavalry fight at Beverly Ford, on the Rappahannock river, Va., in which Gen. Buford's Fed. troops defeated Gen. Stuart's command with heavy loss on both sides.

9. Gen. Carter's Fed. troops defeated Gen. Pegram's army at Monticello, Tenn.

10. An enrolling officer murdered at Manville, Ind.

10. Rebs. repulsed at Lake Providence by negro troops.

11. Preparations in Pa. to repel rebel invasion.

11. Rebel cavalry crossed the Potomac at Poolesville, Md., but were driven back.

11. Peace Democratic meeting in Brooklyn.

11. Vallandigham nominated for Governor of Ohio.

11. Lee's army began to move up the Rappahannock.

11. Rebels attack Triune, Tenn., and are repulsed.

11. Steamer Maple Leaf, while conveying rebel officers as prisoners from Fortress Monroe to Fort Delaware, was seized, and 64 effected their escape.

11-16. Gen. Lee's army crossed the Potomac, and invaded Md. and Pa.

13-20. Forced march of the army of the Potomac from the Rappahannock to Frederick, Md., in which many lives were lost from heat and exhaustion.

12. Union gunboats shell the shores of James river.

12. Darien, Ga., burned by Federalists.

12. Union cavalry captured near Port Hudson.

12. Skirmish near Middletown, Va. Rebels defeated.

12. Rebel privateer Clarence captured 6 vessels off the Chesapeake.

12. Attack on Morris Island by Fed. gunboats.

12. Rebels attack Fed. troops on Folly Island.

13. Rebels plunder a railroad train at Elizabethtown, Ky.

13. Skirmish on Slate creek, Ky. Union defeat.

13. Skirmish and rebel defeat near Boston, Ky.

14. Assault on Port Hudson by Gen. Banks' troops, in which they were repulsed with heavy loss.

14. Capture of Winchester, Va, by reb. troops. Defeat of Gen. Milroy's army, who lost 2,000 men, and all his artillery and stores.

14. English and Austrian consuls sent away from Richmond, Va.

14. Rebel raid upon Maysville, Ky.

15. President Lincoln calls for 100,000 men for six months from Pa., Md., W. Va., and Ohio, to resist invasion, which were promptly furnished.

15. Enrollment resisted in Boone Co., Ind.

15. The rebel troops who attacked Maysville were overtaken; their plunder and one hundred prisoners taken.

15. Rebel troops entered Chambersburg, Pa.

17. Severe cavalry skirmish near Aldie, London Co., Va., in which the rebels were defeated with loss, and eighty-five taken prisoners.

17. Capture of rebel iron-clad ram Fingal, or Atlanta, by monitors Weehawken and Patapsco, in Warsaw Sound, S. C., 180 prisoners taken.

17. Cavalry fight at Thoroughfare Gap, Va.

17. Skirmish on the Blackwater.

17. Rioters in Holmes Co., Ohio, resist the enrollment.

17. Skirmish near Big Black Bridge, Miss.

17. Fight with guerrillas near Westport, Mo.

18. 1700 of Milroy's men arrive safely at Bedford, Pa.

18. Skirmishing near Aldie.

June 18. Rebels burn canal boats at Hancock, Md.

18. Small skirmishes with Lee's invaders in Maryland.

18. Union defeat near Hernando, Miss.

19. Rebel cavalry cross the Ohio into Harrison Co., Ind.; 50 of them captured.

20. Gen. Schenck suppresses disloyal papers in Baltimore.

20. Vicksburg bombarded.

20. N. Y. packet ship Isaac Webb captured by rebel steamer Tacony, and released on bond.

21. Gen. Pleasanton's cavalry engaged rebel cavalry near Middleburg, Va. Feds. victorious, capturing 80, and killing or wounding 150 of the enemy.

21. Brilliant cavalry fight, and rebels whipped at Aldie Gap.

21 Skirmish near New Baltimore. Union repulse.

21. Skirmish at Low Creek, W. Va. Rebels beaten.

21. Rebs. defeated at Lafourche crossing, La.

22. Skirmish at Frederick, Md. Rebs, driven out.

22-23. Twelve fishing vessels destroyed off Martha's Vineyard, Mass., by rebel steamer Tacony.

23. Col. S. H. Saunders arrived at Boston, Ky., with his command, after a successful raid into E. Tenn., having destroyed the railroads and bridges in many places, and captured several cannon, 1,000 stand of arms, and 500 prisoners.

23. Skirmish near Gettysburg.

23. Gunboat Sumter sunk by accident off Cape Henry.

24. Rebels advance to Shippensburg and Hagerstown.

24 Union raid force returned from N. Miss., after much success.

24. Gen. Rosecrans' army in motion. Skirmishes at Guy's Gap and Liberty Pike.

24. Col. Hoover's mounted infantry defeated the rebels at Hoover's Gap, Tenn., routing them with heavy loss. Fed. loss, 45 killed and wounded.

24. Gen. Willich's Fed. brigade defeated rebels at Liberty Gap, Tenn. Fed. loss, 50. The fight renewed next day, and rebs. defeated with severe loss. Fed. loss, 40 killed, 100 wounded.

25. Rebels near Carlisle, Pa.

26. Rebels occupy Gettysburg.

26. Unionists evacuate Carlisle.

26. Skirmish at South Anna, Va. Gen. W. F. Lee (rebel) and 110 men, 300 horses, and 35 wagons captured by Col. Spear, 11th Pa. cavalry.

26. Death of Admiral Foote.

26. Rebels occupy York and threaten Harrisburg.

26. The inhabitants of York, Pa., were levied on by rebel Gen. Ewell for large sums of money, clothing, and provisions.

26. Gen. Meade superseded General Hooker in command of the army of the Potomac.

27. The Potomac army northwest of Baltimore.

27. Cavalry fight at Fairfax. Union defeat.

27. Rosecrans' army occupy Manchester, Tenn., after slight resistance. Also, Shelbyville.

28. Rebels capture a train near Rockville, Va., with 150 wagons and 900 mules. Also, sutler's stores at Annandale, Va.

28. Skirmish at Columbia bridge, on the Susquehannah, Pa. 200 of Col. Frick's Fed. troops captured.

28. Enrollment in Indiana enforced by military.

28. Rebels defeated at Donaldsville, La.

29. Rebels driven from Decherd, Tenn.

30. Mines exploded and rebel outworks breached at Vicksburg.

30. Cavalry fight at Hanover.

July 1. Rebels repulsed in attack on Carlisle, Pa.

1. First conflict at Gettysburg. Rebel advance checked. Gen. Reynolds k.

1. Bragg retreats before Rosecrans. Tullahoma occupied by Fed. advance.

1. Engagement at Hanover Junction, Pa., between Gen. Pleasanton's Fed. cavalry and Gen. Stuart's forces. Rebs. defeated.

2. Skirmish at Bottom's Bridge, Va.

2-3. Defeat of rebel Gen. Lee's army, near Gettysburg, Pa., by Gen. Meade's army, after a sanguinary conflict, in which 40,000 men were k. or w.

4. Surrender of Vicksburg, Miss., to Gen. Grant, with 30,000 men, under Gen. Pemberton, and a large supply of arms and ammunition. The rebel army was paroled.

4. Assault on Helena, Ark., by rebel Gens. Marmaduke, Price and Holmes, with 6,000 men, who were signally defeated by Gen. Prentiss's garrison, who took 1,000 prisoners, and killed or wounded 500 of the enemy.

3-10. Raid of Gen. Morgan into Ind., destroying a large amount of property.

5. Rear-guard of Gen. Johnston's army, numbering 4,000 men, captured by Gen. Grant's forces, near Bolton, Miss.
5. Vallandigham arrives at Halifax.
6. Raid from Newbern to Warsaw, N. C.
7. Great excitement in Louisville. Morgan said to be coming.
7. Two steamboats captured by rebels at Brandenburg, Ky.
7. Bragg retreats across the Tennessee, destroying the Bridgeport bridge.
8. Surrender of Port Hudson, Miss., with its garrison of 5,500 men, under Gen. Gardner, to Gen. Banks.
8. Cavalry skirmish near Boonesboro', Md.
10. Gilmore lands on Morris Island, taking all the rebel works except Forts Wagner and Gregg, which are shelled by the monitors.
10. Union forces occupy Jackson, Miss.
10. Rebels defeated at Big creek, Ark.
10. Cavalry fight on the old Antietam field.
10. Lee in fortifications opposite Williamsport.
10. Morgan burns depot at Salem, Ind.
11. Morgan burns railroad bridge at Vienna, Ind.
11. Repulse of Gen. Gilmore's forces assaulting Fort Wagner, S. C.
12. Col. Hatch's 2d Iowa cavalry defeated a body of rebel cavalry near Jackson, Miss. Fed. loss, 13 killed and wounded. Rebel loss, 175 killed and wounded, and 400 conscripts released.
12. Morgan gets into Ohio.
12. Martial law in Cincinnati, Newport and Covington
12. Fight at Jackson, Miss.
13–17. Great Draft Riot in New York. 25 or 30 buildings destroyed. The *Tribune* office assailed. Colored Orphan Asylum burned, several negroes killed, and 120 stores and dwellings were sacked by the mob. The city railroads were stopped, and all the principal factories and shops compelled to suspend work for several days. The disturbance was quelled by the military and police, after 25 of the military and officers were killed or seriously wounded, and 150 of the rioters.
12. Gen. Lauman's division of Gen. Sherman's army corps incautiously advanced to an exposed position in front of the rebel works at Jackson, Miss., and lost 300 men in killed and wounded.
13. Yazoo City taken by Fed. troops.
13. Union defeat at Bayou Lafourche, La. 210 taken prisoners.
13. Lee's army crosses the Potomac.
14. Fight at Falling Waters, Va. Gen. Kilpatrick's cavalry attacked a reb. force of infantry, artillery, and horse, defeating them, and capturing 1,300 prisoners, and killing and wounding 130. Fed. loss, 29 killed, 36 wounded.
15. Cav. skirmish near Charlestown, Va.
15. Draft riots in Troy and Boston.
15. A universal conscription of all the white men in the Confederate States between the ages of 18 and 45, subject to military duty, ordered by Jeff. Davis.
16. Rebels defeated near Fort Gibson, Ark.
16. Rebel dash upon Hickman, Ky.
17. Orders given to enforce the draft at all hazards.
17. Huntsville, Ala., taken by Union troops.
17. Rebels evacuate Jackson, Miss., which was occupied by Gen. Sherman's forces after severe fighting for 4 days with Johnston's army.
17. Defeat of rebel Gen. Cooper's army at Elk creek, Ark., by Gen. Blunt's forces. Rebel loss, 400 killed or wounded, 60 prisoners. Federal loss, 10 killed and 25 wounded.
18. Raid from Newbern into N. C.
18. 400 rebels captured at Rienzi, Miss.
18–19. Bombardment and assault on Fort Wagner, S. C., in which Gen. Gilmore's troops were repulsed, with the loss of 700 men, k., w. and missing.
19. Engagement at Wytheville, W. Va., by Fed. cavalry under Cols. Tolland and Powell, who destroyed the Va. and Tenn. railroad and defeated the rebel forces. Fed. loss, 65 killed and wounded. Rebel loss, 75 killed, and 150 prisoners.
19. Fighting with Morgan at Buffington Island. 300 of his men taken.
20. Basil Duke and a portion of Morgan's force taken near Pomeroy, O.
21. Joe Johnston retreats to Brandon, Miss.
21. Union raid to Tar river and Rocky Mount, N. C.
22. Skirmish near Nolan's Ferry on the Potomac.
22. Skirmish at Chester Gap, Va. by Gen. Spinola's Fed. brigade.
22. Brashear City, La., recaptured by Union gunboats.
23. Engagement at Manassas Gap, Va. 300 rebels killed or wounded, 60 pris.
24. Skirmish with Morgan's men at Washington, O.
25. The furloughs granted to the majority of rebel paroled prisoners at Vicksburg, rescinded by Gen. Pemberton, and the men ordered to report at headquarters within 15 or 20 days.

July 26. Rebs. defeated at Lexington, Tenn.

26. Capture of Gen. Morgan with the remainder of his cavalry (400) near New Lisbon, O., by Col. Shackleford.

27. Rebels drive Union forces out of Richmond, Ky.

28. Death of Senator W. L. Yancey, near Montgomery, Ala.

29. Capture of 29 wagons with sutlers' stores at Fairfax Court House, Va., by Mosby's guerrillas, which were recaptured by 2d Mass. cavalry on the next day.

29. Defeat of Gens. Pegram's and Scott's rebel forces while attacking Fed troops at Paris, Ky.

30. Death of Brig.-Gen. Strong, in New York, from wounds received in the attack on Fort Wagner, S. C., July 19.

30. Pres. Lincoln by proclamation, ordered the imprisonment at hard labor of rebel prisoners, in retaliation for violation of the laws of war toward colored soldiers.

31. Lee's and Meade's armies again on the Rappahannock.

31. Rebels take Stanford, Ky., but are quickly driven out.

Aug. 1. Severe engagement near Culpepper, Va., by Fed. cavalry, infantry, and artillery, under Gen. Buford, with a similar reb. force, in which the loss was heavy on both sides.

1. 60 wagons loaded with forage were burned by rebs. at Stamford, Ky.

1. Reb. Col. Ashby and 350 men were captured near the Cumberland river, Ky., by Col. Sanders.

2. The Enfans Perdus, of N. Y., capture 500 rebs. at Folly Island.

3. Skirmish near Kelly's Ford.

4. Steamer Ruth accidentally burned below Cairo.

4. Skirmish near Brandy Station.

4. Reconnoissance up the James river, Va., by monitor Sangamon, gunboat Com. Barney, and tug Cohasset. The vessels met with a severe fire from the enemy's troops lining the banks, but returned with slight loss of life; the Barney badly injured.

5. Union raid upon Woodville, Miss.

6. Gen. Sibley reported 3 battles, and defeat of hostile Indians in Minnesota.

6. A day appointed by Pres. Lincoln for National thanksgiving and praise, in gratitude for signal victories obtained by the Fed. armies.

10. Admiral Farragut arrived with his flagship at N. Y.

12. Robert Toombs publishes a letter of this date exposing the bankruptcy of the Confederacy.

14. Several Union signal officers captured near Warrenton, Va.

14. Gen. Gilmore tried the range of his heavy guns toward Fort Sumter.

15. Union cavalry returned to Corinth, Miss., with 250 prisoners just conscripted by Forrest.

16. Explosion of the "City of Madison," ammunition boat at Vicksburg; about 150 men killed.

16. Severe bombardment of Fort Sumter by the monitors and Fed. batteries on Morris Isl. Com. Rogers killed on board the Catskill.

17. Great destruction of railroad property and ordnance stores at Granada, Miss., by Federal troops under Col. Philips.

18. Union raid in North Carolina. 30 rebs. killed near Pasquotank.

19. Union raid upon Grenada, Miss. Great destruction of railroad property.

19. Recommencement of the draft in the city of N. Y., which had been suspended owing to the riot a month previous. 10,000 Fed. troops were stationed in the vicinity of the city, during the drawing, which was completed Aug. 28.

20. The town of Lawrence, Kansas, was sacked by rebs. under Quantrell. 130 citizens murdered, and a large portion of the town burned. Quantrell's band was pursued by Fed. troops, and over 100 of them killed.

21. Brig Bainbridge foundered. Only 1 man saved.

21. Chattanooga, Ala., besieged by Gen. Rosecrans' army.

22. A raid to Pocahontas, Ark. 100 rebs. captured, including Gen. Jeff. C. Thompson and staff.

22. Charleston, S. C., shelled by rebel batteries on Morris Isl.

23. Gen. Blunt crosses Ark. river. Rebs. fall back without fighting.

24. Cavalry skirmish below Fredericksburg, Va.

24. A squad of Union cavalry captur'd near Annandale.

24. Cavalry skirmish near Fairfax, Va.

25. U. S. gunboats Satellite and Reliance captured by rebs. at the mouth of the Rappahannock, Va.

25. Rebs. under Price and Marmaduke defeated at Bayou Metiare, Ark.

26. Union expedition to Bottom's Bridge, Va.; rebs. defeated and bridge destroyed.

27. John B. Floyd died at Abingdon, Va.

27. Belle Boyd, a reb. spy, arrested in Va.

27. An army train captured near Philippi, W. Va., by rebs.

28. Union camp captured at Edwards' Ferry, Va.

28. Fight near Warm Springs, Va. Reb. loss 200.

29. 5 deserters shot in the Army of the Potomac.

30. Rosecrans' army crossed the Tennessee near Chattanooga.

31. Swarms of guerrillas in Western Tenn., and on both sides of the Miss. riv'r, down to Baton Rouge.

31. Fort Smith, Ark., taken by Gen. Blunt.

Sept. 1. Union expedition in W. Va., under Gen. Averill, returns after general success.

1. Knoxville, Tenn., occupied by the advance of Gen. Burnside's army.

1. Rebel raid upon Brownsville, Tenn. The place plundered.

2. Skirmish at the Holston river bridge on the E. Tenn. and Ga. railroad. The bridge burnt by Gen. Burnside's troops.

2. Gunboats Satellite and Reliance, lately taken by the rebels, destroyed by a Union force.

3. Kingston, Tenn., taken by Burnside.

3. Gen. Sully's Fed. troops defeated Indians at Whitestone Hill, on the upper Missouri, many of whom were killed, and 156 taken prisoners. Fed. loss, 20 killed, and 38 wounded.

4. Enthusiastic reception of General Burnside and his army by the inhabitants of Knoxville, Tenn.

5. Skirmish near Moorfield, W. Va. No loss.

5. Women's bread riot in Mobile.

7. Gen. Burnside tendered his resignation, which was not accepted.

7. A magazine exploded in Fort Moultrie by Union shells.

7. Morris Island was evacuated by reb. forces, and Fort Wagner and Battery Gregg were seized by Gen. Gilmore, who took 75 prisoners, and 19 pieces of artillery.

7. An assault was made on Fort Sumter by 450 men in 20 boats from the Fed. fleet, under Commander T. H. Stevens. The sailors were defeated with the loss of 114 men.

8. The gunboats Clifton and Sachem attached to an expedition under General Franklin, grounded on the bar at Sabine Pass, Texas, and were captured by the enemy.

8. Skirmish at Bath, Va.

8. Rebels defeated near Arkadelphia, Ark.

9. Union defeat at Tilford, Tenn. 300 captured.

9. Surrender of Cumberland Gap, Tenn., to Gen. Burnside, with 2,000 prisoners, and a large supply of army stores.

9. Cavalry skirmish at Alpines, near Chattanooga, Tenn. 4 Feds. killed, and 12 wounded.

9. Chattanooga occupied by Gen. Crittenden's corps of Rosecrans' army.

10. Little Rock, Ark., captured by Fed. troops under Gen. Steele, and Gen. Davidson appointed military commander.

12. Gen. Negley's division was attacked and driven through one of the gaps of Pidgeon Mountain, Tenn., by the troops of Witters and Stuart, of Bragg's army. Fed. loss in killed and wounded, 40.

12. Union cavalry raid into Miss'ppi.

12. Sabine Pass expedition returns to N. O., having utterly failed.

13. Cavalry fight beyond Culpepper. 40 rebels and 2 guns taken. Gen. Pleasanton advanced to the Rapidan.

13. Rebel works at Grant's Pass, near Mobile, shelled.

14. Arkansas being rapidly cleared of rebels by Gen. Blunt.

15. The President suspended the writ of habeas corpus.

16. Skirmish along Rosecrans' lines. Little damage.

17. Cavalry fight at Raccoon Ford. Union repulse.

18. White's rebel cavalry routed at Warrenton, Va.

18. Fight at Reid's bridge on the Chickamauga creek, Tenn. Cols. Minty and Wilder's troops were driven back by rebel infantry.

19. Battle of Chickamauga commences.

20. Battle of Chickamauga rages furiously. Union army defeated.

20. Fight at Zollicoffer, Tenn.

21. At night Rosecrans' army withdrew from Chickamauga to Chattanooga. Bragg did not follow.

21. Madison C. H., Va., occupied by Gen. Meade's cavalry.

21. The rebels seized a steam-tug at South-west Pass, but it was rescued by Union troops.

22. Cavalry fight and Union victory at Madison C. H., Va.

22. Confederate cavalry crossed the Potomac near Rockville, but were driven back.

23. Meade's army reached the Rapidan.

23. 1,200 rebel prisoners who were captured at Cumberland Gap, arrived at Louisville.

Sept. 25. Mosby breaks the railroad near Fairfax.

25. Rebels driven out of Donaldsonville, La.

27. Steamer Robert Campbell burned by rebels at Milliken's Bend. 25 lives lost.

28. Rebels attack Burnside's right wing near Knoxville, but are repulsed.

29. Gen. Hooker arrives in Cincinnati

29. Two Union regiments defeated above Port Hudson, La.

30. Delegation from Missouri visit the President to ask a change of commander in the Western Department.

30. Rebel cavalry repulsed in trying to cross the Tennessee near Harrison's Landing.

Oct. 1. Frequent skirmishes with guerrillas south of the Potomac.

2. Battle at Anderson's Cross-roads, Ky. Rebel cavalry whipped.

2 Explosion of an ammunition train near Bridgeport, Tenn.

2. Gen. Gillmore moves his headquarters to Folly Island.

3. Fight at McMinnville, Tenn.

3. Greek fire thrown into Charleston.

3. Guerrillas active near Glasgow, Ky.

4. Four steamers burned at St. Louis by rebel incendiaries.

4. Expedition from Fortress Monroe to break up guerrilla bands.

4. Rebels attempt to destroy Shelbyville, Tenn.

5. Rebels destroy a large railroad bridge south of Murfreesboro'.

5. The rebels bombard Chattanooga from Lookout Mountain.

5. Cavalry fight near New Albany, Ala.

5. Rebels repulsed in an attack on Murfreesboro'.

6. Rebels whipped near Shelbyville, Tenn.

6. Skirmish at Como, Tenn.

6. Rebels attempt to destroy the New Ironsides with a torpedo. They fail; their men taken.

7. Federal cavalry ambuscaded near Harper's Ferry by Imboden.

7. Part of Gen. Blunt's escort whipped by the rebels near Fort Scott. All who surrendered were murdered.

7. Rebel steamers destroyed on Red river.

8. Coffee and Shelby, with rebel guerrillas, plundering in Central Missouri.

8. Fight near Farmingham, Ky. Rebs defeated.

8. Fight at Salem, Miss. Rebels driven off.

9. Rebels make great efforts to cut Rosecrans' communications, but fail.

9. The overland Texas expedition from New Orleans reaches Vermillionville.

10. Skirmish near Madison Court House, Va.

10. Fight at Blue Springs, near Knoxville.

10. Union raiding expedition, under Col. S. H. Mix, leave Newbern, N. C. Return in a few days entirely successful.

11. About this time much fighting along the Memphis and Charleston railroad. Rebels generally defeated.

12. Skirmishing along the lines on the Rappahannock. Gen. Meade withdraws all his army to the north bank.

12. Skirmish at Blackwater, Mo.

12. Fight at White Sulphur Springs, Va.

13. Skirmish at Arrow Rock, Mo.

13. Brisk fight from Catlett's Station to Manassas.

13. Rebels under Shelby, in Missouri, defeated by Gen. Brown

13. Skirmish on the Big Black below Vicksburg

14. Fight at Bristow Station. Rebels defeated. 450 taken prisoners.

15. Skirmishing on the Bull Run battle-field.

15. 300,000 volunteers were called for by the President, the men to receive all government bounties. A draft was ordered, at the same time, for the deficiency in any State quota on January 5, 1864.

16. Rebel raid upon Brownsville, Mo.

16. The Department of the Tennessee, the Cumberland, and the Ohio were formed into the Military Division of the Mississippi, and Maj.-Gen. U. S. Grant appointed the commander.

17. Active volunteering for the Union army in Arkansas.

18. Skirmishing near Stone Bridge and Manassas Junction.

18. Jim Keller, a noted guerrilla, taken near Sharpsburg, Ky., and shot.

19. Lee recrosses the Rappahannock, and marches southward.

19. Secret meetings in New Orleans to revive the rebel State government.

20. Gen. Rosecrans relieved. Gen. Grant takes command.

20. Gen. Blunt relieved of Army of the Frontier, Gen. McNeil taking his place.

20. Kilpatrick's cavalry on a raid toward Warrenton.
21. Fight near Philadelphia, East Tennessee.
21. Fight at Cherokee Station, near Corinth, Miss. Rebels defeated.
22. Skirmishes at Columbia and Kingston Spring, Tenn.
22. Gen. Averill's Union cavalry near Covington, Va.
23. Rebel raid upon Danville, Tenn.
23. Fighting at Beverly Ford, on the Rappahannock.
23. Unionists land at Bay St. Louis, Miss., and recapture some prisoners.
24. Guerrillas driven out of S. Mo.
25. Whole of 1st Ala. cavalry said to have been captured near Tolanda, Miss., about this date.
26. Grant starts his movement upon Lookout Mountain. A flanking force crosses the river.
27. Hooker defeats the rebels at Brown's Ferry.
27. Arkadelphia, Ark., occupied by Union forces about this date.
28. Flanking and capture of Lookout Mountain. It is soon after abandoned, and reoccupied by the rebels.
29. Union prisoners from Richmond, in a state of starvation, arrive at Annapolis. Some die on the trip from Fortress Monroe.
29. 60 rebels taken near Columbia, Tenn.
30. Charleston, Mo., robbed by guerrillas.
30. Guerrillas routed near Piney Factory, Tenn.
30. Burnside's forces cross the river at Knoxville, and occupy Loudon Heights.
30. Heavy bombardment of Charleston, S. C.
31. Banks' expedition lands at Brazos Island.
31. Plot in Ohio to overthrow the government comes to light.
31. Rebel cavalry repulsed at Warrenton.
31. Gen. Hooker wins an important victory at Shell Mound, Tenn.
31. Fight at Leiper's Ferry, Tenn.
Nov. 1. Much anxiety in Richmond about food.
1. Union raid in N. Ala. They reach Florence.
1. Skirmish near Washington, N. C.
1. Collision on Opelousas railroad. 16 soldiers killed and 65 wounded.
2. Rebels routed at Roan Springs, Tenn.
2. Rebels capture 2 trains and destroy railroad, near Mayfield, Ky.
2. Unsuccessful attempt upon Sumter by a boat expedition.
3. Rebel cavalry defeated near Columbia, Tenn.
3. Rebels defeated at Colliersville, Tenn. Their Brig.-Gen. Geary captured.
3. Gen. Washburne's advance attacked.
4. Banks' expedition take peaceable possession of Brownsville, on the Rio Grande.
4. E. Tenn. said to be clear of rebs.
5. Rebels continue to shell Chattanooga.
5. Skirmish at Motley's Ford, E. Tenn.
5. Union camp at Rogersville, E. Tenn., surprised, and 4 guns and nearly 800 men taken.
6. Guerrillas plunder Blandville, Ky.
6. Much excitement about the starvation of Union prisoners at Richmond.
7. Meade's army begins an advance. Sharp fighting at Kelly's Ford and Rappahannock Station. The rebels driven across the river.
7. Rebels break up the Memphis and Charleston railroad near Salisbury.
7. Rebels defeated at Lewisburg, W. Va.
8. Meade advances, the rebels retiring toward Gordonsville.
8. Successful reconnoissance returns from Chowan river, N. C.
8. Banks' expedition in possession of Brazos, Bienville, and Point Isabel.
9. Skirmish near Culpepper. Meade's army in line of battle all day. Lee declines a fight.
9. Rebel dash upon Bayou Sara, La.
9. Fight on the Little Tenn. A rebel regiment repulsed with 50 killed and 40 prisoners.
10. Skirmishing near Culpepper.
10. Rebels concentrate along the south bank of the Rapidan.
10. Supposed conspiracy in Canada to set free rebel prisoners on Johnson's Island.
11. Charleston and Fort Sumter regularly shelled day by day.
12. Union meeting held in Arkansas. Rebellion dying out.
13. Rebel foray across the Potomac at Edward's Ferry.
14. Longstreet crosses the Tenn., and attacks Burnside, who retires toward his works at Knoxville.
14. Banks captures CorpusChristi Pass.
15. Reconnoissance and skirmish on the Rapidan.

Nov. 15. Skirmish near Holston, Tenn. Burnside falls back to Lenoir.

16. Gen. Sherman's corps forms a junction with Thomas at Chattanooga.

16. Figh ing near Mount Jackson, Va.

16. Burnside falls back to Bell's Sta'n.

17. Seabrook Island occupied by Gillmore.

17. Charleston again shelled.

17. Burnside reaches Knoxville.

18. Skirmish at Germania Ford, Va.

18. Capture of Mustang Island by Gen. Banks.

19. Gettysburg Cemetery dedicated.

19. Fighting at Knoxville.

20. Mosby's guerrillas, in Union uniform, attempt to capture Fed. for es at Bealton, Va. The trick discovered in time.

21. Skirmishing along Burnside's and Longstreet's lines.

22. A portion of Knoxville burned. The city closely invested by Longstreet.

22. Successful scouting by negro troops at Pocotaligo, S. C. A grandson of John C. Calhoun killed.

23. Reconnoissance in force by Gen. Thomas. Rebels driven back.

23. Guerrillas whipped in Loudon Co., Va.

24. Storming and capture of Lookout Mountain. Hooker's "fight above the clouds." Defeat of Bragg.

24 Skirmishing near Knoxville.

25. Capture of Missionary Ridge. Bragg's army routed and driven back toward Ringgold.

25. Colored troops doing good service in N. C.

25. Rebel cavalry repulsed at Kingston, Te n.

26. Bragg's army pursued by Fed. victorious troops.

26. Meade's army crosses the Rapidan with no serious opposition.

27. Brisk skirmishing between Meade and Lee. Heavy fighting on the left.

27. Wheeler's rebel cavalry whipped at Cleveland, Tenn.

27. Mosby captures part of one of Meade's trains.

28. John Morgan and 6 of his officers escape from the Ohio penitentiary.

28. A rebel battery discovered, built behind the Moultrie House while they kept a hospital flag flying from the roof.

29. Siege of Charleston progresses regularly.

29. Longstreet attacks Knoxville, and is beaten after a heavy battle.

Dec. 1. Hooker retires from Ringgold, and Army of the Cumberland again concentrates at Chattanooga.

1. Meade recrosses the Rapidan.

2. Bragg superseded by Hardee in command of the rebel army in Georgia.

3. Union cavalry make a foray toward Canton, Miss.

3. Sherman's cavalry near Knoxville.

4. Longstreet raises the siege of Knoxville, Tenn., and retreats toward Va

6. Chesapeake, steamer, seized by reb. pirates on board, engineer shot, and crew landed at St. Johns.

6. The monitor Weehawken founders at Charleston harbor, with all on board.

7. Jefferson Davis issues his annual message.

7. U. S. Congress reassembles.

8. Pres. Lincoln issues his Message and Proclamation of Amnesty.

11. Fort Sumter vigorously bombarded and partly set on fire.

14. Bean Station, Va. Longstreet attacks Union cavalry under Shackelford. Rebels lose 800 killed and wounded. Union loss, 200.

15-20. Extensive destruction of saltworks by vessels from the Eastern Gulf Squadron in West Bay, St. Andrews Sound, Fla. Property of the value of $3,000,000 destroyed.

16. Maj.-Gen. John Buford died at Washington.

16. Averill destroys 15 miles of Va. and Tenn. railroad.

17. Rebel cavalry attack Meade's communications at Sangster's, and are repulsed.

17. Com. G. J. Van Brunt died at Dedham, Mass., aged 64.

17. The Chesapeake recaptured in Sambro Harbor by the Ella and Annie. All of the crew but 3 escape.

18. Col Phillips, with Indian brigade beats and scatters Quantrell's force near Fort Gibson, killing 50.

19. Fort Gibson, Ark., attacked by Standthwaite with 1,600 men. Standthwaite repulsed.

22. Gen. Corcoran killed by a fall from his horse.

22. An expedition from Beaufort starts inland under Gen. Seymour.

22. An expedition of 1 white and 3 colored regiments, starts for Red river from Port Hudson, under Gen. Ullman.

23. Longstreet's soldiers are deserting 20 to 50 per day.

23. Union raid on Luray. Large quantities of leather, bacon, &c., captured.

23. Ferryboat at Memphis attacked by

guerrillas who killed the captain. The boat escaped.

24. Choctaw Indians and their Chief abandon the rebel cause.

24. Reeves, with 150 guerrillas, surprises Centreville, Mo., and captures garrison of 50 men, 3d M. S. M.

24. Legareville, S. C., attacked by rebs., who are driven off.

25. Fight between the gunboat Marblehead, and rebel batteries on Stone river, S. C. Rebels defeated. Fed. loss, 3 killed, 4 wounded.

25. At Pulaski, Tenn., 50 of Forrest's guerrillas captured by Gen. Dodge.

25. Gen. Sullivan's expedition from Harper's Ferry returns with 100 prisoners and 100 horses.

25. Gen. Banks establishes Department of the Frontier on the Rio Grande.

25. British bark Circassian seized in North river by U. S. Marshal.

25. Dr. Sagar, Mr. Perez, and Mr Carter sent to Fort Lafayette for smuggling arms to rebels.

26. The Dictator, turreted iron-clad, launched at New York.

28. At Charleston, Tenn., rebel Gen. Wheeler, with 1,500 men attacks Colonel Liebert and supply train; captures the latter. Col. Long reinforces Liebert and rebels are beaten, losing 121 prisoners.

29. Part of Union train captured by rebels at Williamsport, Va.

30. Great naval expedition leaves N. O., supposed for Mobile.

31. McChesney's expedition meets rebels near Washington, N. C., routs them, kills a lieut. and 5 men, captures 1 cannon and 10 men.

1864 —Jan. 1.

ARMY CORPS COMMANDERS—GENERALS.

1st.	John Newton.	13th.	E. O. C. Ord.
2d.	W. S. Hancock.	14th.	John M. Palmer.
3d.	W. H. French.	15th.	John A. Logan.
4th.	Gordon Granger.	16th.	S. A. Hurlbut.
5th.	George Sykes.	17th.	J. B. McPherson
6th	John Sedgwick.	18th.	B. F. Butler.
7th.	Consolidated with others.	19th.	W. B. Franklin.
		20th. } 21st. }	Consolidated to form the 4th.
8th.	H. H. Lockwood.	22d.	S. P. Heintzelman.
9th	A. E. Burnside.	23d.	G. L. Hartsuff.
10th	Q. A. Gillmore.		Cavalry Corps—George Stoneman.
11th.	O. O. Howard.		
12th.	H. W. Slocum.		

DEPARTMENT COMMANDERS.

Dep't of the Tennessee — Maj.-Gen. W. T. Sherman

" the Cumberland — Maj.-Gen. Geo. H. Thomas.

" the Ohio — Maj.-Gen. J. G. Foster.

" the East — Maj.-Gen. John A. Dix.

" the Gulf — Maj.-Gen. N. P. Banks.

" N. C. and Va. — Maj. Gen. B. F. Butler.

" the Northwest — Maj.-Gen. John Pope.

" Washington — Maj.-Gen. S. P. Heintzelman.

" the Monongahela — Maj.-Gen. W. T. H. Brooks.

" the Susquehanna — Maj.-Gen. D. N. Couch.

" Western Virginia — Brig.-Gen. B. F. Kelly.

" New Mexico — Brig.-Gen. J. H. Carleton.

Dept. of the Pacific—Brig. Gen. George Wright.

" Kansas—Maj. Gen. James G. Blunt

" Middle Department—Brig. Gen. Lockwood.

" the South—Maj.-Gen. Q. A. Gillmore

" Missouri—Maj. Gen. John M. Schofield.

1. Gov. Bramlette of Ky., ordered the arrest of 5 rebel sympathizers for every loyal man captured by rebel guerrillas.

1. Arrest of a contractor of the Confederate government in New York who was engaged in manufacturing notes and bonds. The plates and engraving tools seized, and $7,000,000 in notes and bonds.

1. Departure of a Fed. cavalry reconnoissance to Front Royal, Va.

1. Fed. pickets driven in at Winchester, Va.

2. Gen. Curtis took command of Kansas Military Department.

2. A Fed. train attacked near Moorfield, Va. Rebels defeated, losing 13 killed, and 20 wounded.

3. Fight at Jonesville, Va. 60 Fed. troops killed or wounded, and 300 captured.

3. Death of Archbishop Hughes, in New York.

4. Gen. Grierson pursuing Forrest's rebel troops south of Coldwater, Miss.

4. Trial of the crew of the Chesapeake for piracy.

5. Gen. Stoneman made Chief of cavalry under Gen. Grant.

6. Marmaduke and Price at Arkadelphia, Ark., with 7,000 men.

6. Skirmish at Newtown, W. Va.

6. Gen. Kirby Smith takes command of rebels west of Mississippi river.

7. Death of Caleb B. Smith, U. S. Secretary of the Interior.

7. Gen. Grant made Maj.-Gen. in the regular army.

7. Gen. Thomas made Brigadier in the regular army.

8. Gens. Meade and Sherman made Brigadiers in the regular army.

8. Petersburg, Va., attacked by rebels under Fitz Hugh Lee, who were driven off.

8. Chase and destruction of the Anglo-rebel steamer Dare.

8. Death of Com. Stover, U. S. navy.

9. Madisonville and St. Francisburg, La., occupied by Fed. troops.

9. Gen. Wild's colored troops made a raid into N. C., releasing 3,000 slaves, and capturing or destroying an immense quantity of stores.

10. Gen. Rousseau left Decatur, Ala., for a raid in the rear of Gen. Hood's reb. army.

10. A severe fight at Strawberry

Plains, E. Tenn. Rebels repulsed with severe loss.

Jan. 10. A battalion of Cole's Md. cavalry attacked by rebels under Mosby, in Loudon Co., Va. Rebels defeated.

11. Madisonville, La., captured by Fed. troops.

11. Longstreet's rebel army fortifying Bull Gap, Tenn.

11. Capture of rebel salt-works at Tampa Bay Fla

11. Battle at Smithfield, Va. Federal troops defeated.

11. Gunboat Iron Age aground and under reb. fire in Wilmington Harbor.

12. Raid by Fed. troops under Gen. Marston in Westmoreland Co., Va. Much property destroyed.

12 Rebel cavalry defeated at Mossy Creek, Tenn. by Gen. McCook's troops, who killed 14 and took 49 prisoners.

13. Gen. Herron's troops crossed the Rio Grande into Mexico, and escorted the American Consul to Brownsville with $2,000,000, belonging to Americans and the Government.

14. Fed. pickets at Three Mile Station, Va., attacked by rebel cavalry, who were repulsed.

14 A Fed. train of 23 wagons captured near Tenisville, Tenn., by rebels under Gen Vance, who are pursued by Col. Palmer, who retook the wagons, and captured the rebel general, and a portion of his force.

14. Rebel steamer Mayflower captured in Sarasote Pass, Fla.

14. Skirmish at Bainbridge, Tenn.

14. The American ship Emma Jane captured by the Alabama, off Trivandrum, while on her way from Bombay to Moulmein.

17. Fight near Dandridge, Tenn. National troops defeated, losing 150 killed or wounded.

17. Longstreet's force moving towards Knoxville, Tenn.

17. Rebels attack Union lines at Bainbridge, Tenn., but are defeated with heavy loss.

18. Gen. Butler pronounced an outlaw by rebel Congress.

19. Gen Sturgis' Fed. troops retreated from Strawberry Plains to Knoxville.

19. Mosby defeated at Thoroughfare Gap, Va., by 1st Mass. cavalry.

20. Guerrillas attacked Col. Sweitzer's brigade of 5th Corps, and were repulsed, leaving 8 dead on the field.

21 Extensive conflagration of hospital buildings at Camp Winder, near Richmond, Va.

21. A large number of rebel deserters arrive at Chattanooga.

23. Brandon, Va., on the James river, destroyed by Fed. troops, who captured 100 negroes, and much rebel property.

23. Union raid to Lake Phelps, N. C 200,000 lbs. of pork destroyed.

23. Rebel Gen. Roddy driven south of Tenn. river, by Col. Phillips, with loss of his train, 200 cattle, 600 sheep and 100 horses and mules.

25. Athens, Ala., attacked by 600 rebs. under Col. Harrison, who were defeated.

26. Successful Fed. raid in Onslow and Jones Co., N. C., by Col. Palmer's troops.

27. Rebel cavalry under Armstrong and Morgan defeated near Sevierville, Tenn., by Gen. Sturgis.

27. Rebels defeated in an attack on Florence, Ala.

28. A meeting at Nashville, Tenn., to restore the State Government.

28. Destruction of rebel salt works at St. Andrews Bay.

28. Rebels defeated at Tunnel Hill, Ga. 32 killed and 1 company captured.

29. Skirmish 13 miles from Cumberland Gap, Tenn. Fed. cavalry with reb. troops under Gen. Jones.

29. Bridges and other property destroyed by Union troops at Windsor, N. C.

29 Major Johnson's Ky troops drove rebels out of Scottville, Ky., killing 40 and taking 20 prisoners.

30. A Fed. supply train of 80 wagons, guarded by Col. Snyder's troops, captured near Petersburg, W Va., after a 4 hours' fight. Fed loss, 80 killed or wounded. The Fed. garrison evacuated the place that night.

30. Skirmish near Cumberland Gap, Tenn. Rebels defeated by Col Love.

30. Fight at Smithfield, Va.

Feb. 1. Union repulse at Bachelor's Creek, near Newbern, N. C. Steamer Underwriter destroyed.

1. President Lincoln calls for 500,000 men for 3 years. Draft for deficiency to be made March 10.

1. Burlington, W. Va., occupied by rebels.

1. Fighting in the New Creek (Va.) valley.

1. Fed. outposts at Bachelor's Creek driven in by a rebel force threatening Newbern, N. C.

1. Fighting at Smithfield, Va.

2. Fight at Mechanicsburg Gap, near Romney, W. Va. Rebels retreat.

2. Rebel troops burn a bridge at Pat-

terson's Creek, Va., and were next day driven off by the guard.

2. Union reinforcements arrive at Newbern, N. C., and rebels are driven back to Kinston.

2. U. S. steamer Levi burned in Kanawha river, W. Va., and Gen. Scammon and staff captured by rebels.

3. Sherman's advance defeated rebels in a skirmish at Bolton, Miss. Union loss, 12 killed, 35 wounded. Rebel loss larger.

3. Gen. Smith's cavalry expedition starts from Corinth, Miss.

4. Col. Milligan drove rebels from Morefield, W. Va., after 6 hours' fighting.

4. A party of rebels captured near White Oak river.

4. Gen. Sherman's troops skirmish near Champion Hill, Miss.

4. Cavalry skirmish at Canton, Miss.

4. Gen. Averill defeats rebels at Woodfield, W. Va.

4. Rebel battery defeated at Clinton, Miss. Union killed 15, wounded 30.

4. Gen. Seymour's expedition left Port Royal, S. C., for Jacksonville, Fla.

5. Engagement between Gen. Sherman's troops and rebels, at Bear Creek, near Clinton, Miss.

5. Navajo Indians defeated near Fort Sumner, with loss of 50 killed and 25 wounded.

6. Col. Kit Carson brings 280 Indian prisoners to Santa Fe.

6. Skirmish at Bottom's Bridge, W. Va., by Gen. Butler's troops.

7. Rebels driven across the Rapidan by the army of the Potomac.

7. A Federal expedition returned to Knoxville, Tenn., having defeated a reb. force, killing and wounding 215, and taking 50 prisoners.

8. Rebel regiments at Dalton, and at Decatur, Ala., mutiny when required to re-enlist. Several soldiers are killed.

8. Gen. Seymour's expedition arrived at Jacksonville, Fla.

9. Rebels abandon Jacksonville, Fla., losing 100 men prisoners, and 8 guns.

9. Union gunboats arrive at Sartartia, on the Yazoo river.

10. Col. Streight, and 110 other officers, escaped from Libby prison by tunnelling.

11. Guerrillas rob a train on Balt. and O. railroad, near Harper's Ferry.

11. Gens. Grierson and Smith's Fed. troops start on a raid through Miss.

11. Gen. W. L. Smith's cavalry expedition started in the direction of Colliersville, Tenn.

11. First 20-inch gun cast at Pittsb'g, Pa.

12. Fed. pickets at Manassas attacked by Mosby.

12. Smith's Fed. expedition reaches Okolona, Miss.

12. Passage of the Enrollment bill by the House of Representatives.

13. The line of the Memphis and Ohio railroad evacuated by the Fed. forces.

14. Negro garrison of 400 at Waterproof, La., was attacked by a large rebel force, which was repulsed 3 times, and retired.

14. Rebel Col. Ferguson surprised in Wayne Co., W. Va., losing 60 prisoners, with arms and supplies, and releasing 500 Union captives.

14. Meridian evacuated by the rebels.

14. Guerrilla attack at Tecumseh Landing, Miss.

14. A company of colored troops, save 2, surprised and murdered at Grand Lake, Miss.

14. Gainesville, Fla., attacked by 40th Mass., Capt. Roberts. Rebels routed with loss of 100.

14. Meridian, Miss., occupied by Gen. Sherman's Union forces, who destroyed the State arsenal, and great quantities of ammunition.

15. Chesapeake steamer surrendered to her owners by colonial authorities at St. John's.

16. Rebel Gen. Pickett captured at Newbern, N. C.

14-20. Sherman sends various expeditions from Meridian, Miss., who destroy adjacent towns, and immense quantities of stores.

18. Sherman's army reaches Quitman, Ga., without opposition.

18. Gen. Seymour left Jacksonville, Fla., with 5,000 troops, and established a depot of supplies at Baldwin.

18. Gen. Smith's Union expedition reached Okolona, 75 miles south of Corinth, Miss.

18. Sloop-of-war Housatonic sunk at Port Royal by a rebel torpedo.

20. Longstreet retreats from Bull's Gap to Strawberry Plains.

20. Rebels hang Rev. Dr. Cox, chaplain of Corps de Afrique, near Donaldsonville.

20. Skirmish with Mosby's rebel cavalry, at Piedmont Station, Va. 17 of his men taken.

20. Gen. Smith defeated by Forrest at West Point, Ga., and driven back towards Memphis.

20. Battle of Olustee, Fla. Gen. Seymour's troops encountered a superior

force of rebels 55 miles beyond Jacksonville, Fla. After a severe contest of 3 hours, the Union troops were defeated, and retreated to Sanderson. Union loss, 1,500. Rebel loss about the same.

Feb. 21. A force of Fed. troops left Hilton Head, and proceeded up the Savannah river, without result.

21. Heavy fighting at Pontotoc, Miss.

21. Ringgold, Ga., occupied by Gen. Palmer.

22. Mosby defeats 150 Fed. cavalry near Drainsville, Va., who lose 8 killed, 7 wounded, and 75 missing.

22. 28 of Mosby's men captured near Warrenton by Major Cole.

22. A "Border State Convention," convened at Louisville, Ky., for the purpose of adopting harmonious action on important issues then pending in National affairs. Representatives from six States were present.

22. Rebel train destroyed near Poplar Bluffs, Mo.

22. Louisiana State election. Michael Hahn elected Governor, by 6,830 votes, against Fellows, 2,720, and B. F. Flanders, 1,847.

23. Rebel Gen. Forrest repulsed in an attack on Smith, near Memphis, Tenn.

23. Bombardment of Fort Powell, Mobile Bay, by Fed. mortars.

23. Skirmish near Tunnel Hill, Ga.

24. Passage of a bill by Congress authorizing the appointment of a Lieut.-Gen.

25. Skirmish at Bean Station.

25. Rebel raid on Maysville, Ky.

26. Grierson and Smith's forces return to Memphis. Results of expedition are 200 rebel prisoners, 1,500 negroes, 300 horses taken; 3,000,000 bushels corn, 4,000 bales cotton, 2,000 hides, and 40 miles of Mobile and O. railroad destroyed.

26. Tunnel Hill occupied by column from Chattanooga, after heavy skirmishing.

26. Fire opened upon Fort Powell by Admiral Farragut.

27. Col. Jourdan makes another dash into Jones and Onslow Cos., N. C., captures 3 prisoners, and destroys stores and ammunition.

27. Fed. troops withdrew from Tunnel Hill, Ga., to Ringgold.

27. Sherman's expedition returns to Vicksburg, after 22 days' raid, devastating many towns, burning bridges, seizing or destroying vast quantities of stores, liberating 10,000 negroes, breaking up many miles of railways, and taking 600 prisoners. Union loss, 170 k. and w.

27. Gov. Goodman, of Arizona, with exploring party, fights with Indians, killing 5, and wounding many.

28. Colonel Richardson, a notorious guerrilla, captured near Cumberland river.

28. Seymour's retreating army reaches Baldwin, Fla., which it evacuates, burning stores.

28. Gen. Kilpatrick, with 5,000 picked men, leaves Culpepper for a raid on Richmond, crosses the Rapidan at Ely's Ford, surprising rebel pickets at Spottsylvania Court House, and capturing 15 men and 2 officers.

29. Kilpatrick's exped. passed through Louisa C. H., to Pamunkey Bridge, destroying as he went. A force is sent by Butler to reinforce him.

29. Expedition of Custar's cav. crosses Rapidan and Rivanna, destroys an artillery camp, burns caissons, &c., and recrosses Rivanna bridge, burning it. Reb. cavalry charged and scattered at Burton's Ford and Stannardsville roads, and Custar safely returns with 60 prisoners, horses, &c.

29. Rebels in force attack Newbern, N. C., and were repulsed. Garrison ultimately relieved by reinforcements.

March 1. A lieut. and 15 men of the 5th Pa. cavalry captured while reconnoitering in the Dismal Swamp, Va.

1. A force under Gen. Kilpatrick and Col. Onderdonk, left Yorktown, Va., on an expedition to King and Queens C. H. Near Carlton's store the troops encountered 2 regiments of Virginia cavalry and a body of citizens. The enemy was routed and driven from the town. After penetrating to the inner fortifications of Richmond, Kilpatrick's troops were repulsed.

1. Reb. Government salt works at St. Marks, Fla., destroyed by expeditions from gunboat Tahoma.

1. Gen. Thomas, reinforced, marching against Dalton, from Tunnel Hill.

2. Reinforcements reaching Gen. Seymour at Jacksonville.

3. Kilpatrick's expedition moves to Williamsburg to rest. Many prisoners and stores captured and destroyed during this raid.

4. Kilpatrick returns within Union lines, having destroyed large portions of the Va. Central R. R., and burned several mills on James river. Loss 150, including Col. Dahlgren

4. Gen. Custer, with 500 men, made a reconnoissance to Ely's Ford, on the Rapidan.

5. Reb. cavalry still scouring country E. of Knoxville.

5. Reb. cavalry, in force, attack 93 of 3d Tenn. at Panther Springs. Union loss 2 k. 8 wounded, 22 prisoners. Rebel, 50 k. and wounded.

5. Battle in Yazoo City, between 11th Ill. and 8th La., and 4 reb. brigades. Rebs. defeated with considerable loss. Union, killed 6; wounded 20.

6. Gunboat Peterhoff sunk off Wilmington, N. C.

6. 23 Union soldiers, captured from Gen. Foster's command, hung by rebs. at Kinston, N. C.

6. Sherman's main army at Jackson, commencing to cross Pearl river.

7. Sherman's cavalry enter Brandon, after skirmishing, and camp two miles east.

8. Reb. cavalry driven from camp near Carrollton. Grain mills and stores burned.

9. Sherman at Hillsboro', N. C.

9. 40 of 5th Pa. cavalry captured by guerrillas at Bristow Station, Va.

9. An outpost of national troops near Suffolk, Va., was attacked by 4 regiments of infantry, a squadron of cavalry, and 2 batteries of artillery, and driven to Bower's Hill. A column of national troops arrived to the support, and the enemy in turn was attacked, driven back and pursued. Fed loss 200.

10. Suffolk, Va., captured. Reb. loss 25 killed. Union, 10 k.

10. A body of 10,000 troops under Gens. A. J. Smith and Thomas Kilby Smith, left Vicksburg on transports, destined for the mouth of Red river, at which point a force under Gen. Banks was being rendezvoused, in view of a campaign in the Red river region.

10. A naval expedition from Brashear City captures camp, arms, flag at Atchafalaya river.

10. Palatka occupied by Union forces.

12. Gen. Grant appointed Commander-in-Chief of the armies of the U. S.

13. Indianola evacuated by Union troops.

13. Gen. Smith's army at Simmesport.

13. Alexandria, La., captured by Fed. fleet.

14. Capture of Fort de Russy, on the Red river, by 1st and 3d divisions of 16th corps, under Gen. Mower. The fort was blown up at night.

15. President calls for 200,000 men, and a draft ordered for the deficiency on the 15th of April.

15. Reb plot to assassinate Pres. Lincoln discovered.

15. Sherman repulses rebs. near Chunky Creek.

16. Gov. Bramlette of Ky., remonstrates against employment of slaves as soldiers.

16. Battle near Fort Pillow. Rebs. defeated, loss of 50 k. and w.

16. Arkansas votes herself a free State.

16. Gens. Smith and Banks at Alexandria. Rebs retreat to Shreveport and burn 2 steamers with 3,000 bales of cotton.

16. Rebs. attack a train from Nashville near Estelle Springs, Tenn.

17. Reb. raid on Magnolia, Fla.

19. Reb. attack on Port Royal, S. C., fails.

21. Gen. Mower captures reb. camp at Henderson's Hill, 282 prisoners, guns, &c.

21. Banks captures 306 rebs. near Alexandria.

21. Engagement at Natchitoches, La., between Gen. Mower's troops of A. J. Smith's command, and reb. cavalry under Gen. Lee. 200 rebs. captured, with but small loss in killed or wounded on either side.

22. The gunboat Petrel captured by rebs. on the Yazoo river.

22. Gen. Thayer, with an army of 5,500 men left Fort Smith, Ark., to aid Gen. Steele's army.

23. Union City, Ky., captured by reb. Gen. Forrest. Col. Hawkins, with the 7th Tenn. cavalry, 400 men, surrendered after repulsing 2,000 rebs. 3 times.

25. Reb. Gen. Forrest, with 7,000 men, attacked the Fed. fort at Paducah, Ky., defended by Col. Hicks, with 500 men. Aided by 2 gunboats, Col. Hicks defeated Forrest, who retired with a loss of 1,000 killed and wounded. Fed. loss 14 killed and 46 wounded. The town was nearly destroyed by the bombardment.

26. Col. Clayton captured 370 rebs., 35 wagons, and 300 horses, at Longview, Ark.

29. Battle of Cane river, La. Rebs. defeated.

30. Fight in Arkansas with 1,200 rebs., who are defeated.

30 Riots by disloyalists at Charleston and Mattoon, Ill.

31. Rebs. defeated at Crump's Hill (Piney Woods).

April 1. Fight near Snyder's Bluff, on the Yazoo.

1. S. S. Maple Leaf blown up by torpedo in St. John's river.

1. Rebel ram Tennessee sunk near Grant's Pass.

2. Shelby defeated by Steele near Camden, in Ark.

April 2. Grierson's cavalry engages Forrest near Summerville, and falls back.

4. Fight at Roseville, in Ark.

4. Col. Gooding engages Harrison's guerrillas at Compti, and withdraws with loss.

4. Marmaduke defeated by Steele on Little Missouri river, Ark.

4. N. Y. Metropolitan Sanitary Fair opened.

5. Fight between gunboats and guerrillas at Hickman, Ky.

5. Banks' Texas expedition at Grand Ecore.

5. Gen. W. P. White, reb., of Georgetown, S. C., assassinated by his own men.

6. Fort Halleck, Columbus, Ky., attacked by rebel Gen. Buford. Surrender refused by Col. Lawrence.

6. Maryland Constitutional Convention on Slavery met.

7. U. S. Senate pass the resolution to submit to States' Legislatures the Constitution amendment abolishing slavery.

8. Gen. Franklin's command of Banks' expedition defeated at Mansfield, La., by Gen. Taylor's army, losing 24 guns and nearly 2,000 men, and falling back to Grand Ecore. Gen. Smith, next day, relieved Franklin, defeated the rebels, and captured 36 guns and 2,000 prisoners.

8. Shelbyville entered by 40 guerrillas.

9. Battle of Pleasant Hill, La. After severe fighting the Union troops retreated at night in good order.

10. Cape Lookout lighthouse seized by 40 rebels.

11. Banks retires to Grand Ecore.

11. Rebels repulsed in an attack on Roseville, Ark.

12. Capture of Fort Pillow and massacre of garrison.

12. Admiral Porter's Red river fleet attacked by 2,000 rebel infantry on shore, who are beaten off.

12. Horrible murder of a farmer by guerrillas at Osage river, Mo.

13. A portion of Banks' army attacked near Blair's Landing, La. Rebs. repulsed with loss.

13. New York Soldiers' Voting Bill passed New York Senate. Yeas 29, nays none.

14. Gunboat expedition from Butler's army capture prisoners and stores at Smithfield, Va.

14. Nebraska Constitution and State Government Bill passed by U. S. Senate.

15. Chenango, gunboat, exploded.

16. Gunboat Eastport sunk by snag above Grand Ecore.

17. Bread riot by women in Savannah, Ga.

18. Rebel attack on Fort Wessell, near Plymouth, N. C. Gunboat Southfield sunk. Com. Flusser killed and most of crew drowned. Ram also destroys the gunboat Bombshell.

18. Baltimore Sanitary Fair opened.

19. Guerrillas driven from Burksville.

19. Transports and gunboats aground above Grand Ecore, Red river.

19. Fort Wessells, N. C., evacuated by Feds.

20. Plymouth, N. C., surrendered to rebels by Gen. Wessels, after severe loss by rebels. Gen. Wessells and 2,500 men surrendered.

21. North Carolina salt works, worth $100,000, near Wilmington, destroyed.

22. Rebels captured gunboat Petrel on the Yazoo river, and burnt her.

22. Forrest moving toward Alabama, followed by Grierson.

22. Banks' army left Grand Ecore for Alexandria, La., by land.

23. Brisk engagement near Camden, Ark. Feds. defeated.

23. Rebels capture and murder Union pickets at Nickajack.

23. N. Y. Metropolitan Sanitary Fair closed. Sword voted to Grant by 30,291, against 14,509 for McClellan.

24. Battle at Cane river, La. Rebels losing 1,000 men and 9 guns.

25. A supply train of 240 wagons, and the 26th Iowa, 73d Ohio, and 43d Ind. regiments, under Col. Drake, 2,000 men, were captured after a brave resistance on their return to Pine Bluff, Ark., after an unsuccessful effort to reach General Steele's army.

26. Gen. Steele's army left Camden for Little Rock, Ark.

26. Rebels in strong force attack Admiral Porter's gunboats on the Red river, and were defeated with severe loss.

28. Little Washington, N. C., evacuated by Fed. troops.

28. A detachment of Fed. cavalry under Col. Lowell, encountered a portion of Mosby's command near Upperville, Va., and defeated them, capturing 23, killing 2 and wounding 4. Fed. loss, 3 killed, 4 wounded.

30. Gen. Steele's army in Ark. crossed the Sabine river after a fight with rebs.

30. Madison Court House, Va., was burned by a Union expeditionary force while engaged in a skirmish with a rebel company at that place.

May 1. Death of Commodore W. D. Porter.

1. Gen. Steele's army 40 miles from Little Rock, Ark. His cavalry reached that city.

2. Advance of the Army of the Potomac across the Rapidan towards Chancellorsville and the Wilderness.

2. West Point, Va., occupied by Feds.

2. Gen. Sturgis' cavalry encountered a band of the rebel Forrest's men, near Bolivar, Tenn., and, after a severe fight, defeated them.

3. The crossing of the Rapidan by the army of the Potomac effected, without opposition, at Culpepper, Germania, and Ely's Fords.

3. The Sec. of the Navy sentenced Ad. Wilkes to be reprimanded and suspended for three years, for insubordination, &c.

4. The crossing of the Rapidan by the army of the Potomac continued.

4. Gen. Warren's headquarters at the Wilderness.

4. A fleet of transports on Hampton Roads commenced embarking troops.

4. Rebel raid into Princeton, Ky.

5. Battle of the Wilderness commenced. A day of terrific fighting, on most difficult ground, in the Wilderness, near Chancellorsville, Va. Night closed in without any definite result. Gen. Hayes killed.

5. Gen. Butler's army passed Fortress Monroe in transports, on their way up the James river.

5. Gen. Kautz forced the Blackwater, and burnt the railroad bridge at Stony Creek.

5. Naval engagement between the reb. ram Albemarle and Fed. fleet, near the mouth of the Roanoke river.

5. Skirmish at Thoroughfare Gap, Va. Burnside's cavalry attacked the enemy on their passage through the Gap.

6. Battle of the Wilderness continued. Another day of terrible fighting, resulting in the falling back of Lee's army. Gen. Wadsworth killed. Loss of both armies about 15,000 each in the 2 days' fighting. The rebel Gen. Longstreet wounded. Fed. wounded, who had been removed to Fredericksburg, fired on by citizens.

6. Gen. Butler's forces effected a successful landing near Fort Fisher, N. C., without resistance.

6. Gunboat Com. Jones blown up by rebel torpedo on James river.

7. Gen. Grant's army in pursuit of Lee, having marched 15 miles on the night of the 6th.

7. Tunnel Hill, Ga., taken by Gen. Thomas.

7. Severe fight at Todd's Tavern, between Custar's and rebel cavalry. Loss, 250 on each side.

7. Battle near Petersburg, Va., between Gen. Butler's army and the rebels.

7. Tazewell salt-works destroyed by Gen. Averill.

8. General Hancock's corps passed through Spottsylvania C. H. at daylight, and, at noon, his headquarters were 20 miles south of the battle-field of the 6th.

8. Battle of Spottsylvania C. H., Va., commenced. The armies near Spottsylvania C. H. engaged from 8 to 12 M., at which time Fed. forces gained the point for which they contended. At 6 P.M., 2 fresh divisions were thrown in, and, after a severe engagement of an hour and a half, the rebel position was carried, and their first line of breastworks occupied.

8. General engagement at Mill Creek Gap, Ga.

8. Union troops held possession of Fredericksburg, Va.

9. Battle of Spottsylvania C. H., Va., continued. Lee's army made a stand, but no general engagement occurred in the morning. Maj.-Gen Sedgwick killed. The fight in the evening was brought on by Hancock, who crossed the river Po, and established himself on the south bank.

9. Gen. Butler at Bermuda Landing, in a strong position. His forces defeated a portion of Beauregard's army under Gen. Hill. The fight commenced at noon, and continued till night. The rebels driven back 3 miles.

9. Night attack on Gen. Butler's lines. The rebels repulsed.

9. Gen. Sheridan marched around the rebel right flank, and reached the North Anna river in safety in the evening. In the night he destroyed a great quantity of rebel stores, and recaptured 378 Feds.

9. Battle of Cloyd Mountain. Rebels defeated.

9. U. S. transport H. A. Weed blown up by torpedo near Jacksonville, Fla.

10. Gen. Sheridan crossed the South Anna river.

10. Battle of Spottsylvania C. H. continued. A general advance of Fed. army ordered at 5 A.M. A tremendous conflict ensued. In the afternoon an attack was made on the rebel batteries. After the assault had continued some time it was found that the rebel batteries could not be carried without great loss, and the effort was abandoned. The battle ceased about 9 P.M., and was one of the most terrible and bloody of the war. The 6th

corps carried the enemy's works, and captured 1,000 prisoners. Loss, 10,000 on each side on this day.

May 10. Gen. Sheridan reported that he had turned the rebel right, reached their rear, and destroyed from 8 to 10 miles of railroad and other property.

10. Gen. Averill's force fought a battle near Wytheville, Va., defeating Gen. Jones and destroying railroad.

10. Crooke defeated rebels near Newbern, capturing 7 guns and many pris.

10 Sec. Stanton reported that Gen. McPherson was within 7 miles of Resaca, Ga.

10. Gen. Sherman in front of Buzzard Roost Gap, Ga.

11. The armies under Grant and Lee engaged with varied success until 11 A.M., when Fed. line was somewhat advanced. Gen. Grant reported to the War Department, that, after 6 days' fighting, the result was much in favor of the Union arms.

11. After 3 days of skirmishing Feds. drove the rebels back to Rocky Ridge and Buzzard Roost Mountain, Ga.

11. Gen. Sheridan captured Ashland Station, destroying a large amount of stores. He attacked Gen. Stewart at Yellow Tavern, near Richmond, and penetrated the 1st and 2d lines of the rebel defences.

12. The battle between Grant's and Lee's army renewed 5 miles below Spottsylvania C. H., Va. Gen. Hancock opened the battle, and made a brilliant assault on A. P. Hill's division, which he routed. Gen. Grant reported that the day closed leaving between 3,000 and 4,000 prisoners in his hands, including 2 general officers, and over 30 pieces of artillery. In the night Lee abandoned his position.

12. Gen. Sheridan's army encamped at Walnut Grove and Gaines' Mills.

12. Gen. Butler's army engaged.

12. Rebel position at Dalton, Ga., carried and held by Sherman.

13. Gen. Butler's army advanced toward Petersburg, Va. Skirmishing with the rebels in the afternoon.

13. Gen. Sheridan's forces encamped at Bottom's Bridge.

13. Gen. Sherman's army in line of battle in Sugar Valley.

13. Gen. McPherson captured 9 trains, with rebel military stores, at Dalton.

14. Gen. Smith carried the 1st line of rebel works at Petersburg, Va. The rebels attacked the 5th corps, army of the Potomac, but were finally driven back with severe loss, after a furious cannonade.

14. Gen. Sherman's forces actively engaged Gen. Hooker's corps attacked by the rebel Gen. Hood's division. The rebels repulsed. General battle, which lasted till midnight, each party holding its respective position.

15. Battle of Resaca, Ga. An all-day battle, in which Feds were successful. The rebels forced to evacuate Resaca. Gen. Johnston retreats from Fed. front in the night.

15. Rocky Faced Ridge taken by Sherman.

15. Gen. Sigel fought a battle at Newmarket, Va. The rebels successful. Union forces fell back to Strasburg, Va.

15. Gen. Banks' gunboats arrived at Fort de Russey, La.

16. The rebel army encamped around Spottsylvania C. H, Va.

16. The rebels in force attacked Gen. Smith's lines in Va., and forced them back with considerable loss.

16. Gen. Butler's force attacked by troops from Petersburg Furious fighting. The rebels made a desperate onslaught in a fog, but were repulsed.

16. Resaca, Ga., occupied by Gen. Sherman.

16. Admiral Porter's fleet above Alexandria Falls, released by Col. Bailey's dam.

17. Gen. Kautz reached City Point, Va., returning from his raid on the Danville railroad.

17. Gen. Sherman's army at Colburn, Ga.

17. General Banks' forces reached Semmesport, La.

18. Ewell attacked Union baggage train in rear of Grant's right flank, but was repulsed

18. Heavy engagement between the armies in Va. Gen. Hancock charged the enemy, and carried the first line of rebel intrenchments.

18. Gen. Sherman reached Adairsville, Ga., where he was engaged in skirmishes.

18. Sec. Stanton announced that a draft would be ordered, to take place July 1.

18. A pretended proclamation of the President calling for 400,000 men, and announcing the Spring campaign closed, published in the Journal of Commerce and the World. The 2 papers suppressed for 3 days, and the author of the forgery, Jos. Howard, of Brooklyn, arrested.

19. Gen. Ewell attempted to turn Grant's right, but was repulsed.

19. Gen. Sherman advanced on the enemy, who retreated. Kingston, Ga., reached. General Sherman pushed a column as far as Cassville, Ga.

20. Torpedoes explode at Bachelor's Creek. Many N. Y. soldiers killed and wounded.

20. Sherman in possession of Kingston and Rome, Ga.

20. Rebels attack Ames' division of Butler's army. Heavy losses on both sides.

20. Arrest of Howard, the forger.

21. Gen. Hancock's troops entered Bowling Green, Va.

23. U. S. tugboat Columbine captured on St. John's river by rebs.

24. Rebels destroy bridge over North Anna. Grant's headquarters at Jericho Mills. Sheridan destroyed Danville railroad near Richmond, Va.

24. Fitzhugh Lee repulsed at Wilson's Wharf by Federal negroes under Gen. Wild.

24. Sherman flanks Johnston at Altoona.

24. 1,000 rebels captured by General Grant's army at Mt. Carmel Church, Va.

25. Battle near Dallas, Ga. Hooker drives rebels 2 miles. Union loss, 1,500. Reb. about same.

25. Gen. Birney ascends the Ashepoo river.

26. Grant's army moves toward Hanovertown.

26. La. State Convention abolishes slavery.

27. Eight steamers and several river craft burned at New Orleans Levee, by incendiaries.

27. Lee evacuates position on South Anna, and retreats toward Richmond.

27. Sheridan captures and holds Hanovertown and Ferry.

28. Longstreet attacks Sherman at Dallas, and is driven toward Marietta. Rebel loss, 2,500 killed and wounded, and 300 prisoners. Union loss, 300.

29. Grant's army crosses the Pamunkey river, Va.

30. Trains of refugees attacked near Salem, Ark. 60 men and several women killed.

30. Lee attacks Grant north of Chickahominy, and is repulsed. Hancock drives him out of intrenched line of rifle-pits and holds it.

31. Grant's and Lee's armies confronting each other from Hanover C. H. to Cold Harbor.

31. Gen. Fremont nominated for President and Gen. Cochrane for Vice-Pres. of U. S.

June 1. Expedition under Gen. Sturgis in Miss., defeated, with loss of wagon train, artillery, and ammunition.

1. Reb. attacks at Cold Harbor, Va., repulsed.

1. Rebs. twice attack Butler, and are repulsed.

2. Schofield and Hooker at Marietta. Cavalry take Altoona Pass.

3. Battle of Cold Harbor.

4. Reb. night attack on Hancock repulsed.

4. Grant's cavalry defeated Hampton's cavalry at Howes' Store, Va.

5. Reb. attack on left (Hancock's) repulsed.

5. Sherman's army fall back toward the Chattahoochie and Atlanta.

5. Marmaduke, with 3,000 men, defeated at Columbia, Ark.

5. Battle of Piedmont, Va. Reb. loss 1,500 prisoners, 3 guns, 3,000 stand of arms, and stores, and a large number k. and w.

5. Gens. Crook and Averill entered Lexington, Va.

5. Rebs. driven through Ripley, Miss., by Gen. Sturgis' troops.

6. Reb. midnight attack on Burnside repulsed.

6. Sherman's headquarters at Acworth.

7. Rebs. defeated at Lake Chicot on the Miss. river, by Gen. A. J. Smith's troops.

7. The 9th corps, on Grant's right, attacked briskly, and rebs. driven back.

7. Morgan, with 3,000 men, commences a raid into Kentucky.

7. Philadelphia Sanitary Fair opens.

7. Abraham Lincoln and Andrew Johnson nominated President and Vice-President of the U. S.

8. U. S. troops defeated at Mount Sterling, Ky., by Gen. Morgan's forces.

8. Paris, Ky., taken by a portion of Morgan's forces.

8. Sherman's whole army moves forward toward the Kenesaw range. McPherson occupies Big Shanty, and rebels fall back with left on Lost Mountain, and right on Kenesaw.

8. Gilmore's raid on Richmond fortifications.

9. Gen. Burbridge defeats rebels at Mount Sterling, and captures 700 pris.

10. Gen. Sturgis' Fed. troops defeated at Guntown, Miss., and again at Ripley, by Gen. Forrest. Feds. destroy their supply train, and '0 cannon, and retreat towards Memphis, after spirited contest and severe loss.

10. Lexington, Ky., robbed by Morgan.

June 10. Rebel guerrillas repulsed at Princeton, Ky.

10. Frankfort, Ky., unsuccessfully attacked by 1,200 rebels.

10. Gen. Hunter, with Crook and Averill, moves from Staunton, Va., after destroying over $3,000,000 worth of rebel property.

10. Reb. Congress adjourned.

11. Fed. troops defeated near Cynthiana, Ky., and the town burnt by Gen. Morgan.

11. Gen. Hobson's Ohio militia captured by Morgan, after a short combat near Cynthiana.

11. Battle of Trevillian Station, Va. Rebs. badly beaten by Sheridan.

12. Gen. Burbridge defeats and scatters Morgan at Cynthiana, with great loss.

12. Grant crosses the Chickahominy.

13. Grant's headquarters at Wilcox's Landing.

13. The Fugitive Slave Law repealed in the House of Representatives.

13. Gen. Hobson and staff recaptured.

13. Sheridan recrosses the North Anna.

14. Destruction of reb. canal boats and stores at Buchanan, Va., by Gen. Averill.

14. Grant's army crossed to south of the James.

14. Reb. Gen. Polk killed.

14. Sherman advancing toward Kenesaw.

15. Battle of Baylor's Farm. 16 rebel guns, 300 prisoners taken.

16. Gen. Hunter entered Liberty, Va., and destroyed a long bridge. Also 7 miles of railway.

17. Gens. Crook and Averill routed Imboden's rebel cavalry between Quaker Church and Lynchburg, Va.

16. A portion of the southern defences of Petersburg, Va., carried by Hancock and Smith's corps.

17. Burnside captured 2 redoubts in the Petersburg works, 450 prisoners, and 4 guns.

17. Severe fighting by Gen. Hunter's army, 7 miles from Lynchburg, Va. No decisive result.

18. Simultaneous and desperate assault on the rebel works at Petersburg, by the Armies of the Potomac and the James.

18. Gen. Wilson's Federal cavalry took position on the extreme left of the Union lines at Petersburg.

18. The battle at Lynchburg, Va., renewed. The rebels driven into their works, and Gen. Hunter retreated.

19. The Army of the James reoccupy Bermuda Hundred, and repair the railroad.

19. The rebel privateer Alabama was sunk near the Harbor of Cherbourg, France, after an engagement of over an hour with the U. S. sloop-of-war Kearsarge, Capt. Winslow. 70 of the rebel crew were taken on board the Kearsarge, and 115 reached England and France. 3 persons only were wounded on the Kearsarge.

20. Reb. cavalry defeated at the White House, Va.

21. Rebs. assault Gen. Sherman's army in Ga. several times, and lose 800 men.

21. Gen. Foster crossed the James river, and intrenched near Aiken's Landing.

21. Gen. Hunter's artillery train retreating from Lynchburg, Va., attacked by rebs. He destroys a portion of the guns and caissons. Gen. Hunter retreats to the Ohio river.

22. A sudden attack on the Union lines at Petersburg, which are broken by the enemy with severe loss to both sides.

22. Wilson and Kautz's cavalry destroy 4 miles of the railroad north of Petersburg, Va.

23. Severe battle on the Weldon R. R., Va. 2 rebel trains captured.

23. Railroad junction at Burksville, Va., destroyed by Feds.

24. Battle of Staunton Bridge, Va. Wilson and Kautz's Federal cavalry repulsed.

24. Rebs. attack Gen. Sheridan at White House, Va., and are beaten.

24. Maryland State Convention abolishes slavery.

24. Rebs. attack Feds. at Lafayette, Ga. and are beaten.

25. Reb. night attack on Gen. Burnside's troops on the James river repulsed.

27. Fight near Kenesaw Mountain, Ga. Union loss 1,500.

28. Sherman flanks Johnston at Kenesaw Mountain, Ga.

28. Fight at Stoney Creek, Va. Wilson and Kautz's Fed. cavalry retreat to Reams's Station.

29. Battle at Reams's Station. Fed. cavalry defeated.

30. Johnston evacuates Kenesaw Mountain, Va.

July 1. Gen. Wilson's force reaches Grant's lines, having lost all their guns and wagons.

1. An expedition left Hilton Head, S. C., in direction of North Edisto river.

1. The southern side of James Island, S. C., occupied by Gen. Foster's troops.

1. Col. Hoyt and 137 men captured on Johnson's Island.
2. The expedition from Hilton Head disembark at Seabrook Island.
2. An unsuccessful attempt to take the rebel Fort Johnson on the north end of James Island.
1. W. P. Fessenden accepts Secretaryship of U. S. Treasury.
2. Rebel Gen. Ewell invades Shenandoah valley in 3 columns.
2. Martinsburg, Va., evacuated by Feds.
3. Sherman's army entered Marietta, Ga.
3. A part of the expedition from Hilton Head repulsed.
3. Rebels defeated by Sherman, 2 miles south of Marietta, Ga.
3. Winchester, Va., taken by rebs. and Gen. Sigel falls back to Harper's Ferry.
4. The rebels took possession of Bolivar Heights, half a mile from Harper's Ferry, on their advance into Md., where they were attacked.
4. Sigel arrived at Sandy Hook.
4. Gen. Mulligan evacuated Bolivar Heights.
4. The rebels make a raid to Point of Rocks, Md.
4. Naval operations in Stono river.
5. Slocum's expedition routed rebels east of Jackson, Miss.
5. Ellicott's marine colored brigade attacked by rebels near Port Hudson. Rebels defeated with loss of 150.
5. Martial law declared in Ky. by the President, and the writ of habeas corpus suspended.
6. Hagerstown, Md., evacuated by Union troops.
6. Gen. Wallace's troops repulsed near Middletown, Md.
6. Hagerstown, Md., plundered by rebels.
7. Rebel Gen. Johnston crossed the Chattahoochie.
7. Gen. Sigel's Union forces evacuate Harper's Ferry.
7. Rebel raiders near Frederick, Md.
7. The rebels checked at Monocacy Bridge.
7. Proclamation issued by President Lincoln appointing the first Thursday in August as a Fast Day.
8. Harper's Ferry reoccupied by Fed. forces.
8. The rebel cruiser Florida captured the bark Golconda.
8. Capture of Platte City, Mo., by guerrillas.
8. Rebels enter Fredericksburg, Md.
8. Parksville, Mo., sacked by rebels.
9. Battle at Monocacy, Md., lasting from 9. A. M. to 5 P. M. Fed. forces overpowered and forced to retreat in disorder, losing 1,000 men.
9. Fed. forces on John's Island, S. C., twice repelled a rebel assault.
9. Gen. Sherman reached the Chattahoochee.
9. Gov. Brown, of Georgia, ordered all the militia of the State into active service.
9. Rebels capture Westminster, Md. Couch reoccupies Hagerstown, and Hunter, Frederick.
10. Gen. Rousseau leaves Decatur with 2,700 men on an expedition in rebel Gen. Hood's rear.
10. Gen. Johnston retreats to fortifications around Atlanta.
11. The rebels near Washington, D. C. They capture a railroad train at Magnolia Station, between Philadelphia and Baltimore, and Maj.-Gen. Franklin, who was on the train.
11. Burning of Gunpowder bridge, Md., by the rebels.
11. Rebel salt works at Tampa Bay destroyed.
12. Engagement near Fort Stevens, one of the defences of Washington. The rebels driven off with severe loss.
13. Gen. Rousseau defeated 4,000 rebs. under Clanton, near Coosaw river.
13-15. Gens. Smith and Slocum defeat Forrest in 5 battles in Tenn., driving him from Pontotoc to Tupelo. Rebel loss, 2,000. Union loss, 300.
15. Rebels drive 1,000 horses and 5,000 cattle from Montgomery Co., Md., into Va.
16. A rebel force captured the Fed. stockade at Brownsboro', on the Memphis and Charleston railroad.
17. Gen. Sherman's command moved forward to within 5 miles of Atlanta, Ga. His advance crossed the Chattahoochee river.
17. Gen. Joseph E. Johnston turned over the command of the rebel army at Atlanta to Gen. J. B. Hood.
17. Severe fight near Grand Gulf.
17. Indian raid on Fed. post at Fort Larned.
17. Col. Jacques and Mr. Gilmore visited Jeff. Davis at Richmond, by permission of Fed. authorities.
17. Wirt Adams defeated at Grand Gulf, by Fed. Gen. Slocum, with heavy loss.
17. Gen. Rousseau defeated 1,500 rebs. under Clanton, at Chewa Station.

July 18. Crook defeated by Breckinridge at Island Ford, Va. Loss, 300.

18. Gen. Duffie defeated at Ashby's Gap, Va., losing 200 wagons and many prisoners.

18. Gen. Crook defeats Early at Snicker's Gap, capt'g 300 wagons and many pris.

18. Decatur, Ga., occupied by Federal forces.

18. President Lincoln issued an order for a draft of 500,000 men to take place immediately after Sept. 5, the term of service to be one year.

18. The President sent his famous "To whom it may concern," dispatch.

19. Sherman's forces reached Peachtree creek, 4 miles north of Atlanta, Ga. They were attacked by Hood's troops, who were defeated. Rebel loss, 6,000, including 3 generals. Fed. loss, 1,713.

20. Gen. Smith's forces reached La Grange, Tenn.

20. Gen. "Baldy" Smith took leave of his command before Petersburg, Va., and Gen. Martindale assumed command.

20. Gen. Averill attacked and defeated the rebel Early in front of Winchester, Va. Rebel loss, 300 killed and wounded, and 200 prisoners. Early was reinforced and repulsed the Union troops.

21. Henderson, Ky., attacked by 700 rebels.

21. The rebel lines contracted close to Atlanta.

21. Skirmishing on the James river.

22. Great battle before Atlanta. The rebels assaulted Sherman's lines near Atlanta with great fury seven times, and were as often repulsed after a terrible struggle. Fed. loss was 3,521; the rebel loss estimated at 10,000. Gen. McPherson was killed.

22. Skirmishing in front of Burnside's corps of the Army of the Potomac.

22. Louisiana State Convention abolish slavery.

23. Burial of the dead before Atlanta.

23. Atlanta shelled.

23. Heavy fighting in the Shenandoah Valley.

23. Averill defeated at Winchester.

24. The cavalry expedition which left Decatur, July 10, arrived at Marietta, Ga., having been completely successful in a raid on the Montgomery and West Point railroad.

25. The rebels again occupied Martinsburg, Va.

26. Battle near Helena, Ark. Federal forces at first were unsuccessful, but afterward repulsed the enemy and charged through their lines.

26. Engagement at Point of Rocks Md.

26. The rebels made an attempt to flank Gen. Butler's position.

26. Gen. Stoneman dispatched a cavalry force to destroy the Macon and Western railroad. They succeeded in destroying 18 miles of track, and in capturing 500 rebels, when they were in turn attacked, the prisoners released, and 1,000 of Gen. McCook's troops captured.

27. Fed. army attacked while crossing James river. A spirited engagement in which the rebels were driven back.

27. Gen. O. O. Howard assumed command of the Department and Army of the Tennessee, lately commanded by Gen. McPherson.

21. The siege of Atlanta commenced. The 15th corps of Sherman's army assaulted the rebels in force and defeated them. The rebel army under Hood was repeatedly hurled against Sherman's army, but as often rolled back and cut to pieces. The rebels suffered severely without gaining any advantage.

28. An expedition sent into N. C.

28. Gen. Hooker relieved of his command at his own request.

28. Fed. gunboats in Louisiana destroyed a large amount of rebel lumber and 2 saw mills.

29. The rebels crossed the Potomac on a raid into Maryland and Pennsylvania.

29. Fed. cavalry occupy Fayetteville, Ga. They cut the Atlanta and Macon railroad.

29. Fights with the rebels near Morganzia, La.

30. Explosion of an immense mine by Union troops in front of Burnside's position before Petersburg. Its explosion was the signal for the discharge of every piece of artillery on the line from the Appomattox to the extreme left. After the discharge of the artillery the army advanced and assaulted the rebel works, but after a desperate attempt to carry them was repulsed, with a loss of over 4,000 men.

30. The rebels entered Chambersburg, Pa., where the rebel commander demanded $500,000 under threat of burning the city. His demand not being complied with, the city was burned.

31. Gen. Stoneman and part of his command captured by the rebels in Georgia.

31. The rebels occupied Frederick, Md.

Aug. 1. Bradley Johnson and McCausland defeated at Cumberland, losing part of their plunder from Pennsylvania.

2. Fed. Col. Stout, with 500 men, posted to intercept the retreat of McCausland and Johnson, was captured by them, losing 90 men.

3. Return to Norfolk, Va., of a cavalry expedition sent into N. C., July 28, after having visited 5 counties and captured considerable property.

4. Fast day in the U. S.

4. Exchange of the Union and rebel officers, under fire, at Charleston, S. C.

4. Gen. Kelley repulsed rebels under Johnson and McCausland at New Creek, Md. The fight continued until after dark, the rebels retiring in the night.

5. Great battle at the entrance of Mobile Bay. Fort Gaines opened on Fed. fleet at about 7 A.M., the monitor Tecumseh having opened the attack a short time before. The rebel ram Tennessee captured after one of the fiercest naval battles on record. In the night the rebs. evacuated and blew up Fort Powell. The monitor Tecumseh was blown up by a rebel torpedo.

5. Explosion of a rebel mine near Petersburg, Va. But little damage done. A terrific fight in front of Petersburg, lasting from 5:30 to 7:30 P.M. It commenced by a charge of the enemy, which was repulsed with slaughter.

6. Com. Farragut shelled Fort Gaines, Mobile Harbor.

6. Battle of Atlanta. The rebels made a demonstration on the 16th corps, and were heavily punished, and driven back. The 23d corps were driven from the reb. lines, losing 500 men.

6. Indian massacre near Beaver Creek.

7. Gen. Averill overtook rebels under McCausland, Gilmore, and McNeil, near Moorefield, in the Shenandoah Valley, and attacked them with great success, routing the rebels, capturing their artillery, a large number of prisoners, horses, and arms.

7. Gen. Sheridan assumed command of Middle Military Division.

8. Surrender of Fort Gaines, Mobile Bay, to Com. Farragut.

8. Steamboat Vanderbilt sunk in the Hudson.

8. Indians capture 9 wagons at Plumb Creek, and kill the teamsters. They also burn 21 wagons at Point Ranche.

8. Gen. Burris returns to New Madrid after 17 days' scout in S. E. Mo. and N. E. Ark. 50 rebs. killed, 40 wounded, 57 prisoners.

9. Dutch Gap Canal, Va., commenced by Gen. Butler.

9. Terrible explosion of a boat loaded with ammunition at City Point, Va.

9. Heavy shelling of Atlanta.

10. Gen. Sheridan's army skirmishing near Winchester, Va. Sharp fight near Martinsburg.

10. Steamer Empress fired into by reb. batteries on the banks of the Mississippi.

10. Sharp skirmish near Abbeyville, Miss.

11. The Tallahassee scuttled the sch'r S. A. Boyce, burnt the pilot-boat James Funk, brig Carrie Estelle, bark Bay State, brig A. Richards, and bonded the schooner Carrol for $10,000; burnt the pilot-boat Wm. Bell and the schooner Atlantic.

11. Battle of Sulphur Springs Bridge.

12. The Tallahassee bonded the bark Suliote, burnt the schooner Spokelane and ship Adriatic, scuttled the brig Billow, bonded for $30,000 the schooner Robert E. Pecker.

12. Attack of guerrillas on the gunboat Reliance in Northumberland Co., Va.

13. Gen. Grant threw a powerful force, under Gen. Hancock, across the river at Deep Bottom. Hancock took position 10 miles from Richmond. Gen. Birne assaulted the rebel works in his front.

13. Gen. Burnside relieved.

13. Guerrillas attacked Selma, Ky.

13. Gen. Smith attacked the rebels at Hurricane Creek, Miss., and defeated them.

13. The Tallahassee scuttled the bark Glavomore, and burned the sch'r Lamot Dupont.

13. Mosby attacks Sheridan's supply train near Snicker's Gap, Va.

13. Rebel cavalry captured 5 steamers with governm't cattle at Shawneetown.

14. The rebel Gen. Wheeler demanded the surrender of Dalton, Ga., which was refused by Col. Siebold. The rebels entered the town, but were kept at bay by the garrison.

14. The Tallahassee scuttled the ship James Littlefield.

14. Battle of Strawberry Plains, Va. 10th corps take rebel line of breastworks, 4 guns, and 100 prisoners.

15. Gen. Sheridan falls back toward Charlestown, Va.

15. Fighting near Richmond.

15. The Tallahassee scuttled schooners M. A. Howe, Howard, Floral Wreath, Restless, Etta Caroline, and bonded sch'r S. K. Harris.

15. Gen. Steadman reinforces Dalton,

and rebels are driven out of town in confusion.

Aug. 15. Kilpatrick cut West Point, Ga., road at Fairburn, and burned depot.

15. 19th corps threaten Malvern Hill.

16. Fighting on the north bank of the James at Deep Run. The engagement resulted favorably, though not decisively, for the Feds. The enemy somewhat driven back from their position.

16. Cavalry fight between a division of Sheridan's army and the rebels, near Front Royal, Va.

16. Fight near Chattanooga.

16. The Tallahassee scuttled the bark P. C. Alexander, and burned the sch'rs Leopold, Pearl, Sarah Louisa, and Magnolia.

17. The Tallahassee scuttled the sch'r North American, and bonded the brig Neva for $17,500.

18. A furious attack on Burnside's corps at Six Mile Station, on the Weldon railroad, near Petersburg, which was repulsed with great loss to the rebels.

18. General Warren moved his corps across the Weldon railroad, in doing which he was engaged in considerable fighting.

18. The Tallahassee arrived at Halifax, after having burned the schooners Josiah Acorn, Diadem, Sea Flower, and brig Roan.

19. The rebels drove in Warren's pickets and forced back 2 divisions of Fed. army at Six Mile Station. A heavy fight took place, resulting in re-establishing Union lines and capturing 1,500 prisoners. Fed. loss, 3,000.

19. Martinsburg robbed by rebels.

20. Guerrillas raid on Woodburn, and set fire to depot.

21. Rebels attack Union position on Weldon road, and after great loss (over 2,000) withdraw. Union loss about 600.

21. Battle of Summit Point, Va. Early driven 2 miles.

21. Memphis entered by Forrest with 9 regiments and 4 guns; took 250 prisoners. Union forces arriving, Forrest left; was overtaken near Lanes', and severely punished in a 2 hours' battle.

22. Cannonade of Fed. works near Petersburg. The rebels charged, but finding themselves in a trap, retreated in confusion.

22. Rebel force on Weldon road withdrawn from front of 5th and 9th corps, and intrenches 3 miles from Petersburg.

22. Rebel Johnson's forces whipped at Canton, Ky., by Col. Johnson, and himself killed.

22. Action at Rogersville, Tenn.

23. Rebels fall back to their lines 2 miles from Petersburg, and Gen. Warren's lines advanced.

23. Shelby captures nearly all 54th Ill. near Duval's Bluff.

23. Fort Morgan, Mobile Bay, surrendered unconditionally. By its surrender Feds. captured 200 prisoners, 60 pieces of artillery.

24. Skirmish on Sheridan's left.

24. Reconnoissance of Gen. Crook's command in the Shenandoah Valley.

24. Clinton, Miss., taken by Generals Herron and Lee.

25. Severe battle on the Weldon railroad near Reams' Station. A desperate attempt of the rebels to retake the road. Hancock's corps was several times attacked, the enemy being each time repulsed. At 5:30 P.M., a combined attack on his centre and left was repulsed, the enemy withdrawing, leaving their dead and wounded on the field. Union forces afterward fell back. Fed. loss, 1,000 killed and wounded, 3,000 prisoners and 9 guns. Rebel killed and wounded 1,500.

25. Gen. Butler's picket-line driven in, but re-established.

25. Torbert encounters Early's forces at Leetown, narrowly escaping flanking. He falls back to near Shepardstown.

26. The rebel Gen. Early attempted to cross the Potomac, but was driven back by Averill.

26. Kilpatrick destroyed 14 miles of Macon railroad, and stores, capturing 6 guns, 4 flags, and 200 prisoners; afterwards forced to abandon most of his captures.

26. Rebels fall back from Sheridan's front toward Smithfield.

27. Guerrillas defeated at Shelbyville, Ky.

28. Early driven through Smithfield.

28. Gen. Sherman's army reached the West Point railroad at Red Oak, 13 miles from Atlanta, and began the destruction of the road from that point.

29. McClellan nominated for President and Geo. H. Pendleton for Vice.

30. Sherman interposed his whole army between Atlanta and Hood's army intrenched at Jonesboro'.

31. Great battle near Atlanta. During the afternoon, Fed. artillery kept up a cannonade to provoke the rebels to an assault. In the afternoon the rebels assaulted Union lines, but were repulsed with great loss. The rebel loss in the attack on Ransom's and Logan's lines estimated at 3,000. In the evening the

14th corps struck the railroad, 5 miles south of Jonesboro'. The work of destruction commenced immediately.

Sept. 1. The battle of Atlanta continued. A brilliant charge was made at 5 P. M. by Gen. Davis' force, resulting in the discomfiture of the rebels and surrender of a large number. Great destruction by the rebs. of large magazines of stores accumulated at Atlanta. They blew up, in addition to other things, 80 car-loads of ammunition. Gen. Slocum's corps assaulted the enemy's works around the city, in the afternoon.

1. Panic and evacuation of the city.

1. Rebels driven from Jonesboro' to Lovejoy's Station, losing 1,000 prisoners and 10 guns.

1. Gen. Rousseau drives 10,000 rebels, near Murfreesboro' pike 3 miles.

2. Atlanta, Ga., occupied by Sherman's army at 11 A. M.

2. Sharp fighting near Martinsburg, Va.

3. Milroy attacks 3,000 rebel cavalry near Murfreesboro', and drives them toward Triune.

3. Sheridan's army again moves forward from Charlestown. Battles of Darkesville and Perryville, Va. Rebels were repulsed, losing 70 pris. Union loss, 300. Mosby captured an ambulance train which had left the field.

4. John Morgan's forces routed, and Morgan killed by Gen. Gillem, at Greenville, Tenn. Killed, 100; prisoners, 75, including Morgan's staff.

5. Steamer Elsie captured in running the blockade at Wilmington.

5. The President issued a proclamation, recommending that Sunday, Sept. 11, be observed as a day of Thanksgiving.

6. Battle of Matamoras.

7. Dibbel's rebel brigade surprised at Readyville, Tenn., by 220 of 9th Pa. cavalry, losing 130 prisoners.

8. Rebel Col. Jessie and 100 men captured near Ghent, Ky.

8. Brownsville, Texas, attacked by Cortinas, and the rebels driven from the town.

8. Gen. McClellan accepted the nomination for the Presidency.

8. Gen. Sherman ordered the removal of the inhabitants of Atlanta, and proposed a truce of ten days.

9. Spirited attack on the rebel pickets near Petersburg, in the night.

10. Gen. Sheridan's forces in the Shenandoah Valley attacked at Darksville, Va.

10. Grant drives picket line across Plank Road, and advances his permanent line half a mile.

10. Steamer Fawn burned by rebels on Dismal Swamp Canal.

11. An expedition left Fort Morgan, near Mobile, and proceeded up White river, destroying a large amount of lumber at Smith's Mills.

13. Attack on the rebels near Occoquan creek by some of Sheridan's forces. A South Carolina regiment captured.

14. Secretary Stanton ordered the draft to be commenced Sept. 19.

14. Price, with about 10,000 men, crosses White river, en route for Mo.

14. Gov. Brown, of Ga., withdraws 15,000 Ga. militia from Hood's army.

16. 2,500 cattle, the 13th Pa. regiment, with arms, wagons and camp, captured at Sycamore Church, Va.

18. Averill drives rebels out of Martinsburg.

19. Battle at Powder Mill, on Little Rock river.

19. Steamer Island Queen captured and sunk on Lake Erie, and the Philo Parsons burned by rebels on British soil.

19. Battle of Bunker Hill, near Winchester, Va. A great battle fought by Sheridan in the Shenandoah Valley. Sheridan made the attack and won a splendid victory, capturing over 2,500 prisoners, together with 9 battle-flags, and 5 pieces of artillery. The reb. Gens. Gordon and Rhodes were killed, and 3 other general officers wounded. All of the rebel killed and most of the wounded fell into Fed. hands.

20. Gen. Sheridan crossed Cedar creek, having pursued the enemy 30 miles.

20. Athens, Ala., captured by Forrest. 500 Union soldiers forced to surrender.

21. Fremont and Cochrane withdrew their names as candidates for President and Vice-President.

21. Battle of Fisher's Hill, Va. Sheridan's army defeated the rebels. Early loses 1,100 prisoners and 16 guns.

21. Torbert's cavalry defeats Wickham at Luray, capturing some prisoners.

23. Rebel Gen. Price occupies Bloomfield, Mo.

23. Montgomery Blair resigned his office of Postmaster-General.

23. A part of the rebel Gen. Forrest's force, about 400 strong, crossed the Tennessee river, at Bates' Landing.

25. Gen. Sheridan's advance passed beyond New Market. His forces drove the enemy from Mount Jackson.

25. Athens, Ala., occupied by the rebel Gen. Forrest's troops.

Sept. 25. The rebels at Luray attacked.
25. A force of rebel cavalry occupied Frederickstown, Mo., 20 miles east of Pilot Knob.
26. Battle at Pilot Knob.
26. Gen. Sheridan's headquarters at Harrisonburg, Va. His cavalry entered Stanton, Va., and destroyed a large quantity of rebel government property. They then proceeded to Waynesboro', destroying an iron bridge over the Shenandoah and a large amount of property. Gen. Early's reb. army routed and demoralized, fled through Brown's Gap toward Gordonsville. Gens. Merritt and Powel were driven back when they attacked Early at Brown's Gap.
27. Skirmish with Forrest's troops in Tenn.
27. The rebels attacked Fed. forces at Mineral Point, Mo.
27. Gen. Ewing arrives at Rolla, Mo., after being surrounded at Harrison by Price's forces.
28. Rebel night attack on Hancock's front, on Jerusalem Plank Road repulsed.
29. Gen. Ord's corps of Grant's army advanced and carried a very strong fortification and line of intrenchments below Chapin's Farm, taking 15 pieces of artillery and 200 or 300 prisoners.
29. Gen. Barney advanced from Deep Bottom and carried the Newmarket road.
30. Gen. Butler's forces assaulted the rebels in 3 columns near Chapin's Farm.
30. Warren captures first line of rebel works at Preble's Farm, capturing 50 men, and 1 gun. Rebels retired half a mile back to strong positions, and repulsed an attack thereon, capturing 1,500 prisoners, and killed and wounded 500.
30. The 10th and 18th corps concentrated at Newmarket Heights, furiously attacked by rebels, and swept back with terrible loss 3 times, losing 1,000, beside 200 prisoners and 2 flags.
Oct. 2. The rebels attacked at Saltville, Va., and were driven into their works.
2. Rebels in front of Warren fell back to their main lines, from Petersburg lead works, to Southside Road.
3. Lieut. Meigs murdered by guerrillas in Shenandoah valley.
3. Sherman's forces crossed the Chattahoochie with 15 days' rations, moving toward Marietta.
3. Gen. Thomas ordered to Chattanooga after Forrest, and Gen. Corse to Rome.
5. Hood captured small garrisons at Big Shanty and Ackworth, and burned 7 miles of railway; then moving on Allatoona.
6. Gen. Sheridan commenced moving back from Port Republic, Mount Crawford and Harrisonburg, Va., previous to which the whole country from the Blue Ridge to the North Mountain was made untenable for the rebel army by destroying an immense quantity of stores, grain, &c.
6. Allatoona unsuccessfully attacked by Hood.
6. Fed. Gen. Lee captures Clinton, La., and 30 prisoners.
7. Battle at Darleytown Road and New Market Heights. Rebel loss 1,000; Union 500. Gen. Kautz's cavalry attacked by rebels, who suffered considerably. They afterwards attacked Birney's division, who also repulsed them with very heavy loss. In the afternoon Gen Butler took the offensive and recaptured some of the intrenchments which had been taken from Kautz.
7. Reb. privateer Florida captured at Bahia, Bay of San Salvador, by U. S. S. Wachusett, Commander Collins.
7. The advance of the rebels from Osage river, Mo., spiritedly contested by Union cavalry.
7. Gen. Sheridan's forces reached Woodstock, Va.
7. A band of 200 rebels captured a steamboat and crossed into Ky.
8. Rebels at Woodville attacked by expedition from Gen. Dana, killing 40, and capturing 3 guns and 56 men.
8. The Fifth and Ninth Corps, Army of the Potomac, advanced their lines half a mile, driving the rebel skirmishers into their breastworks.
8. The rebels drew up in line of battle near Jefferson City, Mo., but afterwards moved off toward the west.
9. An engagement took place near Fisher's Hill, Va., in which the rebels were defeated, leaving 11 pieces of artillery and other munitions of war.
10. Engagement with the rebel Gen. Forrest at East Point, Tenn.
11. Gen. Curtis drove the rebels out of Independence, Mo.
11. Bloody fight with guerrillas near Winchester, Va.
11. Successful reconnoissance from the Army of the Potomac to Stony Creek.
11. Reb. Gen. Buford, with 1,200 cavalry, crosses Cumberland River, Tenn., at Harpeth Shoals.
11. Col. Weaver, with 90 colored troops, attacked by 200 rebels near Fort

Nelson, Tenn. Defeats them, and kills and wounds 27.

12. Death of Chief-Justice Roger B. Taney.

13. Reconnoissance in force from the Army of the James.

13. Attack on Resaca, Ga., by rebel Gen. Hood. The rebs. repulsed.

13. Engagement at Greenville, East Tenn.

15. The rebel army under Longstreet having appeared near Strasburg, Va., Gen. Sheridan advanced and found them drawn up in four lines of battle, but, on charging, the rebels fled.

16. Hood's army at Lafayette.

16. Gen. Sherman took Ship's Gap.

18. Maj.-Gen. Birney died at Philadelphia.

18. Gen. Blunt, with 2,000 cavalry and 4 howitzers, entered Lexington, Mo.

19. Battle of Cedar Creek, Shenandoah Valley. Gen. Sheridan's army was attacked before daylight and its left turned and driven in confusion, with a loss of 20 pieces of artillery. Gen. Sheridan afterward arrived on the field and drove the rebels, taking 48 pieces of artillery and many prisoners, gaining a great victory. Sheridan pursued the rebels to Mount Jackson, which he reached in the night.

19. The rebel Gen. Price attacked Gen. Blunt at Lexington, Mo., with an overwhelming force, and after a sharp fight drove him from the city. Gen. Blunt fell back to the Little Blue river, fighting desperately, and retarding the advance of the enemy.

19. The rebels entered Mayfield, Ky.

20. Capture of 10 of the St. Albans robbers.

20. Skirmishing between the Little and Big Blue river, Mo.

21. A very gallant fight between Little Blue river and Independence, Mo. Fed. troops fought Price's army 5 hours. The Union forces evacuated Independence, falling back on the Big Blue.

22. Col. Emmerson was attacked at Bryan Ford, Mo., by a heavy column of rebels, at 10 A. M. At 3 P. M. the rebs forced the ford. Fed troops fought the rebels until after dark, driving them 4 miles. Gen. Pleasanton pursued Price with 2,000 men, fought him on the battle-field of the day before, drove him from Independence, and pursued him sharply Pleasanton captured a large number of prisoners and 3 pieces of artillery.

25. Price defeated at Fort Scott Road, losing camp equipage, 20 wagons of plunder, 1 gun, and cattle.

25. Price driven from Mine Creek by Pleasanton, and loses 1,000 prisoners, and 1,500 stand of arms. Gens. Marmaduke and Cabell captured.

27. An advance in force on a reconnoissance, made by Warren's corps of Grant's army. In the evening the enemy attacked Hancock's corps vigorously, but were repulsed. Feds. retire. Union loss 3,000. Reb. loss 1,500.

27. The reb. ram Albemarle sunk by Lieut. Cushing, in the Roanoke river.

27. Arrest of Col. North on charges of fraud in the matter of soldiers' votes.

27. Price forced to retreat from Marais des Cygnes, Ark.

28. Reb. Gen. Forrest captured a Fed. gunboat and 3 transports at Fort Hieman, on the Tennessee river.

28. Price again defeated at Newtonia, destroying more wagons, and losing 250 men.

28-30. Rhoddy's cavalry attack Col. Morgan's colored troops at Decatur, and lose 400 prisoners and many killed and wounded. Union loss 100.

28. Gen. Gillem had a fight with the rebels under Vaughn at Norristown, East Tenn., completely routing them, and capturing 200 prisoners and 8 pieces of artillery.

28. A reb. force of 2,500 attacked Fayetteville, Ark., but was repulsed with heavy loss.

29. Maryland proclaimed a Free State by Gov. Bradford.

30. Fed. fleet shelled Plymouth, N. C.

31. Nevada admitted as a State by proclamation of the President

31. Capture of reb. batteries and their ordnance and ordnance stores, at Plymouth, N. C.

Nov. 3. The rebel army under Hood attempted to cross the Tennessee, near the mouth of the Blue Water, and were repulsed by Gen. Sherman.

3. The rebels bombarded Fayetteville, Ark.

4. Johnsonville, Tenn., a depot for Fed. supplies on the Tennessee river, was attacked and destroyed by rebels under Col. Forrest, and $1,500,000 value of property destroyed. 3 "tin-clad" gunboats and 7 transports were destroyed by the rebels.

4. The siege of Fayetteville, Ark., by the rebels, raised.

4. Revelation by one of the conspirators of a plot to overthrow the Govern

ment, release and arm the rebel prisoners, and kill Gov. Morton, of Ind.

Nov. 5. Gen. Butler assumed command of the troops arrived and to arrive in New York city to protect the city during election.

5. Rebels unsuccessfully attack Fort Sedgwick, on Jerusalem Plank Road, south-east end of Petersburg, Va. Union loss, 70. Rebel, 120.

6. Rebels attack Mott's and Gibson's pickets; capture 30 and a mile of intrenchments, but are driven out and lose 47 prisoners. Several such attacks and repulses at this time.

7. A rebel attack on Fed. pickets south of Atlanta.

8. Atlanta attacked by the rebs. under Gen. Iverson.

8. President Lincoln reelected, and Andrew Johnson elected Vice-President of United States. Hon. Reuben E. Fenton elected Governor of New York, over Seymour.

8. Gen. McClellan resigns his commission in the U. S. army.

8. Sheridan created Major-General of regular army.

9. Sheridan moved all his army back to Newtown from Cedar Creek.

9. Advance and repulse of a small reb. force near Fort Steadman, army of the Potomac.

10. Arrest on board of the vessel, of a party of rebels, conspiring to seize the Panama Railroad Co.'s steamship Salvador, on the Pacific.

10. Rebels engaged 2d corps' pickets all night, without success, on this and 2 next nights.

11. U. S. S. Tulip destroyed by boiler explosion off Ragged Point. 49 officers and men killed (all of crew but 10).

11. Reconnoissance by the rebels in the Shenandoah Valley.

11. Commencement of the burning of Atlanta, Ga.

12. Burning of Atlanta continued. The public buildings destroyed.

12. About 10,000 prisoners exchanged near Fort Pulaski.

12-16. Several unimportant skirmishes between Gen. Sheridan and rebel Gen. Early. Both armies looking for winter quarters.

12. Rebel Gen. Lomax defeated near Nineveh, Va., by Powell, losing 150 prisoners and 2 guns.

12. Custer captures 150 and Merritt about 200 prisoners on reconnoissance from Cedar creek.

13. Battle of Bull's Gap. Gen. Gillem defeated with loss of baggage train, and all his artillery.

13. Gen. Sherman's right wing, under Gen. Howard, moved out of Atlanta and began its march through Ga.

14. Gen. Sherman's left wing left Atlanta.

14. A division of Price's rebel army assaulted the works at Fayetteville, Ark., but were repulsed.

15. The last of Sherman's army left Atlanta.

16. Gen. Sherman's right wing passed through Jonesboro', Ga.

16. The rebel cavalry under Wheeler, engaged Fed. cavalry at Bear Creek Station, Ga.

16. Jackson, Ga., reached by Sherman's right wing.

16. Howard drives rebel Gen. Iverson at Rough and Ready.

17. Part of Butler's picket line captured, at night, near Chester's Station, Va.

17. A column of Sherman's army occupied McDonough, Ga.

17. Fed. cavalry occupied Griffin, Ga.

17. Sherman's left wing reached Covington, Ga., the cavalry pushing on to Social Circle.

18. Sherman's cavalry drove Wheeler out of Barnesville, Ga.

18. Gov. Brown and the Georgia Legislature fled from Milledgeville, Ga.

18. Exchange of prisoners at Savannah.

18. Macon railroad cut by Slocum at Forsyth.

19. Gov. Brown, of Georgia, issued a proclamation, ordering a levy *en masse* to oppose Sherman.

19. The advance of Beauregard's army at Waynesboro', Tenn. Beauregard's headquarters at Corinth, Miss., and Hood's at Florence.

19. Mosby's force captured a party of Union cavalry in Va.

19. Madison captured by Sherman. Depots, &c., burned.

20. Gen. Gillem's retreating force arrives at Knoxville.

20. Sherman crossed the Oconee, arriving at Greensboro'.

20. Gen. Sherman attacked East Macon, Ga. His troops crossed the Ocmulgee river, and his cavalry advanced to Griswoldsville, 8 miles E. of Macon, Ga.

21. Thomas' army at Pulaski.

21. Rebels badly whipped at Liberty, La., losing 3 guns and 200 prisoners.

21. Heavy skirmishing near Cumberland Gap.

21. Gen. Sherman's right wing captured Milledgeville, Ga. Gordon, Ga., occupied. Slocum's column reached Etonville, Ga.

22. Battle of Rood's Hill, Va., between Sheridan's and Early's forces. Union troops retreated.

22. The rebel armies under Hood and Beauregard, having been reinforced by 9,000 men, advanced and encamped 20 miles from Pulaski, Tenn. Gen. Thomas fell back to Franklin.

22. Sherman's rear guard at Griswoldville attacked. Gen. Slocum's column reached Milledgeville, Ga., where both wings united.

22. Sheridan reconnoiters towards Rood's Hill, where rebels are found in force. Rest of Early's army at Mt. Jackson and Newmarket.

23. Fed. forces withdrew from Pulaski, Tenn.

23. Gen. Sherman's cavalry occupied Toomsboro', on the Georgia Central railroad.

23. Fight near Griswoldville, Ga.

23. Hood's infantry at Waynesboro' and Lawrenceburg.

23. Fight at the Oconee river, Ga.

24. Second day of fighting up the Oconee river, Ga.

24. Severe skirmishing near Columbia, Tenn.

24. Sherman's rear guard left Milledgeville, Ga.

24. Slocum's column at Devereaux, Ga.

24. Fed. troops made a flank movement on Jackson, Miss.

24. Potomac, James, and Valley armies celebrate Thanksgiving with aid of thousands of turkeys and other delicacies from New York, &c.

25. Severe fighting west of Columbia, Tenn., between Hood's and Thomas' armies. Thomas falls back to Franklin.

25. A large number of Fed. prisoners confined at Salisbury, N. C., attempted to escape, but were overpowered by the guard, who opened upon them with grape and canister.

25. Cavalry battle at Sandersville, Ga.

25. Rebel attempt to burn New York. 15 hotels, Barnum's Museum, and shipping fired.

26–29. Decatur besieged by Beauregard, who is repulsed, losing 500 men.

26. Columbia, Tenn., evacuated by Gen. Thomas' army.

26. Gen. Slocum's column of Sherman's army at Warrenton, Ga.

26. Gen. Howard's column reached Sandersville, Ga., and cut the railroad.

27. Fed. stores and sick and wounded removed from Columbia, Tenn., to Nashville.

27. Capture of Roger A. Pryor near Petersburg, Va.

27. Gen. Canby's troops reached and destroyed Big Black bridge on the Mississippi Central railroad.

27. Steamer Greyhound burned on James river.

28. Rosser captures Fed Fort Kelly, at New Creek, Va., with guns and prisoners.

28. Fed. forces evacuate Columbia, Tenn.

29. Sharp fight at Spring Hill, 12 miles south of Franklin, Tenn. Fed. cavalry were driven back on the infantry, who checked the progress of the rebels.

29. Gen. Foster's expedition, cooperating with Sherman, landed at Broad river.

30. Battle of Franklin, Tenn. The rebels under Hood attacked Thomas' army at Franklin, but were repulsed at all points. The rebels commenced advancing on Fed. lines at 4 P. M. They charged furiously on the lines, but were driven back and a great victory gained. Rebel loss, 5,000 killed and wounded, and 1,000 prisoners. Fed. loss, 1,000. Gen. A. J. Smith's army passed through Nashville and reinforced Thomas.

30. Battle of Grahamsville, on the Charleston and Savannah railroad.

30. Howard's column of Sherman's army passed through Louisville, Ga.

30. A cavalry expedition arrived at Tangipahoe, La.

30. Hon. Joseph Holt appointed Attorney-General U. S.

Dec. 1. The army near Nashville engaged in heavy skirmishes.

1. Death of Hon. Wm. L. Dayton, U. S. Minister to France.

1. Blockade of Norfolk, Fernandina, and Pensacola ceased.

1. Gen. Banks resumes command of Department of the Gulf.

1. Creek Station, Va., captured by Gen. Gregg. 2 guns, 190 prisoners, depot burned, &c.

2. Sherman's army passed through Millen, Ga.

3. Sherman attacked by Wheeler near Haynesborough, Ga.

3. Portions of Hood's army cross the Tenn., between Florence and Decatur.

3. An expedition sent from Roanoke Island, N. C., which met with perfect success in destroying rebel property.

Dec. 3. Heavy skirmishing before Nashville, Tenn.

4. Merritt's expedition in London Valley, Va., returns with 2,000 cattle and 1,000 sheep. The Valley stripped of stock and forage.

4. Lieut.-Com. Fitch defeated and drove the left wing of Hood's army on the Cumberland river, with heavy loss to the rebels. He also recaptured 2 transports.

4. Capture of rebel works and cannon near Pocotaligo, S. C., by Gen. Foster's troops.

4. Cavalry battle in Ga. Sherman's army started for Savannah.

5. U. S. Houses of Congress meet in 2d Session, 38th Congress.

5. Blockhouses at Murfreesboro' unsuccessfully attacked by rebels.

5. Brig Lizzie Freeman captured by pirates off Warwick river. Passengers robbed; 1 murdered.

6. Ex-Secretary Chase appointed Chief Justice Supreme Court.

6. Hood skirmishing 5 miles from Nashville.

6. Rebels defeated near the Charleston and Savannah railroad.

7. Rosseau routs Forrest near Murfreesboro', capturing 207 prisoners and 14 cannon.

8. Rebels establish a battery on Cumberland river. Gunboats fail to dislodge it.

8. Five divisions, under Maj.-Gen. Warren, made a raid on the Weldon (N. C.) railroad. The Nottoway was reached about midday, Dec. 8th, and destroyed; thence the railroad track was destroyed nearly to Bellfield Station, 20 miles south.

9. 500 Indians killed near Fort Lyon by Col. Chivington's force.

9. 4,000 rebels, under Gen. Lyon, cross the Cumberland river, 20 miles above Fort Donelson.

9. Reconnoissance of Gen. Miles to Hatcher's Run, on the right of the rebel forces defending Petersburg. He captures the rebel works and holds them during the night.

9. Direct communication with Sherman re-established. His army in the vicinity of Savannah.

9. A reconnoitering expedition, under Col. Frencle, leaves Plymouth, N. C.

10. Gen. Sherman's troops 5 miles from Savannah.

10. Rebel reconnoissance toward the army of the Potomac.

10. Gen. Warren commences starting homeward, and in the evening reaches Sussex C. H. Destroyed, during the trip, over 20 miles of the Weldon railroad, all the stations and depots along the line of march, numerous mills, barns, and dwellings. Entire loss in the expedition about 40 killed and wounded, and a few missing.

10. Gen. Miles returns to his camp. The rebels attack him, but are repulsed.

10. The gunboat Otsego sunk by a rebel torpedo in the Roanoke river.

12. Arrival of Gen. Howard's messengers at Hilton Head, S. C.

12. Skirmishing between the National and rebel forces before Nashville. The rebels fall back to their main line.

12. Expedition under Gen. Burbridge starts from Bean's Station, E. Tenn.

12. Fight at Kingston, E. Tenn. The rebel Col. Morgan and 85 of his men captured.

13. The St. Albans robbers released by the Canadian Judge Coursol.

13. The rebels before Nashville reoccupy their advance works.

13. Gen. Burbridge routs the rebel brigade under Basil Duke, at Kingsport, E. Tenn. Rebel loss, 150 men and the train.

13. Gen. Hazen's division, of the 15th corps, captures Fort McAllister, commanding the entrance of the Ogeechee river, 15 miles southwest of Savannah.

13. Sherman's report on his great march. "Not a wagon lost on the trip." 200 miles of railroad destroyed. Total loss during the march about 1,000.

13. Departure from Hampton Roads of land and naval forces under Gen. Butler and Ad. Porter.

13. A raiding expedition under Gen. Robinson leaves New Orleans for Ala.

14. An expedition threatening Mobile reached Pascagoula.

14. Gen. Thomas assumes the offensive.

14. Capture of Bristol by Gen. Burbridge. 300 rebels captured.

15. The St. Albans raiders ordered by the Attorney-Gen. of Canada to be rearrested.

15. Raid of Gen. Stoneman in Southwest Va. Surprise and capture of Glade Springs, 13 miles from Abingdon.

15. Defeat of Forrest near Murfreesboro'. Loss, 1,500 killed and wounded.

15. Raiding expedition of General Granger into Alabama starts from East Pensacola, Fla.

15. Battle of Nashville commenced. Gen. Thomas attacked Hood's army at 2 A.M. Fed. lines advanced on the right

5 miles. The rebels were driven from the river, from their intrenchments, from a range of hills, on which their left rested, and forced back upon the right and centre. The rebels lost 17 cannon and 1,500 prisoners, and a whole line of earthworks. In the night Hood withdrew his right from the river.

16. Another battle near Nashville. Hood completely routed. Prisoners and cannon captured on every part of the field. Hood's loss before Nashville, 13,189 prisoners, 2,207 deserters, 30 guns, 7,000 small arms. An entire rebel division (Ed. Johnson's) captured. Union loss, about 6,500. Total loss of the rebs. about 23,000.

17. Gen. McCook defeated rebel Gen. Lyon in a sharp fight at Ashbyville, Ky.

17. Fed. troops entered Wytheville, S. W. Va., destroyed the depot and other buildings, and injured the lead mines in the vicinity.

17. A detachment of Union artillery cut up near Millwood, Va.

17. The rebel army of Hood driven through and beyond Franklin. 1,500 wounded rebels captured in the hospital of Franklin.

18. Hood's army driven as far as Spring Hill, 30 miles from Nashville. The rebel Gen. Quarles captured.

18. The rebel raiders in Ky. defeated at Hopkinsville by Gen. McCook. All their cannon captured.

19. Gen. Custer's cavalry started on an expedition up the Shenandoah Valley.

19. A call and draft for 300,000 men. All soldiers fit for duty ordered to join their regiments.

19. Hood driven to Duck river. 9,000 rebels captured from Dec. 15 to Dec. 19, and 61 (out of 66) pieces of artillery.

20. Gen. Sherman demanded the surrender of Savannah. The city was evacuated by Hardee's army in the night. The rebels blew up their rams at Savannah.

20. Capture of rebel salt-works at Saltville, Va.

21. Admiral Farragut appointed Vice-Admiral.

21. Gen. Custer's force in the Shenandoah Valley engaged with rebel cavalry.

21. Occupation of Savannah by Sherman. He captures 800 prisoners, 150 pieces of artillery, 33,000 bales of cotton, 3 steamers.

21. Madison C. H., Va., occupied by Gens. Torbert and Powell.

21. Gen. Grierson starts from Memphis for a raid on the Mobile and Ohio R. R.

22. Loss of the U. S. transport North American, by foundering, at sea. 194 lives lost.

23. Fight near Gordonsville, Va.

24. The fleet of Ad. Porter before Fort Fisher, N. C. Furious attack on the fort.

25. Attack on Fort Fisher renewed. 3 brigades of Union infantry landed 2 and a half miles above the fort. They are repulsed, and reembark.

25. Heavy cannonading on Broad riv., between Sherman's and Hardee's forces.

26. Ensign Blume cuts loose and takes out from Galveston harbor the blockade running schooner Sallie.

26. The blockade-runner Julia, with 450 bales of cotton, captured by the gunboat Accacia.

26. A dispatch from Hood reports his army south of the Tenn.

27. Destruction of a fort and artillery at Chickasaw, Ala.

28. Hood's rear guard crosses the Tenn. river at Bainbridge.

1865.

Jan. 1. The head of Dutch Gap Canal, Va., blown out, but without effect.

1. Admiral Farragut commissioned Vice-Admiral.

1. San Jacinto, sloop-of-war, wrecked on Bahama Banks.

2. Passport system established on U. S. frontier.

2. Steamship George Washington burned at New York. Loss $500,000.

3. Hood's pontoon train captured.

4. Rebel powder and torpedoes destroyed on the Rappahannock.

5. John Thompson expelled, for disloyalty, from the Missouri Legislature.

5. Gen. Grierson arrives at Vicksburg, having destroyed on his raid 70 miles of the Mobile and Ohio railroad, and 30 miles of the Miss. Central, and captured 600 prisoners and 1,000 negroes.

5. "Sue Munday," a guerrilla, murders 5 soldiers near Lebanon, Ky.

6. Owensboro', Ky., evacuated by the rebels.

6. Magruder's guerrillas burn the Lebanon train, and murder 4 discharged soldiers.

6. Gen. Sherman and his army crossed the Savannah river.

6. Missouri Constitutional Convention organized.

6. Steamship Knickerbocker, of N. Y., sunk on the Chesapeake.

6. Steamer Potomac, of N. Y., burned off Cape Elizabeth.

6. Gen. Terry's expedition sailed for Wilmington from Fortress Monroe.

Jan. 7. Gen. Thomas appointed Maj.-Gen. U. S. A., vice Fremont, resigned.

7. Julesburg, Colorado Territory, attacked by Indians, who were defeated, after killing 19 soldiers and citizens, and destroying much property.

7. Hon. F. P. Blair left for Richmond, on a self-constituted Peace mission.

8. Gen. Butler relieved from command of the Army of the James.

8. Steamer Venango captured and burned by guerrillas on the Mississippi river.

8. The steamship Melville foundered at sea; over 60 drowned.

8. Gen. Terry's expedition arrived off Beaufort, N. C.

9. Picket line of Second Division A. C. Potomac army attacked.

10. Rebel storehouses, &c., at Charlotte, N C, burned.

11. Foraging party on Jerusalem Plank Road, Va., repulsed by bushwhackers.

11. Beverley, W. Va., captured and partially burned by Gen. Rosser. 200 Fed. soldiers captured.

11. Gov. Thomas Swan, of Md., inaugurated.

11. H. S. Foote arrested by rebel authorities while attempting to escape from Richmond.

12. Missouri declared a Free State.

13. Disembarkation of troops to attack Fort Fisher.

14. A reconnoissance pushed within 500 yards of Fort Fisher, and small work captured.

14. Gen. Sherman recommences movement from Savannah.

14. Pocotaligo, S. C., captured by Fed. Gen. Blair.

14. Slavery abolished by Tenn. State Convention.

14. Steamship Rebecca Clyde sent from N. Y. with relief for Savannah.

15. Gens. Sherman, Sheridan, and Thomas confirmed Maj.-Gens. U. S. A. and Gen. Hancock, Brig.-Gen. U. S. A.

15. Rebs. defeated at Dardanelle, Ark.

15. Grand assault on Fort Fisher, which is captured with entire garrison. Union loss 110 killed, 536 wounded. Reb. loss 2,500 prisoners, 72 guns.

16. Fort Fisher magazine explodes, with great loss of life.

16. Rebels blow up and abandon Fort Caswell and works on Smith's Isl., N. C.

16. S. S. Cox's Peace Resolution tabled by House.

16. Reb. Congress debate question of Peace.

16. Mr. Blair returns from Richmond.

16. The monitor Patapsco sunk by a rebel torpedo in Charleston Harbor. 60 of the officers and crew were lost.

17. Steamers Chickamauga and Patapsco blown up by rebels.

18. Gen. Ord placed in command of the Army of the James.

18. Smithville, N. C., captured.

18. The Harriet Lane, rebel vessel, destroyed at Havana.

18. 200 of rebel Gen. Forrest's cavalry defeated, 10 miles from Columbus, Ky.

18. Gen. Terry appointed Maj.-Gen.

19. Fatal explosion at Hazard Powder Mills.

19. Gen. Schofield captured Fort Anderson, the main defence of Wilmington.

20. Rebel Secretary Seddon resigns.

20. Gen. Schofield fighting on this and next day at Wilmington.

21. Rebel Gen. Roddy pardoned by Pres. Lincoln.

22. Wilmington captured by Gen. Schofield; rebels retreat towards Goldsboro'.

23. Rebel Gen. Hood superseded by Dick Taylor.

23. Charles A. Dana appointed Assistant-Secretary of War.

24. Rebel ironclads attempt descent of the James; are driven back, and the Virginia blown up.

24. H. S. Foote expelled by the rebel Congress.

24. The Smithsonian Institution destroyed by fire.

25. Mr. Blair returns from Richmond, his Peace Mission having failed.

25. Reb. Gen. Lee appointed General-in-Chief by Jeff. Davis.

26. Steamer Eclipse explodes her boiler on the Tennessee, killing 140 persons.

26. The steamer Dai Ching attacked by rebels on the Combahee river; gets aground, is abandoned and burned.

26. Emancipation Acts of Missouri and Tennessee celebrated in New Orleans.

26. Part of the 75th Ohio captured by treachery.

27. Gen. Robert E. Breckinridge appointed rebel Secretary of War.

28. Rebel House resolves to arm negroes.

28. Valley Station, Omaha, attacked by Indians; 12 men killed and 650 head of cattle stolen.

30. Messrs. Stephens, Campell and Hunter enter Union lines as Peace Commissioners.

30. Jackson Burroughs, a Treasury clerk, shot by Miss Mary Harris.

31. The Anti-Slavery Constitutional Amendment passed by House, 19 to 56.

Feb. 1. Secretary Seward leaves for Fortress Monroe to meet rebel Commissioners.

1. Sherman's whole army in motion for Savannah.

1. Constitutional Amendment ratified by Maryland House and Illinois.

2. President Lincoln proceeds to meet rebel Commissioners.

2. Constitutional Amendment ratified by Michigan and Rhode Island; also by New York Senate.

2. Julesburg, Omaha, fort attacked by Indians, and station burned.

2. Midway, Ky., robbed and partially burned by guerrillas.

3. Sherman's advance crosses the Salkchatchie river.

3. Constitutional Amendment ratified by Massachusetts, West Virginia and Pennsylvania; also by New York Assembly and Maryland Senate.

4. Failure of the peace negotiations. President Lincoln and Secretary Seward return to Washington.

4. Rebels flanked at Branchville by Gen. Sherman.

4. Lieut. Cushing with 4 boats and 50 men takes possession of All Saints, on Little river, S. C., capturing a large amount of cotton.

4. Great battle at Mud Springs, Mo., between Col. Livingstone and 2,000 Indians, who are defeated with loss.

5. The New York pilot-boat Favorita sunk by collision at sea.

5. Rebels driven from rifle-pits at Rowanty creek, Va., by 5th Corps; and the 2d Corps advance to Hatcher's Run. Severe fighting at both places. Repulse of rebels.

6. Harry Gilmer, the notorious guerrilla, captured near Moorfield, Va.

6. Constitutional Amendment ratified by Missouri.

6. Severe fight at Dabney's Mills. The rebels driven back, but in their turn force back Crawford's division, to be again finally driven back. Casualties in 5th Corps, in 2 days, 500. In the 2d Corps, 750.

6. Jefferson Davis makes a great war speech at Richmond.

6. Gen. Ord assigned to command Department of Virginia.

6. 2 blockade runners captured at Galveston by Ensign French.

7. Rebels attack the 5th Corps, and are repulsed.

7. Kilpatrick's cavalry drives rebels from Blackville, S. C.

7. Constitutional Amendment ratified by Maine.

7. Rebel Senate votes against arming negroes.

7. 225 rebel prisoners at Camp Chase refuse to be returned to the rebel army by exchange.

8. Occupation of Branchville, S. C.

8. Lieut. Cushing, with 15 men, captures Shallotte, N. C.

8. Ohio, Minnesota and Kansas ratify Constitutional Amendment. Delaware refuses.

8. The electoral vote for President and Vice-President counted in the House of Representatives, the result being 212 votes for Lincoln and Johnson, and 21 for McClellan and Pendleton.

8. Great fire in Philadelphia, commencing in petroleum oil warehouse. 47 buildings destroyed, and about 15 persons burned.

9. A large force of Indians at Mud Springs again defeated by Col. Livingston.

10. Constitutional Amendment ratified by Indiana.

10. Rebels repulsed from Fort Meyer, Fla.

10. Gen. Gillmore resumes command Department of the South.

10. Gen. Grierson confirmed Major-General by Senate.

10. Gen. Sherman's troops occupy James Island, 2 miles from Charleston.

11. Gen. Terry advances towards Wilmington, N. C., and engages rebel works. Rebel loss, 100. Fed., 60.

11. Wheeler defeated by Kilpatrick at Aiken, S. C. Feds. occupy the town.

11. Gen. Lee assumes command of the rebel armies.

11. Gen. Terry commences his advance toward Wilmington.

13. Louisiana House ratified the Constitutional Amendment.

15. Destruction of Charlotte Iron Furnace, on Water Lick creek, by 1st and 6th Michigan cavalry.

15. F. W. Smith, a Boston merchant, fined $25,000 for frauds on government.

16. Slavery Constitutional Amendment ratified by Nevada.

17. Charleston evacuated by rebels, who burned vast quantities of stores, &c.; an explosion of powder kills 200 persons. 2 rebel ironclads blown up.

17. Columbia, S. C., captured by Gen. Sherman.

17. Rebel flag of truce boat, William

Ailison, blown up by rebel torpedo on the James river.

Feb. 17. Charlotte, N. C., crowded by rebel refugees and placed under martial law.

17. Pres. Lincoln ordered an extra session of Congress, to commence March 4.

17. Louisiana Senate ratifies the Constitutional Amendment.

18. Charleston occupied by Union forces. 200 pieces of artillery and much ammunition captured.

18. Gen. Lee calls upon rebel House for negro soldiers.

19. Gen. Schofield and Admiral Porter capture Fort Anderson, N. C., after severe bombardment. Fed. loss, 30.

20. Gen. Cox routs rebels 4 miles from Wilmington, N. C.

20. Repulse of rebel attack on Fort Myers, Fla.

21. The rebels evacuate Wilmington at night, after burning cotton, resin, &c

21. Gens. Crook and Kelly captured in their beds at Cumberland, Va.

21. Wisconsin ratifies the Constitutional Amendment.

21. Bridgeport, Ky., almost destroyed by fire.

22. Gen. Schofield occupies Wilmington.

22. Constitutional Amendment rejected by Kentucky.

22. Georgetown, S. C., surrenders.

23. Capture of Camden, S. C.

23. Gen. Johnston appointed to command troops operating against Sherman.

23. A passenger train from Nashville captured by guerrillas.

24. Columbia, S. C., burned.

25. Fatal explosion at Dupont's Powder Mills, at Wilmington, Del.

26. 20 guerrillas captured in Ky., tried by drum-head court martial, and shot about this date.

27. Sheridan moved from Winchester with 10,000 men.

27. Hickman, Ky., robbed and partly burned by guerrillas.

27. Flagship Arizona burned at New Orleans.

28. Six hundred million loan bill passed by House.

28. Lord Lyons resigns as British Minister to Washington, and is succeeded by Sir Frederick Bruce.

28. Admiral Thatcher takes command of the West Gulf Squadron.

March 1. Sheridan secures the bridge over the Shenandoah at Mt. Crawford.

1. The 600,000,000 loan bill passed by Senate.

1. The Constitutional Amendment rejected by N. J. House.

1. Lovelaceville, Ky., robbed by guerrillas.

1. Gen. Bailey starts on a cavalry raid from Baton Rouge.

2. Sheridan captures nearly the whole force of Early, consisting of 1,800 men and 11 guns, between Charlottesville and Staunton.

2. Steamer James Watson sunk with government stores on the Miss. 30 lives lost.

3. Skirmish between Sherman's cavalry and that of Wade Hampton. The rebel Col. Aiken killed.

3. Occupation of Cheraw, S. C., by Sherman's advance.

3. Close of the 38th Congress.

3. Charlottesville, Va., captured by Sheridan.

3. Ten soldiers killed by train on the Opelousas railroad. 40 wounded.

4. Reinauguration of Pres. Lincoln.

4. U. S. transport steamer Thorne blown up by a torpedo in Cape Fear riv.

4. Parson Brownlow elected Governor of Tenn.

4. Rebels worsted at Natural Bridge, Fla.

6. Expedition up the Rappahannock. Capture of 400 prisoners and 95 tons of tobacco at Fredericksburg. Extensive contraband trade broken up.

7. Hugh McCulloch confirmed Secretary of the Treasury, succeeding Hon. W. P. Fessenden.

7. Five persons killed by collision on the Camden & Amboy R. R.

8. Sherman at Laurel Hill, N. C.

8. The rebel Senate passes the negro enlistment bill.

8. Engagement between Cox and Bragg 4 miles from Kinston, N. C. Bragg captures a large number of prisoners and 3 pieces of artillery, but is ultimately driven back.

8. The passport restrictions to Canada removed.

9. A transport, with 2,000 Union troops, enters Mobile Bay through Grant's Pass.

9. Steamboat Munroe captured by rebels on the Big Black river.

9. Senator Harlan confirmed Sec. of the Interior, vice Mr. Usher, resigned.

10. Jefferson Davis' fast day celebrated by the rebels.

10. Gen. Sheridan at Columbia, Fluvanna Co., Va., 50 miles west of Richmond. He reports having destroyed all the locks for a considerable distance on

the James river canal, an immense number of bridges, many miles of railroad, mills, factories, and vast quantities of merchandise; also, having captured 12 canal boats, 14 pieces of artillery, and an abundance of provisions.

10. Desperate attempt of Bragg to break the National lines at Kinston, N. C. The rebels lose 1,200 killed and wounded, and 400 prisoners. 2,000 rebs. captured from March 8 to 10. The entire Union losses about 1,000.

10. Gen. Lee urges the work of raising and organizing negro troops.

10. Gen. Stoneman, with 4,000 men, starts on a cavalry raid from Knoxville, Tenn.

10. Engagement between the cavalry forces of Wade Hampton and Kilpatrick near Fayetteville, N. C. Nearly all the members of Kilpatrick's staff captured. The rebels finally beaten back, and most of the officers recaptured.

11. Extra sesions of the U. S. Senate closed.

11. Sheridan at Beaver Mills Aqueduct, 20 miles north of Richmond.

11. Hoke's division of rebels repulsed at Kinston. Loss, over 2,000. Union loss, 300.

11. 21 Union vessels in sight of Mobile, Ala.

11. Sherman arrives at Fayetteville. Reports having captured at Columbia, S. C., 43 pieces of artillery; at Cheraw, S. C., 25 pieces, and 3,600 barrels of gunpowder; at Fayetteville, N. C., 20 pieces, and large quantities of ammunition.

12. Occupation of Kinston by Schofield. The rebels throw many pieces of artillery into the river, and burn the ram Neuse.

12. Gen. Stoneman at Wytheville, Chriansburg, and Salem, Va.

13. Sheridan tears up the railroad between Richmond and Hanover.

15. Fight at Brandenburg, Ky., between a small Union garrison and a party of rebels.

15. Sheridan reports having rendered useless the James river canal as far as Goochland.

16. Rebels blow up Fort Hell at Petersburg, with little effect.

16. Sue Monday (Jerome Clark), the notorious guerrilla, hung at Louisville.

16. Lieut.-Com. Eastman destroys 3 rebel schooners in Mattox Creek, Va.; large stocks of tobacco, guns, ammunition captured.

16. Fight at Averasboro', N. C., (20 miles north of Fayetteville), between a portion of Sherman's army and the rebs. under Hardee. Union loss, 74 killed, 477 wounded. Rebel loss, 327 killed and wounded, and 373 prisoners.

17. Mr. Bigelow succeeds Mr. Dayton as Minister to France.

17. Mohawk Valley inundated. Immense damage to property.

17. Formal notice of the termination of the Reciprocity Treaty given by Mr. Adams to the British government.

17. Gen. Canby's movement against Mobile commences. Portions of the 13th and 23d corps in motion.

17. Gen. Wilson leaves Nashville with 15,000 men on a cavalry expedition into Central Ala. and Ga.

18. Joe Johnston attacks Sherman's advance at Bentonville, captures 3 guns, and drives it back on main body.

18. Reb. Congress adjourns in a panic.

18. Gen. Sheridan's advance reaches White House, on the Pamunkey river. His entire loss during the raid 50 men and 2 officers.

19. The rebel Congress issue a despairing appeal to the people.

19. Engagement at Bentonville, N. C., between Gen. Sherman and Gen. Johnston. Repulse of the rebels. Union loss, 1,646. Rebel loss, 167 dead, 1,625 prisoners.

19. The rebel schooner Anna Dale, in Matagorda Bay, cut loose from under 2 rebel batteries and burned.

20. Gen. Stoneman's expedition moves from E. Tenn., and pushing to Salisbury, defeats Gardiner, capturing 14 guns and 1,364 prisoners.

20. Gen. Steele's forces leave Pensacola, Florida.

21. Goldsboro', N. C., occupied by part of Schofield's army.

21. Johnston retreats at night from Bentonville, leaving his wounded.

21. The rebels flanked and overpowered at Mount Olive, N. C.

21. Roddy's division of Forrest's cavalry routed by Gen. Wilson's forces at Marion and Plantersville.

22. Sherman forms junction with Schofield at Goldsboro'.

22. McDougal's gang of Ky. guerrillas broken up west of Paducah. He and 20 others killed.

22. Gen. Wilson moves from Chickasaw, Ala., toward rebel Gen. Forrest.

23. Passenger train on Nashville railroad burned by Harper's guerrillas. 16 persons wounded.

24. Sheridan moved from White House toward Petersburg.

Mar. 25. Capture of the Union Fort Stedman, of Gen. McLaughlin and 500 men, in front of Petersburg, by 3 reb. divisions under Gordon. They are driven out again by Gen. Hartrauft, with a loss of 1,758 prisoners, and total loss of 2,500. Total Union loss about 1,500.

25. Assault on the rebel lines by the 2d and 6th corps. The first line of the rebel works captured and held.

25. Engagement between the Union cavalry and the 6th and 8th Ala. cavalry at Mitchell's Creek. The rebel General Canton, with 275 men, captured.

25. Robert C. Kennedy, the rebel spy and incendiary, hung at Fort Lafayette.

26. Judge Radcliffe, of Madison Co., Ark., hung by rebels near his own home.

26. Sheridan's cavalry reaches City Point.

27. Sherman visits Grant at City Pt.

27. Spanish Fort and Fort Blakely, Mobile, invested by Union troops.

27. Boone, N. C., captured by General Stoneman.

27. Gen. Getty's division, of the 6th corps, attacked by 400 reb. sharpshooters. Repulse of the rebels.

27. Sheridan's cavalry takes position in Gregg's old cavalry camp, on the left and rear of Grant's army.

27. Portions of the 24th and 25th corps cross the James to join Meade's army.

28. The monitors Milwaukee and Osage sunk by torpedoes in Mobile Bay.

29. The St. Albans raiders are released at Montreal.

29. Grant's army in motion.

29. Sheridan's command makes a detour to Dinwiddie C. H. Occupation of the town. Further advance on the Boydton Road. 2 corps of the infantry (2d and 5th) thrown across Hatcher's Run, the former on the Vaughan road, the latter on the Halifax road. Battle of Quaker road, near Gravelly Run, between Bushrod Johnson's rebels and the 5th corps. Rebels retire. Loss, 500 on each side.

30. The 2 armies before Petersburg, after severe skirmishing, confront each other their whole length.

30. A railway train robbed and burned by guerrillas near Cumberland, Va.

31. Gen. Warren attacked the enemy at White Oak road, but, after severe fighting, is forced back to his 3d division. The rebels are driven back with heavy loss, and White Oak road gained. Sheridan captures Five Forks, but is forced back to Dinwiddie C. H. Fed. loss, 2,500; rebs. less.

31. The transport Gen. Lyon burned off Hatteras, over 500 lives being lost.

April 1. Sheridan, reinforced by Warren, drives rebels to Five Forks, carries the position and captures over 5,000 prisoners and all their artillery. Fed. loss, 3,000. This night Davis flies from Richmond.

1. Forrest defeated by Gen. Wilson at Ebenezer Church, Ala., losing 300 prisoners and 3 guns.

1. Boone, N. C., captured by Stoneman's advance.

1. Hazard Powder Mills, at Canton, Conn., blew up.

2. Rebel lines assaulted at Five Forks, and forced near Hatcher's Run; then the main line carried, and two strong works commanding south of Petersburg, were captured. The rebels south of Petersburg were severely beaten, and fled toward the Appomattox. At night, Lee evacuated Petersburg and Richmond, retreating toward Danville. Many thousands of prisoners were captured by the Union forces on this day.

2. Selma, defended by Forrest, captured by Gen. Wilson, with 3,000 prisoners, stores, &c. Forrest and Roddy taken prisoners.

3. Gen. Weitzel, with his colored troops, enters Richmond.

3. Richmond fired by rebels, and one-fourth of the city destroyed.

3. Fed. cavalry pursue rebels 20 miles from Richmond, Va. 2,000 prisoners taken.

4. Skirmishing by McKenzie's division with rebels at Bethany, Va.

4. Tuscaloosa captured and destroyed by Gen. Wilson.

4. The Harriet Deford captured by rebels on the Pawtuxet.

4. President Lincoln holds a levee in Jeff. Davis' house at Richmond.

5. Secretary Seward thrown from his carriage at Washington, breaking his arm and jaw.

5. Lee is intercepted by Sheridan at Burkesville, Va.

6. Lee is struck near Farmville, and gains partial success, but Sheridan defeats him at Sailors' creek, capturing over 6,000 prisoners, 16 guns, 400 wagons, &c. Rebel Gens. Ewell, Kershaw, Corse, and Custis Lee captured.

6. H. S. Foote returns to New York by the Etna.

6. Hedges and Downes, guerrillas, executed at Louisville.

6. J. L. Clinton, of Texas, robbed of $54,000 in gold by highwaymen.

7. Pursuit of Lee continued; he crossed to the north of the Appomattox, and is constantly harrassed. He is attacked by the 2d corps at Farmville. Gen. Grant writes him that escape is impossible, and proposes to receive his surrender.

8. Lee replies, inquiring terms of surrender. Sheridan makes more captures at Appomattox Station.

8. Spanish Fort, Mobile, bombarded. The rebels evacuate at night.

9. Gens. Grant and Lee meet at Appomattox Court House, and the rebel army of Northern Virginia, numbering 26,115 men, is surrendered, with its arms and material of war, and the officers and men paroled.

11. Mobile evacuated by the rebels.

11. Engagement at Sumter, S. C., between guerrillas and Union troops.

11. Fort Blakely, at Mobile, taken by assault, with 300 prisoners, and 32 cannon. Rebel loss in siege of Mobile, 500 in killed and wounded. Union loss, 2,000.

11. Lynchburg, Va., captured by Union scouting party.

12. Mobile occupied by Union forces.

12. Montgomery, Ala., surrenders to Gen. Wilson, with 2,700 prisoners and 100 guns.

12. A rebel force defeated at Grant's creek, near Salisbury, N. C., by General Stoneman. 1,400 rebels, and 14 cannon taken.

13. Sherman pushes forward against Johnston and occupies Raleigh.

13. The draft and recruiting ordered to cease.

14. President Lincoln shot at Ford's Theatre, by John Wilkes Booth, an actor. Secretary Seward attacked at his house, while in bed, and seriously wounded by another assassin, who also dangerously wounded Mr. Frederick Seward.

14. Correspondence opened between Sherman and Johnston on the latter's surrender.

14. Wilberforce University, Green Co., Ohio, burned.

14. The anniversary of the capture of Fort Sumter celebrated by imposing ceremonies at the fort, and replacing the flag by Gen. Anderson.

15. President Lincoln died at 7:20 o'clock, A. M., having remained insensible since his wound.

15. Vice-President Andrew Johnson becomes 17th President of the U. S.

16. Columbus and West Point, Ala., captured by assault of Gen. Wilson. 1,500 prisoners and 100,000 bales of cotton taken.

16. 1,500 prisoners, 52 guns, 2 gunboats and vast stores taken at Selma, and much railroad stock, &c.

17. Capture of Mrs. Surratt and Lewis Payne. Edward Spangler arrested, implicated in the murder of Pres. Lincoln.

18. Sherman agrees to suspension of hostilities with Johnston.

19. A. G. Atzeroth arrested near Germantown, Md.

19. Steamship blown up by torpedo in Dog river.

19. Funeral of President Lincoln in Washington.

20. Occupation of Macon, Ga., by Gen. Wilson. Gens. Howell Cobb, Gustavus W. Smith, Robertson, Mercer, and McCall, made prisoners. 132 guns in position, and 200 in arsenals, with immense amounts of ordnance and stores captured.

20. The War Department offers $50,000 for the arrest of Booth, and $25,000 each for the arrest of Atzeroth and Harold.

20. Rebel Secretary Mallory surrendered to the navy at Pensacola.

21. Sherman's agreement with Johnston disapproved by the President.

21. Proclamation of Gen. E. Kirby Smith. He asserts his ability to continue the rebellion.

22. Gen. Banks resumes command of the Gulf Department.

22. The Constitutional Amendment ratified by the New York Assembly.

22. The Mississippi Squadron flagship Black Hawk burned at Mound City.

22. Reception of the remains of President Lincoln at Philadelphia.

23. Jeff. Davis leaves Charlotte, N. C., for Georgia.

23. The rebel ram Webb escapes past the Union fleet on the Red river; is run ashore, deserted and blown up.

25. A collision on the Potomac, occurring between the steamer Massachusetts and a barge; many soldiers jump overboard in a panic, and 50 are drowned.

25. R. B. Hamilton, steamer, sunk by torpedo near Mobile. 15 persons killed.

26. Surrender of Gen. Johnston and his army, numbering about 27,500 men.

26. Funeral ceremonies of Pres. Lincoln in N. Y., and departure of his remains.

26. John Wilkes Booth and David C. Harrold, discovered in a barn of Garrett's farm, near Fredericksburg, Va. Booth refuses to surrender, and is killed by Sergt. Boston Corbett, of the 16th N. Y. cavalry; Harrold surrenders.

27. Railroad track near Charleston, S. C., torn up by guerrillas.

Apr. 28. Danville, Va., occupied by Gen. Wright. 13 locomotives, 117 box cars, ironwork, machinery, etc., were captured.

28. The boilers of the steamship Sultana, with 2,000 paroled soldiers, burst near Memphis; she then took fire; over 1,500 persons were burned to death or drowned.

29. Pres. Johnson removes trade restrictions over most of the south.

29. Armistice agreed upon between Gens. Dana and Dick Taylor.

30. The paroling of Gen Johnston's troops commenced at Greensboro'.

May 1. Reception of the remains of President Lincoln at Chicago.

1. Surrender of 1,200 of Morgan's old command to Gen. Hobson, at Mt. Sterling, Ky.

1. Tenn. Senate offer $5,000 reward for Ex-Gov. I. G. Harris.

2. Surrender of Jeff. Thompson to Capt. Mitchell, U. S. N.

2. Reward offered for the arrest of Jeff. Davis, J. Thompson, C. C. Clay, B. Tucker, G. N. Sanders and W. C. Cleary.

4. Burial of Abraham Lincoln in Oak Ridge Cemetery, near Springfield, Ill.

4. Rebel Gen. Dick Taylor surrendered to Gen. Canby all the remaining forces west of the Miss.

5. A train on the Ohio and Miss. railroad, 14 miles from Cincinnati, captured by 20 guerrillas.

9. The Confederate Com. Farrand surrenders 12 vessels, and all his command to Commander Edward Simpson, fleet Captain of the West Gulf squadron, at Nanna Hubba Bluff.

9. Pres. Johnson announces the war at an end, and rebel belligerent rights ceased.

9. Rebel Gen. Forrest disbands his troops, advising them to go home peaceably.

10. The trial of Pres. Lincoln's assassins commenced.

10. Jeff. Davis and the Confederate Postmaster, Gen. Reagan, captured at Irwinville, Ga., by Lieut.-Col. Pritchard, commanding the 4th Mich. cavalry.

10. The Confed. Gen. Sam. Jones surrenders his forces to a division of Gen. Wilson's cavalry.

10. Surrender of Capt. Mayberry, commanding the irregular bands of Confederates in Arkansas and Monroe Cos., Ark., at Pine Bluff.

11. A rebel camp at Palmetto Branch, Texas (15 miles above Brazos), captured and burned by Col. Barrett.

12. Engagement near Boco Chico between 400 Union troops under Col. Barrett and 500 Confed. cavalry under Gen. Slaughter. This was the last engagement of the war. Union loss, 70 men.

12. Surrender of the rebel forces under Gen. Wofford, in N. Ga., at Kingston.

13. R. M. T. Hunter, Ex-U. S. Senator, arrested for treason.

13. Over 30,000,000 of the Seven-Thirty Loan subscribed for on this day.

18. Dr. Luke P. Blackburn arrested at Montreal for plotting to infect N. Y. and other cities with yellow fever.

19. Jeff. Davis and his fellow prisoners arrived at Fortress Monroe.

20. Surrender of the ram Stonewall to the Spanish authorities in Cuba.

22. Belligerent rights withdrawn, and all ports opened, but Texas, by President's proclamation.

23. The army of the Potomac, nearly 100,000, passed in review at Washington, before the President.

24. Capt. Mayburn, commanding all irregular bands of Confeds. in Jackson, Prairie, and White Cos., Ark., surrenders at Duvall's Bluff.

24. The main ordnance department at Mobile exploded, killing about 300 persons and wounding many others. The whole city injured by the explosion.

25. Forts Mannahasset and Griffin, and the defences of Labone Pass, occupied by Rear-Admiral Thatcher.

26. Surrender of Gen. E. Kirby Smith and his army (about 20,000).

27. Military prisoners ordered released by the President.

27. Sabine Pass forts surrendered to U. S. troops.

29. Amnesty proclamation issued by President Johnson.

31. Brazil withdraws belligerent rights from the rebels.

31. Rebel Gen. Hood and staff surrendered.

31. Gen. Sherman bade farewell to his army.

June 1. Occupation of Brownsville, Texas.

1. Day of humiliation and prayer on account of the murder of Pres. Lincoln.

2. Kirby Smith and Magruder formally surrender their forces at Galveston.

2. The British Government officially withdraws belligerent rights from the rebels.

2. Occupation of Alexandria, La. Capture of 22 pieces of artillery.

3. The rebel ironclad Missouri, in Red river, surrenders to Com. W. E. Fitzhugh.

In testimony whereof, I have hereunto set my hand and caused the seal of the Department of State to be affixed. Done at the City of Washington, this 18th day of December, in the year of our Lord 1865, and of the Independence of the United States of America the 90th.

WM. H. SEWARD, Secretary of State.

LIST OF FEDERAL VESSELS CAPTURED BY THE CONFEDERATE NAVY.

By the Alabama.

Name of Vessels.	*Where from.*	*Date of Capture.*	*Tonnage.*
Alert, bark	New London	Sept. 9, 1862	391
Altamaha, brig	Sippican	Sept 13, 1862	300
Amanda, bark	Manilla	Oct. 6, 1863	595
Amazonian, bark	New York	June 2, 1863	481
A. F. Schmidt, ship	St. Thomas	July 2, 1863	784
Ariel, steamer	New York	Dec. 7, 1862	1295
Avon, ship	Houland's Island	Mar. 29, 1864	930
B'n de Castine, brig	Castine	Oct. 29, 1862	267
Benj. Tucker, ship	New Bedford	Sept. 14, 1862	800
B. Thayer, ship	Callao	Mar. 1, 1863	896
Brilliant, ship	New York	Oct. 3, 1862	839
Charles Hill, ship	Liverpool	Nov. 25, 1863	699
Chastelain, brig	Guadaloupe	Jan. 27, 1863	240
Conrad, bark	Montevideo	June 20, 1863	347
Contest, ship	Yokahama	Nov. 11, 1863	1098
Corsair, schr	Provincetown	Sept. 13, 1862	200
Crenshaw, schr	New York	Oct. 23, 1862	278
Dorcas Prince, ship	New York	April 26, 1863	699
Dunkirk, brig	New York	Oct. —— 1863	293
E. Dunbar, bark	New Bedford	Sept. 18, 1862	300
E. Farnham, ship	Portsmouth	Oct. 3, 1862	1119
Emma Jane, ship	Bombay	Jan. 14, 1864	1096
Express, ship	Callao	July 6, 1863	1072
Golden Eagle, ship	Howland's Isl	Feb. 21, 1863	1273
Golden Rule, bark	New York	Jan. 26, 1863	250
Har't Spaulding, bark	New York	Nov. 18, 1863	299
Hatteras, gunboat	Galveston	Jan. 13, 1863	800
Henrietta, bark	Baltimore	—— 1863	4[illegible]9
Highlander, ship	Singapore	Dec. 26, 1863	1149
Jabez Snow, ship	New York	Mar. 25, 1863	1070
John A. Park, ship	New York	Mar. 2, 1863	1050
Justina, bark	Rio Janeiro	May 25, 1863	400
Kate Cory, brig	Westport	April 15, 1863	125
Kingfisher, schr	Fairhaven	Mar. 23, 1863	125
Lafayette, ship	New York	Oct. 23, 1862	945
Lafayette, bark	New Bedford	April 15, 1863	300
Lamplighter, bark	New York	Oct. 15, 1862	279
Loretta, bark	New York	Oct. 28, 1862	284
Levi Starbuck, ship	New Bedford	Nov. 2, 1862	376
Louisa Hatch, ship	Cardiff	—— 1863	835
Manchester, ship	New York	Oct. 11, 1862	1075
Martha Wenzell, bark	Akyab	Aug. 9, 1863	578
Martaban, ship	Maulmain	Dec. 24, 1863	807

Name of Vessels.	Where from.	Date of Capture.	Tonnage.
Morning Star, ship	Calcutta	Mar. 23, 1863	1105
Nora, ship	Liverpool	Mar. 25, 1863	800
Nye, bark	New Bedford	April 24, 1863	300
Ocean Rover, bark	Mattapoisett	Sept. 8, 1862	766
Ocmulgee, ship	Edgartown	Sept. 6, 1862	300
Olive Jane, bark	Bordeaux	Feb. 21, 1863	300
Oneida, ship	Shanghae	April 24, 1863	420
Palmetto, schr	New York	Feb. 3, 1863	172
Parker Cook, bark	Boston	Nov. 30, 1862	130
Punjaub, ship	Calcutta	Mar. 15, 1863	760
Rockingham, ship	Callao	April 23, 1864	976
Sea Bride, bark	New York	Aug. 5, 1863	447
Sea Lark, ship	Boston	May 3, 1863	974
S. Gildersleeve, ship	Sunderland	May 25, 1863	847
Sonora, ship	Singapore	Dec. 26, 1863	707
Starlight, schr	Fayal	Sept. 7, 1862	205
Talisman, ship	New York	June 5, 1863	1239
T. R. Wood, ship	Calcutta	Nov. 8, 1863	599
Tonawanda, ship	Philadelphia	Oct. 9, 1862	1300
Tycoon, bark	New York		735
Union Jack, bark	New York	May 3, 1863	300
Virginia, bark	New Bedford	Sept. 17, 1863	300
Washington, ship	Callao	Feb. 27, 18 3	1655
Wave Crest, bark	New York	Oct. 7, 1862	409
Weather Gauge, schr	Provincetown	Sept. 4, 1862	200
Winged Racer, ship	Manila	Nov. 10, 1863	1767

By the Shenandoah.

Name of Vessels.	Where from.	Date of Capture.	Tonnage.
Abigail, bark	New Bedford	May 25, 1865	375
Adelaide, bark	Boston	Oct. 13, 1864	437
Alina, bark	Newport, Eng.	Oct. — 1864	470
Brunswick, bark	New Bedford	June — 1865	226
Catharine, bark	New Bedford	June 26, 1865	226
Charter Oak, schr	Boston	Oct. — 1864	140
Congress 2d, bark	New Bedford	June 28, 1865	375
Covington, bark	Warren, R. I.	June 28, 1865	300
Delphine, bark	London	Jan. 13, 1865	698
D. Godfrey, bark	Boston	Dec. —, 1864	299
Edward, bark	New Bedford	Dec. 4, 1864	420
Edward Cary, bark	San Francisco	April 1, 1865	370
Euphrates, ship	New Bedford	June 21, 1865	597
Favorite, bark	Fairhaven	June 28, 1865	360
Gen. Pike, bark	New Bedford	June 22, 1865	425
Gen. Williams, ship	New London	June 25, 1865	469
Gipsy, bark	New Bedford	June 26, 1865	390
Harvest, bark	Honolulu	April 1, 1865	350
Hector, ship	New Bedford	April 1, 1865	—
Hillman, ship	New Bedford	June 27, 1865	600
Isabella, bark	New Bedford	June 27, 1865	394
I. Howland, ship	New Bedford	June 28, 1865	900
James Maury, bark	New Bedford	June 28, 1865	400
Jireh Swift, bark	New Bedford	June 23, 1865	360
Kate Prince, ship	Cardiff	Nov. 12, 1864	997
Lizzie M. Stacy, schr	Boston	Nov. 13, 1864	140
Martha 2nd, bark	New Bedford	June 28, 1865	298
Milo, ship	New Bedford	June 28, 1865	500
Nassau, ship	New Bedford	June 28, 1865	450

Name of Vessels.	*Where from.*	*Date of Capture.*	*Tonnage.*
Nile, bark	New London	June 22, 1865	380
Nimrod, bark	New Bedford	June 25, 1865	340
Pearl, bark	New London	April 1, 1865	275
Sophia Thornton, ship	New Bedford	June 23, 1865	400
Susan Abigail, bark	San Francisco	June 23, 1865	159
Susan, brig	San Francisco	June 4, 1865	—
Waverley, bark	New Bedford	June 28, 1865	450
W. Thompson, ship	New Bedford	June 22, 1865	600
Wm. C. Nye, bark	San Francisco	June 26, 1865	388

By the Florida.

Aldebaran, schr	New York	Mar. 13, 1863	187
Anglo Saxon, ship	Liverpool	Aug. 21, 1863	868
Arabella, brig	Aspinwall	Jan. 12, 1863	291
B. F. Hoxie, ship	Mazatlan	June 16, 1863	1387
Clarence, brig	Bahia	— 1863	253
Commonwealth, ship	New York	April 17, 1863	1245
Corris Ann, brig	Philadelphia	Jan. 22, 1863	235
David Lapsley, bark	Sombrero	—	289
Electric Spark, str	New York	July 10, 1864	1400
Estella, brig	Manzanilla	Jan. 17, 1863	300
F. B. Cutting, ship	Liverpool	Aug. 6, 1863	796
Geo. Latimer, schr	Baltimore	May. 18, —	198
Gen. Berry, bark	New York	July 10, —	469
Golconda, bark	Talcahuana	July 8, 1864	331
Greenland, bark	Philadelphia	July 9, 1864	519
Har't Stephens, bark	Portland	——	500
J. Jacob Bell, ship	Foochow	Feb. 12, 1863	1382
Kate Stewart, schr	Philadelphia	June –, 1863	387
Lapwing, bark	Boston	Mar. 27, 1863	590
Mary Alvina, brig	Boston	June –, 1863	266
M. A. Schinler, schr	Port Royal	June 12, 1863	299
Mary Y. Davis, schr	Port Royal	July 9, 1864	270
M. J. Colcord, bark	New York	Mar. 30, 1863	374
Mondamin, bark	Rio Janeiro	Sept., 1864	386
Red Gauntlet, ship	Buena Vista	May 26, 1863	1038
Rienzi, schr	Provincetown	July 7, 1863	95
Southern Rights, ship	Rangoon	Aug. 22, 1863	830
Southern Cross	Boston	June 6, 1863	938
Star of Peace, ship	Calcutta	Mar. 6, 1863	941
Sunrise, ship	New York	July —, 1863	1174
Tacony, bark	Port Royal	June 12, 1863	296
Varnum H. Hill, schr	Provincetown	June 27, 1862	90
Wm. B. Nash, brig	New York	July 8, 1863	299
Wm. C. Clark, brig	Machias, Me	June 17, —	338
Windward, brig	Matanzas	Jan. 22, 1863	199
Zealand, bark	New Orleans	June 10, 1864	380

By the Sumter.

Abbie Bradford, schr	——	July 25, 1861	180
Albert Adams, brig	Cuba	July 5, 1861	192
Alvarado, bark	Cape Town	June —, 1861	299
Arcade, schr	Portland	Nov. 20, 1861	122
Benj Dunning, brig	Cuba	July 5, 1861	284
B. F. Martin, brig	Philadelphia	June 16, 1861	293
California, bark	St. Thomas	1861	299
Cuba, brig	New York	July 4, 1861	199

Name of Vessels.	*Where from.*	*Date of Capture.*	*Tonnage.*
D. Trowbridge, schr.	New York	Oct. 27, 1861	200
Eben Dodge, bark	New Bedford	Dec. 8, 1861	1222
Glen, bark	Philadelphia	July, 1861	287
Golden Rocket, ship	Havana	July 13, 1861	608
Henry Nutt, schr.	Key West	Aug., 1861	235
Jos. Maxwell, bark	Philadelphia	July 27, 1861	295
Joseph Parks, brig.	Pernambuco	Dec. 25, 1861	300
J. S. Harris, ship	Cuba	– 1861	800
Louisa Kilham, bark	Cienfuegos	July 6, 1861	468
Machias, brig.	——	July 4, 1862	250
Naiad, brig.	——	July 6, 1861	390
N. Chase, schr.	New York	Sept., 1861	150
Neapolitan, bark	Messina	Feb., 1862	322
Ocean Eagle	Rockland	Feb., 1861	290
Santa Clara, brig.	Porto Rico	Feb., 1861	189
Sebasticook, ship	Liverpool	Feb., 1861	549
Vigilant, ship	New York	Dec. 3, 1861	650
West Wind, bark	New York	July 6, 1861	429
W. S. Robbins, bark	Arroya	June, 1861	460

By the Tallahassee.

Name of Vessels.	*Where from.*	*Date of Capture.*	*Tonnage.*
Adriatic, ship	London	Aug. 12, 1863	998
A. Richards, brig.	Glace Bay, C. B.	Aug. 11, 1863	240
Arcole, ship	New Orleans	Nov. 3, 1863	663
Atlantic, schr.	Addison, Me.		240
Bay State, bark	Alexandria, Va.	Aug. 11, 1863	199
Billow, brig.	Calais, Me.	Aug. 10, 1863	173
Carrie Estelle, brig.	Machias, Me.	Aug. 11, 1864	200
Castine, ship	Callao	Jan. 25, 1863	962
Coral Wreath, brig.	—	Aug. 11, 1863	260
Etta Caroline, str.	—	Aug. 10, 1863	175
Flora Reed, schr.	—	Aug. 15, 1863	150
Glenavon, bark	Glasgow	Aug. 13, 1863	795
Goodspeed, schr.	Boston	Nov. 2, 1864	280
Howard, bark	—	Aug. 15, 1864	598
Jas. Littlefield, ship	Cardiff	Aug. 14, 1864	599
J. H. Howen, schr.	Gloucester	Aug. 14, 1864	81
L. Dupont, schr.	Wilmington, Del.	Aug. 13, 1864	194
Magnolia, schr.	—	Aug. 15, 1864	170
Mercy Howe, schr.	Chatham	Aug. 15, 1864	143
N. America, schr.	Connecticut	— 1864	95
P. C. Alexander, bark	New York	— 1864	284
Pearl, schr.	—	Aug. 16,	183
Rasselas, schr.	Boothbay, Me.	Aug. 23, 1863	90
Roan, brig.	Salisbury	Aug. 20, 1864	127
S. A. Boyce, schr.	Boston	Aug. 11, 1864	220
Sarah Louisa, schr.	—	1864	61
Spokane, schr.	Calais, Me.	Aug. 12, 1864	126

By the Tacony.

Name of Vessels.	*Where from.*	*Date of Capture.*	*Tonnage.*
Ada, schr.	Gloucester	June 23, 1863	90
Arabella, brig.	Gloucester	June 12, 1863	200
Archer, schr.	Gloucester	June 24, 1863	100
Byzantium, ship	London	June 16, 1863	1048
Elizabeth Ann, schr.	Gloucester	June 22, 1863	100
Florence, schr.	Gloucester	June 22, 1863	200
Goodspeed, bark	Londonderry	June 23, 1863	629

Name of Vessels.	Where from.	Date of Capture.	Tonnage.
Isaac Webb, ship	Liverpool	June 20, 1863	1300
L. A. Macomber, schr.	Noank	June 20, 1863	100
Marengo, schr.	Gloucester	June 22, 1863	200
Ripple, schr.	Gloucester	June 22, 1863	150
Rufus Choate	Gloucester	June 22, 1853	100
Shattemuc, ship	Liverpool	June 24, 1863	849
Umpire, brig	Laguna	June 15, 1863	196
Wanderer, schr.	Gloucester	June 22, 1863	125
By the Clarence.			
A. H. Partridge, schr.	Gloucester	June 7, 1863	100
C. Cushing, cutter	Portland	June 24, 1863	150
Whistling Wind, bark	Philadelphia	June 6, 1863	349
By the Sallie.			
Betsey Ames, brig	Cuba	Oct. — 1861	265
Grenada, brig	Neuvitas	Oct. 13, 1861	255
By the Georgia.			
Bold Hunter, ship	Dundee	Dec. 9, 1863	797
City of Bath, ship	Callao	June 28, 1863	79
Constitution, ship	Philadelphia	June 25, 1863	97
Crown Point, ship	New York	May 15, 1863	1053
Dictator, ship	Liverpool	April 25, 1863	1293
Geo. Griswold, ship	Cardiff	June 18, 1863	1280
Good Hope, bark	Boston	June 22, 1863	436
John Watt, ship	Maulmain	Oct. 1863	947
J. W. Seaver, bark	Boston	June 22, 1863	340
Prince of Wales, ship	Callao	July 16, 1863	960
By the Jeff Davis.			
D. C. Pierce, bark	Remedios	June, 1861	306
Ella, schr	Tampico	1861	92
Enchantress, schr.	Boston	July 16, 1861	200
Jno. Crawford, ship	Philadelphia	Aug., 1861	
John Welsh, brig	Trinidad	July 16, 1861	275
Rowena, bark	Laguayra	June, 1861	340
S. J. Waring, schr	New York	July 16, 1861	372
W. McGilvery, brig	Cardenas	July, 1861	198
By the Winslow.			
Herbert, schr.		June 18, 1861	100
Itasca, brig	Neuvitas	Aug. 4, 1861	300
Mary Alice, schr.	Porto Rico	July, 1861	181
Priscilla, schr.	Curacoa	July, 1861	144
Transit, schr.	New London	July 15, 1861	195
By the Chickamauga.			
Albion Lincoln, bark	Portland	Oct. 29, 1864	237
Emma L. Hall, bark	Cardenas	Oct. 31, 1864	492
Mark L. Potter, bark	Bangor	Oct. 30, 1864	400
Shooting Star, ship	New York	Oct. 31, 1864	947
By the Olustee.			
A. J. Bird, schr.	Rockland	Nov. 3, 1864	178
Empress Teresa, bark	Rio Janeiro	Nov. 1, 1864	316
E. F. Lewis, schr.	Portland	Nov. 3, 1864	197
T. D. Wagner, brig	Fort Monroe	Nov. 3, 1864	390
By the Retribution.			
Emily Fisher, brig	St. Jago,	Mar. 1863	230

Name of Vessels.	*Where from.*	*Date of Capture.*	*Tonnage.*
Hanover, schr	Boston	Jan. 31, 1863	200
J. P. Ellicott, brig	Boston	Jan. 10, 1863	221
By the St. Nicholas.			
Mary Pierce, schr	Boston	July 1, 1862	192
Margaret, schr		June 29, 1862	206
Monticello, brig	Rio Janeiro	July 1, 1862	300
By the Calhoun.			
John Adams, schr	Provincetown	May, 1861	100
Mermaid, schr	Provincetown	May, 1861	200
Panama, brig	Provincetown	May 29, 1861	153
By the Nashville.			
Harvey Birch, ship	Havre	Nov. 19, 1862	800
R. Gilfillan, schr	Philadelphia	Feb. 26, 1862	240
By the Boston.			
Lenox, bark	New York	June 12, 1863	370
Texana, bark	New York	June 12, 1863	588
By the Savannah.			
Joseph, brig	Cardenas	June 15, 1861	171
By the Lapwing.			
Kate Dywer, ship	Callao	June 17, 1863	1278
By the Echo.			
M. E. Thompson, brig		July 9, 1862	210
Mary Goodell, schr		July 9, 1862	200
By the York.			
G. V. Boker, schr	Galveston	Aug. 9, 1861	100
By the Conrad.			
Santee, ship	Akyab	Aug. 5, 1863	898
By the Tuscarora.			
Living Age, ship	Akyab	Sept. 13, 1863	1193
Miscellaneous.			
A. B. Thompson, ship	Savannah	May. 19, 1861	800
Alleghanian, ship	Baltimore	Oct. 21, 1862	1142
Alliance, schr	Philadelphia	Sept. 1863	190
Boston, tug		June 9, 1863	100
Chesapeake, steamer	New York	Dec. 7, 1863	460
Golden Rod, schr	Holmes' Hole	Sept. 1863	130
Hannah Balch, brig	Cardenas	July 6, 1862	149
Harriet Lane, gunbt	Galveston	Jan. 11, 1863	325
James L. Gerity	Matamoros	Oct. 1863	90
J. R. Watson, schr	New York	July 13, 1861	200
Lydia Francis, brig		June 15, 1862	262
Pearl, schr	Moriches	1862	183
Protector, schr	Cuba	June, 1861	200
Sea Bird, schr	Philadelphia	1863	200
Sea Witch, schr	Baracoa	1861	95
Union, schr	Baltimore	Dec 5, 1862	115

www.ingramcontent.com/pod-product-compliance
Lightning Source LLC
Chambersburg PA
CBHW020138170426
43199CB00010B/797

* 9 7 8 3 3 3 7 4 0 9 5 1 7 *